RASPUTIN
AND
THE FALL OF THE ROMANOVS

By the same author

The 'Outsider cycle'

THE OUTSIDER
RELIGION AND THE REBEL
THE AGE OF DEFEAT
THE STRENGTH TO DREAM
ORIGINS OF THE SEXUAL IMPULSE
BEYOND THE OUTSIDER: THE PHILOSOPHY OF THE FUTURE

RASPUTIN AND THE FALL OF THE ROMANOVS
AN ENCYCLOPEDIA OF MURDER (WITH PAT PITMAN)

Novels

RITUAL IN THE DARK
MAN WITHOUT A SHADOW
ADRIFT IN SOHO
THE WORLD OF VIOLENCE
NECESSARY DOUBT

Autobiography

VOYAGE TO A BEGINNING

RASPUTIN

AND
THE FALL OF THE ROMANOVS

Colin Wilson

The Citadel Press
New York

Acknowledgements

I owe a debt of gratitude to many people, including Margaret
Lane, Baroness Budberg, Alan Moorehead, C. J. P. Ionides,
Martin Delany, Harry Edwards and Professors Jackson Knight
and Wilson Knight. The original ideas for this book originated
in discussions with the late Negley Farson, a friend whom I
constantly remember with affection. I would also like to thank
the London Library, and the Librarian of the St Austell Library,
for taking so much trouble to obtain for me books that would
have been otherwise unobtainable, and Mr Ian Willison of the
British Museum Reading Room for translating various works in
German that I had to consult.

C.W.

First Paperbound Edition, 1967

Published by Citadel Press, Inc., 222 Park Avenue South, New
York, N. Y., by arrangement with Farrar, Straus & Giroux, Inc.
Manufactured in the United States of America.

CONTENTS

List of Leading Characters   vii

Introduction   11

1   THE POSSIBILITARIAN   23

2   THE WANDERER   44

3   HISTORY AS NIGHTMARE   58

4   'GOD HELP RUSSIA'   71

5   CITY OF DREAMS   87

6   THE RISE TO POWER   111

7   THE ENEMIES MULTIPLY   129

8   THE STORM GATHERS   144

9   THE RAIN OF FIRE   158

10 RASPUTIN AS TSAR   169

11 THE END   185

12 THE LEGEND AND THE PROBLEM   203

    Bibliography   218

    Appendix: Thaumaturgy and Pre-Vision   221

    Index   232

LEADING CHARACTERS

ANDRONIKOV, Prince: Homosexual intriguer, for a brief period Rasputin's 'Public Relations Officer'.

BARNABY (or Varnava): Rasputin's early companion, later Bishop of Tobolsk.

BELETSKY: Chief of Police under Hvostov (nephew).

ELIZABETH: Grand Duchess, sister of Tsarina.

GILLIARD: Tsarevitch's tutor.

GOLOVINS, mother and daughter: disciples of Rasputin.

GOREMYKIN: Reactionary nonentity, twice Prime Minister.

GUCHKOV: Ex-President of Duma, hated by Tsarina.

HERMOGEN: Bishop of Saratov, one of Rasputin's earliest supporters, later his enemy.

HVOSTOV (nephew): Rasputin sycophant, later Minister of Interior.

HVOSTOV (uncle): Minister of Justice, Rasputin's enemy.

ILLIODOR: Monk, later Rasputin's bitterest enemy.

JOHN OF CRONSTADT: Saintly priest, early supporter of Rasputin.

KERENSKY: Left-wing member of Duma, later leader of government after Revolution (March 1917).

KOKOVTSEV: Minister of Finance, later Prime Minister, Rasputin's enemy.

LOKTIN, Olga: Rasputin's disciple, credited with having taught him to read and write.

MANASEVITCH-MANIULOV: Blackmailer and secret agent, Rasputin's business adviser.

'THE MONTENEGRINS': Grand Duchesses Militsa and Anastasia (Stana—not to be confused with Tsar's youngest daughter); responsible for bringing Rasputin to St Petersburg.

NILOV, Admiral: Court functionary, friend of Rasputin.

NICHOLAS, Grand Duke: Husband of Anastasia (see Montenegrins) later C.-in-C. of army, and Rasputin's enemy.

PETER, Grand Duke: Husband of Militsa.

PHILIPPE, Doctor (surname Vachot of Nizier): Quack brought to St Petersburg by Militsa.

PLEHVE: Chief of Police and Minister of Interior, assassinated by bomb.

POLIVANOV: Minister of War after Sukhomlinov's dismissal.

PROTOPOPOV: Nonentity who was made Minister of Interior by Rasputin.

PURISHKEVICH: Right-wing member of Duma, Rasputin's enemy and finally his murderer.

RASPUTIN, Maria: Rasputin's daughter, born 1898.

RODZIANKO: President of Duma, Rasputin's chief opponent.

SERGIUS, Grand Duke: Brutal Governor of Moscow and husband of Elizabeth. Assassinated by bomb.

SIMANOVICH: Rasputin's business manager and 'secretary'.

STÜRMER: Intriguing reactionary, later made Prime Minister on advice of Rasputin and Maniulov.

SUKHOMLINOV: Minister of War, dismissed for incompetence, 1915.

THEOPHAN, Bishop: Early Rasputin supporter.

THE TSAR, Nicholas II.

LEADING CHARACTERS

THE TSARINA: Alexandra, German-born grand-daughter of Queen Victoria, formerly Alix of Hesse-Darmstadt.

THE TSAREVITCH: Alexis (usually shortened to Alexey) their son. Born August 1904, murdered July 1918 (suffered from haemophilia).

OLGA

TATIANA

MARIE

ANASTASIA

} Their daughters, the Grand Duchesses.

VYRUBOV, Anna: Tsarina's confidant since 1905.

WITTE, Sergius: First Prime Minister, later friend of Rasputin.

YUSSUPOV, Prince: Rich playboy, murderer of Rasputin.

INTRODUCTION

No figure in modern history has provoked such a mass of sensational and unreliable literature as Grigory Rasputin. More than a hundred books have been written about him, and not a single one can be accepted as a sober presentation of his personality.

Mr Alan Moorehead writes: 'Grigory Efimovitch Rasputin has been so blackened and discredited in the forty-odd years since his death that it is almost impossible to see him any more. Like Richard III of England or Italy's Cesare Borgia, he is all villain, the pure quintessence of wickedness, a monster with the cunning of Iago and the brutishness of Caliban. Nothing is good about him; he seldom washed and he smelt vilely; at the table he plunged his greedy hands into his favourite fish soup, he was the kind of drunkard who smashes the furniture, he was blasphemous, vicious and obscene, and his lechery had a barbaric Mongolian quality that made him more like a beast than a human being. "I had at my disposition", wrote Rodzianko, one of the presidents of the Duma, "a whole mass of letters from mothers whose daughters had been dishonoured by this insolent rake." '[1]

Mr Moorehead is a reliable and unbiased historian; but here, after admitting that the real Rasputin has been overlaid by his myth, he proceeds to restate every element in the myth. There is not a single statement that is not open to question. Several writers have mentioned Rasputin's fondness for the *baniaé*, or

[1] Alan Moorehead, *The Russian Revolution* (Collins, 1958).

steam bath, so it is unlikely that he smelt vilely. The description of him plunging his hands into his fish soup comes from an unreliable book by Simanovich; it has been frequently quoted, but no one seems to have reflected that no one could eat soup in this way. The rest of this description presents a completely misleading picture of Rasputin as a barbaric drunkard and rapist. His daughter Maria, who lived with him in St Petersburg during the years of his greatest influence, records that he began to drink too much only in the final year of his life. He never at any time drank vodka, but was fond of sweet wine; in earlier years he was able to drink large quantities of this without showing any sign of it. He was fond of sex, but seems to have had no difficulty in finding fashionable ladies and actresses to share his bed. Rodzianko was one of Rasputin's enemies; mothers do not write letters about their daughter's 'dishonour' without some prompting. Rasputin may or may not have seduced young girls; but Rodzianko's assertion is no proof.[1]

This is the kind of difficulty encountered by anyone who writes about Rasputin. There is an enormous amount of material on him, and most of it is full of invention or wilful inaccuracy. Original source material is scanty. The Revolution came shortly after his death, and the historians of the Soviet government were more interested in denigrating Nicholas II than in historical accuracy. Most of the books about Rasputin that were published outside Russia were cheap sensational biographies that make no pretence of detachment. T. Vogel-Jørgensen's *Rasputin: Prophet, Libertine, Plotter*, published immediately after his death, begins: 'Rasputin was not his real name; he was rightly called Grigory Yefimovitch. He was born in Petronovskoye . . .,' and a footnote explains that *rasputny* means dissolute or profligate. But Rasputin *was* his real name; it was his daughter who pointed out that *rasputi* merely means a cross-road (or fork) and that more than half the inhabitants of the village of his birth bore the name because the village lies on a cross-road of Tobolsk and Tioumen.

---

[1] Even the quotation from Rodzianko illustrates the inaccuracies that creep into accounts of Rasputin. Rodzianko did not write 'dishonoured by this insolent rake' but 'dishonoured by Rasputin'. Trotsky, in his book on the Russian Revolution, alters 'Rasputin' to 'insolent rake', for obvious reasons, and Mr Moorehead seems to have quoted Trotsky.

Yefimovitch, of course, is a patronymic, not a surname, as any reader of Russian literature knows; finally, Rasputin's village was called Pokrovskoe, not Petronovskoye. It can be seen that, even for a sensational biography, this one manages to pack an unusual number of inaccuracies into its first sentence. But Vogel-Jørgensen's book is no worse than a score of others that appeared at about this time.

The definitive book, then, is still to be written; but it would have to be undertaken by a Russian-speaking historian who could sort through the mass of original documents—the diaries and letters of the Royal Family, the archives of the secret police—and travel in northern Siberia searching for information about Rasputin's early life.

This present book is an attempt at a reassessment of Rasputin's personality. It is not my intention to produce a defence of Rasputin. I doubt whether such a book would be worth writing. There have been a few attempts to whitewash Rasputin, and they are uninteresting. But the real objection to the profligate monk with the 'cunning of Iago' is that he is not half as interesting as the real Rasputin, the man who thought of becoming a monk at sixteen, who became a wandering preacher with strange healing powers, and who may have believed himself to be a reincarnation of Christ.

As the reader tries to create for himself a picture of this 'real Rasputin' who is so obviously absent from the books about him, he becomes aware that the problem is to grasp something essential, the inexpressible, living quality of the man. Great writers succeed in leaving their living quality behind; if we turn from Shelley's poetry to a biography, we are only *adding* something to the basic truth of the man, which we already possess in his poetry. But Rasputin was not a great writer, and his biographies are like the outer layers of Peer Gynt's onion; one always has the frustrating sense that the core is missing.

It is also Rasputin's misfortune that he belongs to history—and, moreover, to the sensational history of the last Romanovs. He is an interesting figure, but his historical background is even more interesting. History has a way of reducing individuals to flat, two-dimensional portraits. It is the enemy of subjectivity, which is why Stephen Dedalus called it 'a nightmare from which I am trying to awake'. If we think of Kierkegaard, of Nietzsche, Hölderlin, we see them standing alone, outside history. They are spotlighted by their intensity, and the background is all darkness. They intersect history, but are not a part of it. There is something anti-history about such men; they are subject to time, accident and death, but their intensity is a protest against it. I have elsewhere called such men 'Outsiders' because they attempt to stand outside history, which defines humanity in terms of limitation, not of possibility.

Religion is also, by its nature, anti-historic. Rasputin was a man who was obsessed by religion; a messianic self-belief was his mainspring, not sexual voracity or a will to political power. But Russia is somehow all history—wars, massacres, murders, revolutions, persecutions. R. D. Charques has written: 'Nemesis visibly stalks the twenty-three years of the reign of the last of the Romanov csars. Neither for this nor for any other period of the past will a determinist reading of history satisfy the imagination.' Here he expresses the feeling one gets on reading the history of Russia; there are times when one seems to become almost aware of the 'spirit of history' pulling the strings like a puppet master. But Rasputin has the 'outsider' quality, the revolt against being defined by the spirit of time, which separates one from one's reality. The essence of the 'outsider' quality is caught in Nietzsche's phrase: 'how to become what one is'. For the first forty years of his life, Rasputin struggled to achieve this form of internal reality, and in so doing, gained remarkable powers, a certain inner-momentum that allowed him to resist the current of history. Then he came to St Petersburg, and found himself in the fastest part of the current, and being swept towards a waterfall; the 'Nemesis' that stalked the Romanovs. His inner strength served him well, but he was not strong enough to save the Romanovs as well as himself. The Tsarina was aware of the truth of the situation. Rasputin was not a peasant who had been taken up by the Royal Family; he was *their* patron. This explains why Rasputin could irritably rebuke the Tsar and make him submit like a scolded child; it also explains the Tsarina's letters to him, with their pleading and sense of submission:

My beloved unforgettable teacher, redeemer and mentor! How tiresome it is without you! My soul is quiet and I relax only when you, my teacher, are sitting beside me. I kiss your hands and lean my head on your blessed shoulders. Oh how light, how light do I feel then! I only wish one thing: to fall asleep, to fall asleep, for ever on your shoulders and in your arms. What happiness to feel your presence near me. Where are you? Where have you gone? . . . Come quickly, I am waiting for you and I am tormenting myself for you. . . . I love you forever.

This sounds like a love letter; but Rasputin's power over her was stronger than that of a lover over his mistress; sex could only have weakened it. In this relation Rasputin was the giver; they had nothing to give. Rasputin knew they were asking for sacrifice. They had a twofold claim: the claim of their weakness, and the claim of their royalty. The first would probably have been powerful enough; but Rasputin was also a peasant who believed in the divine right of kings, and this made refusal impossible. His peasant vitality revolted against this self-immolation, and he fled from it several times, and each time returned. Finally, after about 1910, there appears a new element in Rasputin's personality, an element which it is difficult to define, and that would be better expressed by a shrug of the shoulders than by words. He accepted that he was in it to the end, and that he was accepting self-destruction. A new kind of self-division appears, which sometimes gives way to a terrible peace, the peace of a man who knows that he has agreed to commit the worst crime against himself. He could never be sure whether it was the duty of his inner-being to leave the Romanovs to their involvement in the futility of history; pity, and another kind of duty, held him. But having negated his own deepest values, a new personality emerges: cynical and violent, with an element of self-torment. He was like a man who has taken his most treasured possession to a pawnbroker, only to have it rejected; the devaluation reflects on himself; the injured pity becomes a kind of masochism. He knew he was going to die; his last letter makes this clear. He also knew that his destruction was involved with that of the Romanovs; he had told the Tsar that his death would mean the downfall of the throne. His daughter records that, after 1914, he became nervous and irritable, and began to get drunk. When his daughters remonstrated with him, he said: 'Why shouldn't I? I'm a man like the others.' The Rasputin who was murdered in the basement of Yussupov's palace was not the man who came to St Petersburg in 1905, the Rasputin who knew he was not 'a man like the others'. *That* Rasputin had been dying of slow poison since 1910. Perhaps this was why Yussupov's cyanide took no effect, and he had to be finished with revolvers.

Rasputin's life, then, is not 'history'; it is the clash of history with subjectivity. The Rasputin of the St Petersburg years is a Laocoon being strangled by history. But all writers on Rasputin so far have been either historians or popular journalists; it is not surprising that the Rasputin of these books is a Peer Gynt's onion without a centre, a man who is a puppet of history and whose driving force is cunning. Rasputin's centre is his religious obsession. This is the only way to approach his life.

We might cite as a parallel case the example of T. E. Lawrence. Lawrence was also an 'outsider' caught in history, and *Seven Pillars of Wisdom* is perhaps the only major document of such a conflict. Like Rasputin, Lawrence had turned himself into a great man before he became the leader of the Arab revolt. (It is a curious thought that Lawrence and Rasputin might easily have met in Palestine before the war, since they were there at the same time.) He was also obsessed with asceticism and the idea of pilgrimage. He also came to feel that, in serving history he was somehow prostituting himself. He never regained the subjectivity that he had lost in the war. *Seven Pillars of Wisdom* is dominated by a feeling of revulsion against history, a kind of squirming revolt, an attempt to escape the vice that held him. When Eric Kennington showed the book to a clairvoyant old man who knew nothing of Lawrence, the man commented: 'Reading this book has made me suffer. The writer is infinitely the greatest man I have known. . . .' But the clairvoyant also sensed Lawrence's surrender to history, the sense of inauthentic existence: 'He is never alive in what he does. . . . He is only a pipe through which life flows. . . .'

Yet although Lawrence's complete honesty and his greatness seem obvious enough from the *Seven Pillars*, it is still possible for Richard Aldington to produce a debunking biography that proves the mainspring of Lawrence's life to be his passion for lying. It is still possible; even though in the *Seven Pillars* we possess the essential Lawrence; the core of the onion.

Under the circumstances, then, no one need be surprised if no book on Rasputin has even begun to tell the truth about him. The inaccuracy is not so much in historic fact—although there is plenty of that—but in the approach, the understanding of what made Rasputin live as he did.

To begin with, Rasputin was a Russian. Very few of his biographers have been Russians, or understand what it means to be Russian. Of the Russians who have written about Rasputin, most have been communists, or have written from the Marxist point of view.

Like Lawrence's arabs, the Russian is a creature of contradictions. He is lazy, and lacks will-power in the sense of tenacity of purpose. On the other hand, he possesses astonishing powers of endurance and recovery. Most of the 'contradictions' of the Russian character are simply reactions to this basic characteristic of laziness and inefficiency. Berdyaev writes: 'There has been a vast elemental strength in the Russian people, combined with a comparatively weak sense of form'—that is to say, the Russian possesses strength, but doesn't know what to do with it. It is impossible to understand Russian history if one judges Ivan the Terrible and Peter the Great—or even Stalin—as if they were Englishmen. If a western European had committed their atrocities, he would be a paranoiac. But Russia is a land of vagueness and sluggishness, of inefficiency and lack of purpose; the violence of Russian history is the inevitable reaction to these qualities, the reaction of men trying to get something done.

It has been suggested that the inertia of the Russian is part of his Asiatic heritage; John Gunther writes: 'The Mongols . . . are responsible for several characteristics that we call "eastern" or "Asiatic" in the Russia of today; like cruelty, fatalism and sloth.'

But it is possible that Russian sluggishness and inefficiency are not true national characteristics, but are the products of backwardness. Countries as unlike as Ireland and India share these qualities; industrialization tends to eradicate them. In that case, the present century may see their disappearance in Russia.

Religious superstition is another characteristic of backward countries. This may also be a reaction against the inertia, the craving for powerful conviction. Here again, Russia is closer to Asia than to Europe; its Greek Orthodox Christianity has a distinctly Buddhist flavour. In Buddhist countries, a man who decides to leave his family and become a religious mendicant is called a 'tathagata'; in Russia, he is called a *staretz* (pilgrim). Rasputin became a *staretz* when he was thirty.

But there is another characteristic of the Russian that must be understood: when he is religious he takes God for granted. God is an external force. George Fox's concept of God as the 'inner light' is completely foreign to a Russian. Europe has had three centuries in which to get accustomed to a new concept of God—since the scientific revolution of Newton and Galileo. Newton taught European man to trust his intellect, and so produced an invisible revolution. Nietzsche announced the death of God three centuries after it had taken place in Europe. But Russian man has never acquired this complete confidence in the intellect and the 'inner light'. For the Russian, God is always a burning question. In his autobiography, Berdyaev tells how he belonged to a group of intellectuals that used to meet in St Petersburg in the early years of this century. On one occasion when they had been discussing metaphysics all night, someone suggested that it was time to go home. Someone else replied: 'No, we can't go yet. We haven't decided whether God exists.'

It is impossible to imagine a Russian saying, as unconcernedly as Zarathustra: 'Hasn't he heard yet that God is dead?', or taking his atheism for granted in the manner of Sartre. Dostoevsky's Stavrogin, in *The Devils*, is the Russian Zarathustra, and it is instructive to compare him with his German counterpart. Stavrogin is a rich young man who has discovered the death of God, but the discovery produces no Dionysian celebration of his freedom. He finds the world without God boring and meaning-less, and commits crimes in an effort to shock himself into moral response. Stavrogin is all emotion; he gets no pleasure from his intellect. It is impossible to imagine him, like Shelley, plunging into the study of chemistry or political economy. If there is no God, then the world 'out there' is meaningless. But there would be no point in looking inside himself for meaning; his inner world is dead. Life for him means strong emotion or nothing. Intensity has to come from an external stimulus; he cannot imagine it rising from *inside*. His response to the death of God is suicide.

All this must be understood in order to understand what religion meant to Rasputin. Compared to any of the great religious figures of Europe—Pascal, William Law, Newman, Kierkegaard —his religion is curiously unintelligent, curiously literal and objective. This is difficult for a European to grasp—for Rasputin himself was far from unintelligent. He was also monumentally self-reliant. But it was not the intellectual self-reliance of a Nietzsche. If the least grain of Zarathustra's scepticism had ever found its way into Rasputin's mind, the whole structure of his personality would have collapsed. The Tsarevitch nicknamed Rasputin 'the novik', the new man. But he was not a new man; intellectually, he was the last of the Old Believers, and it is fitting that he should have died before the October revolution.

A word should be said, at this point, about the books dealing with Rasputin. These can be divided into three classes: the more-or-less reliable, the reliable but ill-informed, and the totally unreliable. Too many, unfortunately, belong to this latter class.

The best book dealing with the whole period is Sir Bernard Pares' *Fall of the Russian Monarchy*. But, like most historians dealing with the whole period, Pares is concerned mostly with Rasputin's influence at the court of the Tsar, and makes no effort to be fair to him.

Typical of the highly biased accounts of the court life of the period is the anonymous *Fall of the Romanoffs*, sub-titled: 'How the ex-Empress and Rasputine caused the Russian Revolution',[1]

[1] Herbert Jenkins, 1918.

evidently written by some member of the court with an intense personal dislike for the Tsarina. This book presents the Tsarina as a hysteric and Rasputin as an ordinary swindler.

Fülöp-Miller's book *The Holy Devil* is usually regarded as the most important work on Rasputin; it is certainly the largest. Pares summarizes its faults: 'though embodying a whole lot of good spade work, it is unfortunately written up in a journalistic style, entirely misplacing some of the chief episodes of the story and even transforming parts of the record into imaginary conversations for which the author alone is responsible'. Fülöp-Miller also offers very few dates, and does not bother to mention most of his sources.

There are several books by people who knew Rasputin, the chief of which are Yussupov's account of the assassination, his daughter's two 'biographies', and the book by Rasputin's 'secretary' Simanovich. All these books can be regarded as reliable when they speak of personal contact with Rasputin, but are otherwise curiously ill-informed. Simanovich's book reads like a particularly malicious gossip-column, and gives the impression that his main concern is to offer his readers good value for their money. Yussupov's book gives an impression of honesty, but is inevitably concerned with justifying the murder by presenting Rasputin without a single redeeming characteristic.

The two short books by Marie Rasputin are probably, on the whole, the most reliable portraits, but they contain all too little information on dozens of points about which she must have been well-informed. And even these books are not free of contradictions. For example, she mentions that Rasputin saw his vision of the Virgin of Kazan when he was thirty. But earlier on the same page, she had stated that it took place at about the same time that he lost his eldest son, which was presumably in the year after his marriage, when he was twenty. (She mentions that he married at the age of nineteen.)

In the year after Rasputin's murder, appeared two short books on him; one by T. Vogel-Jørgensen, the other by Charles Omessa. Vogel-Jørgensen admits frankly that he is drawing largely on Russian newspapers for his material; therefore, although it is full of the inaccuracies that one would expect, it is at least a reliable picture of the reaction of the Russian press to Rasputin.

Omessa's book, on the other hand, is the first of the blatantly and immorally inaccurate studies of Rasputin. It begins by alleging that the Tsarina began her reign by having a love affair and continues in this vein of free invention, even offering exact dates and newspaper paragraphs to support his fabrications.

The novelist William LeQueux has also written three untrustworthy books on Rasputin, to which I shall refer in the chapter on the Rasputin legend (Chapter 12).

The most recent book on Rasputin, Heinz Liepman's *Rasputin, Saint or Devil* (1957), is written in the same journalistic manner as Füllöp-Miller's, but is far less reliable. It begins by implying that it will supersede all previous books on Rasputin by drawing upon new material published by the Central Historical Archive in Moscow. In fact, a great deal of its material seems to be invented. For example, he describes circumstantially how Rasputin's father was beaten to death by angry peasants when Rasputin was seventeen; and yet Maria Rasputin mentions that her grandfather visited St Petersburg during Rasputin's residence there—that is, when Rasputin was over forty. On the whole, Liepman's book must be placed on the same level as Omessa's. I have, nevertheless, quoted it at intervals where it has been possible to check its information against some other source.

Finally, one of the literary curiosities on Rasputin—and an example of his power to create myths—is George Sava's *Rasputin Speaks*, which the writer claims was dictated to him by the spirit of Rasputin through the mouth of a medium in 1940. The spirit of Rasputin seems to have studied Füllöp-Miller's book, for he repeats many of Füllöp-Miller's stories almost word for word, and also repeats some of his inaccuracies. In the second half of Sava's book, the spirit of Rasputin is made to utter a long prophecy about the future of Russia, which has so far proved notably wide of the mark.

A mere citation of the titles of some of the books on Rasputin is enough to indicate their approach: *Rasputin, Tool of the Jews* (Rudolph Kummer), *Rasputin and the Women* (René Füllöp-Miller), *The Minister of Evil, The Secret History of Rasputin's Betrayal of Russia* (William LeQueux), *Rasputinism in London* (again LeQueux—Rasputin was, of course, never in London), *Rasputin, Monk, Satyr, Criminal* (Auguste Lescalier), *Rasputin and the Bloody Dawn* (Princess Murat), *Rasputin, the All-Powerful Peasant* (A. Simanovich).

It can be seen why, in spite of the immense amount already published, I still consider there is room for another book on Rasputin.

CHAPTER ONE

THE POSSIBILITARIAN

'THERE is something in the Russian soul that corresponds to the immensity, the vagueness, the infinitude of the Russian land', writes Nicholas Berdyaev.[1] The part of Russia to which these adjectives are most applicable is Siberia, the land that lies beyond the Urals. It is a land of great rivers; the Lena, the Amur, the Yenisei and the Ob, rivers so wide that their banks are sometimes invisible from the middle, and which are navigable by ocean liners. The winters are severe, with temperatures of thirty below zero; but the dry, windless air makes them endurable. The summers can be so hot that the Steppe becomes a desert of baked earth.

The south and east are mountainous, but in the north—where Grigory Rasputin was born—there are rolling Steppes fringed with tundra—flat expanses of swamp covered with reindeer moss and lichen.

The exact date of Rasputin's birth is not certain, but it is convenient to assume that it took place in the late 1860s in Pokrovskoe, a small town in the Tioumen district, near Tobolsk. Since the time of Peter the Great, Siberia has been used as a place of exile and imprisonment, and one writer asserts that Pokrovskoe was founded in the 1820s by discharged convicts. If so, the convicts chose their ground wisely. Prince Yussupov describes it:

Straggling along the high, bare banks of the River Tura

[1] *The Russian Idea* (Geoffrey Bles Ltd., 1947).

23

lies the village of Pokrovskoe. From the hill in the heart of it, where the church stands, the roads stretch away in all directions; they are laid out straight, and are bordered with roomy peasant cottages.

Everything seems to breathe prosperity. The streets are full of fowl. The farmyards abound with cows, sheep and pigs, and sturdy little horses of local breed that look as if they are cast in steel. The cottage interiors are spotlessly clean. The wide window-sills are bright with flowers.

If you leave the village, to stand for a moment on the banks of the Tura, you are confronted with the spaciousness of Siberia, a spaciousness the like of which is probably not to be found the whole world over. Meadows and Steppes dotted with birch groves stretch away into the distance, and beyond them lies the *urman*, and endless forest of fir and pine.[1]

Rasputin's father was a well-to-do peasant, a coachman and owner of horses; like his son, he has also been accused of being a horse-thief. This is possible, for he apparently served a year in gaol at one point. He has variously been described as a hard-working peasant and an abominable drunkard. Both descriptions may well be true. It has been asserted that he drank heavily immediately after his marriage, when employed as a coachman of the Imperial Russian Mail, but that the year in prison— following the loss of one of his horses—made him change his ways.[2] Some time in the 1860s, he moved eastward, and found a pleasant spot at the junction of the rivers Tura and Tobol, where there was a hundred-foot-high waterfall. Here Yefimy Rasputin built his home, among a few other cottages that became the village of Pokrovskoe. He worked hard and developed his land into a prosperous farm. In due course, he was elected the head man of the village. It was during this period that his second son, Grigory, was born.

Rasputin's childhood was happy. He loved the horses, and he loved the steppe. He had little schooling; although his father taught him the rudiments of reading, he could see no point in learning to write. He hated discipline; he preferred fishing or

[1] *Rasputin, His malignant influence and his assassination*, p. 28.
[2] Heinz, Liepman: *Rasputin, Saint or Devil?*

24

swimming to sitting over books. (He never learned to write properly; letters in his handwriting show an awkward, childish scrawl.) But the freedom of his childhood and the openness of the steppe gave him the basis of a strength that lasted all his life, and that even the unhealthy intrigues of court life could only undermine to a small degree. Brecht has a poem with the line: 'The cold of the forests will be in me until I die'. The cold of the forests was also in Rasputin, and also an optimism that was the result of a childhood without serious frustrations.

From an early age, Grigory Rasputin had one curious characteristic that distinguished him from the other village boys; he possessed a degree of second sight. His daughter quotes him as saying: '. . . I never dared to steal or pilfer the smallest thing. I used to believe that everybody would at once see that I had stolen something, since I myself was aware of it as soon as one of my comrades had stolen. Even when he had stolen in a distant place and hidden the object, I could always see the object behind him.' To illustrate his second sight, his daughter tells a story of St Petersburg days, when an unknown woman called on Rasputin, carrying a muff. As soon as she came in, Rasputin snatched at the muff, calling, 'Drop that.' A revolver fell to the floor, and the woman collapsed in hysterics.

One of the most persistent legends of Rasputin's childhood concerns a stolen horse. The animal had disappeared from the barn of a poor peasant, and the villagers met to discuss it in the home of the head man, Yefimy Rasputin. At this time, Grigory was ill with a kind of fever, and was lying on a bed or settee in the room. Suddenly he sat up, pointed at one of the peasants, and said: 'This is the thief.' The man was furious—he was one of the richer peasants—and Rasputin's father had to placate him by pointing out that the boy was in a fever and could not be held responsible for what he said. But two of the peasants were suspicious about the man's manner when the boy had accused him. They were curious enough to follow him home. Concealed near his barn in the darkness, they saw him lead out the stolen horse and set it free. They beat him severely, and returned the horse to its owner.

When Grigory was about twelve, misfortune descended on the family. His mother died, and at about the same time a fire destroyed most of the house. One day, when Grigory and his brother, Micheal, were playing on the banks of the river, Micheal fell in and was swept away by the current. Grigory dived in and managed to keep his head above the water until a passing peasant rescued them. Micheal died the next day—one account says of an inflammation of the lungs, another of a cracked skull. Some time after, Rasputin's sister, an epileptic (as was Rasputin's own son later), fell into the river when she was washing clothes, and was drowned. Rasputin and his father were now the only two left on the farm.

At this point, Grigory took a job as a wagoner, working for a contractor in Tobolsk. (Presumably the family fortunes were at such a low ebb that Yefimy Rasputin no longer owned horses.) His job involved carrying goods, and sometimes passengers, all over Siberia. He was often away for several days, sleeping at night under his wagon, or at some small post station. It was probably at this time—when he was not yet sixteen—that he discovered that he was attractive to women. There seems to be a rare unanimity among all his biographers on the question of his sexual prowess in his teens. Sir Bernard Pares writes: 'What is clear is that he shocked the whole village with his sexual licence.' Grigory Rasputin never did things by halves; moreover there was about his character a naïve element of show-off which remained to the end. Probably he set out to acquire the reputation of a rake. He enjoyed being known, being pointed out. But it is doubtful whether he was invariably—or even usually—successful. His methods were not refined, as many St Petersburg ladies later bore witness. If he liked a woman, he would try and grab her and kiss her, and then proceed to undo her buttons. Even in later life, this method brought a great number of rebuffs. Rasputin had a peasant's philosophical outlook, and took them as a matter of course. He was not thin skinned. And no doubt he met many peasant girls at remote post stations who were not inclined to snub him.

But although Pokrovskoe was a pleasant enough village, and Rasputin had the flattering sensation of being a big fish in a small pond, he was not happy there. This may have been partly because he was looked on as a suspicious character (one account describes him as 'the terror of the village'); but since he was the son of a

man who had been village head man, it cannot have been entirely
social non-acceptance that made him dissatisfied. He was a split
personality. Part of him was a Russian peasant with an uncom-
plicated desire for pleasure and notoriety. But part of him felt
revulsion at his own exhibitionism, and at the dislike he incurred
from the more respectable peasants. He felt they were not important enough to dislike him. He was driven by a will to power
that was stifled in Pokrovskoe.

One idea had probably occurred to him several times: to go
into the world and wander. He had occasionally seen pilgrims
passing through his village, on their way to some distant monastery. But he had a certain amount of freedom as a carter, and
was also probably unwilling to desert his father, who had shown
signs of demoralization since the death of his wife and two
children.

When he was sixteen, he was hired to drive a young novice
to the monastery of Verkhoture, about a hundred miles away.[1]
The novice's name was Mileti Saborevski. He talked with the
driver, and was impressed by him. Rasputin was open and
forthcoming, and a good talker. In the days of his prosperity,
his father had been deeply religious and often spent whole
evenings reading the Bible to his family. There were a few
other religious books in the house: lives of the saints, and
probably the *Life of the Arch Priest Avvakum*, the first classic of
Russian literature, written by the leader of the Old Believers.
Rasputin knew these; but he was not naturally religious—probably with the usual rejection of the father. Still, saints and martyrs
can be inspiring reading, particularly to a youth who feels stifled
in his home environment. Saborevski talked about religion, and
Rasputin began to take a sympathetic interest that turned to
excitement. No doubt he told Saborevski something about his
own life, about his sexual conquests—and perhaps about a few
underhand deals with which he was able to supplement his
income as a carter. Saborevski urged him to stay at the monastery, confess his sins and seriously consider becoming a monk.
Finally, after several days of excited discussion, they arrived at

[1] I am presuming he was sixteen at the time—although most writers
accept a later date for his stay at the monastery—because his daughter
mentions that he paid his first visit to Verkhoture when he was sixteen.

Verkhoture, and Rasputin was impressed by it. The monastery stands on a hillside above the river Tura, a white building among the green of the woods. The village lay below, surrounding the church which housed the bones of Saint Simeon the Just. The legend of St Simeon has some resemblance to that of St Francis—he was a rich young man who gave up his position to become a monk. His bones were believed to possess healing properties, so that many pilgrims came.

A strict monastic discipline might have repelled Rasputin; but the monastery of Verkhoture was more like a farmhouse in certain respects; and since the church was in the middle of the village the monks were by no means cut off from ordinary human contact. They also farmed the land and helped the people of the surrounding countryside.

There was another, and even more interesting, aspect of monastery life that attracted Rasputin. The monks were divided into two communities, and one seemed to act as gaolers to the other. Verkhoture was a place of detention for members of certain heretical sects, of which Russia has many. The chief of these were the Khlysty and the Skoptzy (of whom more must be said later). It was probably Rasputin's first contact with heretical sects, and it excited him. The heretics at Verkhoture were chiefly of the Khlysty, or flagellants; men who believed that the kingdom of God can be attained on this earth by the elect. Rasputin talked with these men, and found that in many respects he preferred their religion to that of the orthodox church. At least there was real passion and belief here.

Apart from Saborevski, Rasputin made at least one other friend in Verkhoture; this was a remarkable old hermit called Makary, who lived on the edge of the woods in a hut. Readers of Dostoevsky's *The Brothers Karamazov* will recollect Father Ferapont, the monk who lives apart from all the others in a solitary hut, who seldom speaks to anyone, and is not required to keep the rules of the monastery. Dostoevsky adds: 'Many of the visitors looked upon him as a great saint and ascetic, although they had no doubt that he was crazy. It was just his craziness that attracted them.'

The hermit Makary was not crazy, but he was in the same kind of privileged position as Father Ferapont. Many pilgrims came to pray over the holy bones of St Simeon, and most of them also asked the blessing of Makary. The hermit was also impressed by something about Rasputin, and advised him to learn to write and to improve his reading.

Rasputin spent four months in the monastery, and impressed many people there—at least, we may presume so, since he was presented with a generous sum of money on leaving. At the end of this time, he had decided that monastery life was not a great improvement on village life. He wanted experience and change. So, regretfully, he took his leave of Saborevski and the hermit Makary, and returned to Pokrovskoe, where his father was glad to see him back. He took up his old occupation of wagoner. The monastery had left him convinced that he had no vocation as a monk, so he went back to his pursuit of village girls and any minor illegal activities for which opportunity occurred in the course of his work.

But the great change had occurred, without Rasputin fully understanding what had happened. Life in his native village would never again satisfy him. Pokrovskoe was small, and its way of life was narrow. Russian literature of the nineteenth century offers any number of portrayals of such villages; they can be found in Pisemsky, in Chekhov, in Schredin, in Tolstoy, and later in Gorki and Sologub. In fact, perhaps the most powerful evocation of all is in Sologub's *Melky Bes*, *The Demon of Triviality*, whose title summarizes the whole way of life in such places. Their main characteristics are always the same: a stupidity that takes itself for granted, and that accepts spite and malice as fundamental constituents of human nature, a certain boorishness and brutality; and finally, stagnation, an incredible, soul-destroying stagnation. When Dostoevsky wrote about the Russian peasant in later life—hailing the *moujik* as the saviour of Russia—he had forgotten about these characteristics. He had forgotten about the peasants who murdered his own father by crushing his testicles (so that there would be no marks on the body) and leaving him to die.

The brutality and narrowness might have been redeemed by religion; but the Russian peasant is not naturally religious, in spite of Dostoevsky. The historian Kostamarov writes: '. . . there hardly ever was, in all Christendom, a land less inclined to

religious movements, less prepared for them than Russia. . . .
That such movements were not in keeping with the coldness of
their temper in such matters is often revealed in our history.
We hear nothing but complaints of the alienation of the people
from the church, of its indifference thereto. . . . It is the last
thing that one would have expected, that among people whose
leading trait has for so long been religious indifference, heresy
and dissent should appear.'[1] Schapov also points out, in his
book on Russian Dissent, that, 'popular indifference to religion
was so strong that the Tsars, Micheal and Alexis . . . had to
force people to go to church by means of decrees . . .' Several
other writers have testified to the Russian indifference to religion.
Russia had its monasteries and places of pilgrimage and holy
men, but the average Russian peasant cared as much about
religion as he did about the higher mathematics.

For Rasputin, it was not the atmosphere of religion that was
so important in Verkhoture; his father had always been a reader of
the scriptures. It was the intelligence and friendliness, the revelation of a disinterestedness that he had never encountered before.

'Outsider' is not the ideal word for describing the temperament
of a Rasputin; it applies too easily to weaklings and misfits, to
men who, under more propitious circumstances, would be as
mediocre as the people they despise. Rasputin was not a misfit in
this sense; but he had in him the possibility of self-expression
that could find no outlet in his own village. Robert Musil
suggested a more satisfactory word for Rasputin's type—a
possibilitarian. Human life always involves accepting certain
things; even the most violent rebel must base his life on accept-
ance, on stability. The greater the rebel, the more he needs a
solid basis on which to work. The rebel without such a basis is
usually the criminal. But there is another extreme: too many
human beings are too well adjusted; they accept the world
exactly as they find it and their act of living is an act of minimum
adjustment. They feel no interest in the possibilities of the
universe. Stupid and brutal people are usually of this type.

Rasputin grew up among such people, and Verkhoture was a
revelation. Overnight he became a 'possibilitarian'; vague

[1] Quoted in *Russian Dissenters*, Frederick C. Conybeare (Harvard Theological Studies, 1912).

dissatisfaction became an active questioning, the beginning of a need for a complete shedding of his old personality.

Much of the old personality remained after the first stay at Verkhoture. Shortly after he left the monastery, he was in trouble with the police. One of his horses was missing; the contractor called in the police, who searched Rasputin and found twenty-one roubles, a large sum for a sixteen-year-old youth. Rasputin explained that the money was a gift from the monastery of Verkhoture. The missing horse, he said, had broken away from its tethering by night, slipped into a swollen river, and been drowned. He was finally discharged for lack of evidence.

On a later occasion, he was not so lucky. A load of furs was stolen from his wagon, and Rasputin claimed that he had been attacked by robbers. Later, it was discovered that the furs had been stolen when he had left the wagon untended during the midday halt. He was sentenced to a flogging and a short term of imprisonment. This was at Tobolsk on February 14, 1891.

At the age of nineteen, Rasputin attended a religious festival in the Aballakask convent, near Pokrovskoe. Rasputin enjoyed religious festivals; all his life he liked to sing and dance. Visitors who went to see him in St Petersburg at the height of his power record that he would be carried away by his own talk about religion until he would suddenly burst into song, and then begin to dance. It was probably while he was dancing at the Aballakask convent that he met Praskovie Fedorovna Dubrovine, a girl from a neighbouring village. She was slim and blonde, and four years his senior. One writer speculates that Rasputin decided to marry her because she refused to give herself to him. This is not in keeping with Rasputin's character. What is more probable is that the girl's character was so unlike his own that he felt she would make an ideal wife. Russian peasant girls are inclined to be buxom and dark; she was slim and blonde; she also had boundless admiration for her husband, and a docile, yielding character. Whether she gave herself to him or not—and she probably did—he felt she was not the kind of girl he could desert. The date of his marriage was probably about 1890.

Marriage at first made no difference to Rasputin's character. His job as a carter brought him into contact with many peasant girls, and he continued to take advantage of them. He also spent much time drinking with certain cronies—a close friend called Petcherkine, and a gardener called Barnaby, who later became the Bishop of Tobolsk through Rasputin's influence. He was not a drunkard, but his enormous vitality needed some form of self expression. His wife accepted his extra-marital excursions with docility, probably aware that Rasputin would never leave her for another woman. She was a good housewife, and was soon, with the help of Rasputin's father, running the farm efficiently. Yefimy Rasputin was probably glad to have a woman around the house again. He was getting old and drinking too much.

In late 1890 came an event that changed the course of Rasputin's life. His wife bore him a son, and Rasputin became a fond father. At six months, the baby died, and the father felt shattered. He had already known tragedy, but had not been deeply marked by it, since it came at the end of a happy childhood. But this tragedy came closer, and made him wonder whether his own life was destined to be as pointless as his father's. He was inclined to wonder whether it was some kind of a sign from heaven—at least, we may presume that this was the interpretation he placed on it, since he immediately decided to go and see the hermit Makary, to ask him what the death meant. Accordingly, Rasputin again made the journey to Verkhoture. The monk comforted him and sent him home. But Rasputin was troubled, and that winter he spent much time brooding over the scriptures. He also began to spend a great deal of time on his knees in prayer. The villagers noticed his changed character, and often came in to talk to him about his visits to the monastery. Rasputin also paid visits to the monastery of Balik. He began to acquire something of a reputation as a 'God seeker'. The village priest, Father Peter, heard about Rasputin's new reputation, and the gatherings at his house, when he talked about the scriptures, and was irritated. He suspected that Rasputin had only found another method for making mischief. He had known Rasputin for many years, and regarded him as a malcontent and a rake. No doubt the mention of Verkhoture did nothing to allay his suspicions. He knew it to be a stronghold of the Khlysty, and the Khlysty rites were generally believed to involve sexual orgies. If Rasputin had suddenly become religious, it was probably some new plan for seducing village girls. However, for the time being, Father Peter took no action.

In the spring, a strange thing happened. Rasputin was ploughing one day when he saw a vision. It seemed to be an image of the Virgin, hanging in the sky, and gesturing to him with her hand. Rasputin set a cross in the place where he had seen the vision, and returned to tell his family about it. He explained that the Virgin was not dressed as in the garments he usually saw in ikons, and that he felt she was trying to communicate something to him. His wife was impressed; his father, apparently, was not. Rasputin decided to go and consult Makary again. (His father remarked: 'Grigory has turned a pilgrim out of laziness'.)

Whether Rasputin's vision was a hallucination is beside the point. He had spent a whole winter praying and brooding on religion; he was a man of great nervous force and energy, capable of extremes of joy or depression. Everything about his way of life dissatisfied him; he felt the need for some great change, and wanted an excuse for leaving his home. It is doubtful whether he invented his vision; whatever trick his unconscious mind played him, he really believed that it was a sign from heaven.

The hermit Makary apparently agreed; he told Rasputin: 'God has chosen you for a great achievement. In order to strengthen your spiritual power, you should go and pray to the Virgin in the convent of Afon' (Mount Athos). Rasputin returned home and informed his wife that he had decided to go on a pilgrimage; she apparently made no effort to dissuade him. Some time in 1891, Rasputin set out with his friend, Petcherkine, to walk the 2000 miles to Greece. They dressed in the robes of pilgrims, and knocked on the doors of peasant cottages at night to ask for a corner of the floor to sleep on. It is not known how long the journey took them; it can hardly have been less than three months. Rasputin's first impression of Mount Athos was a good one. This group of monastic communities is among the oldest in Europe, and the rule is of great severity. Petcherkine decided to become a novice immediately; Rasputin was more cautious, remembering his first experience at Verkhoture. And in fact, he discovered a scandal in the monastery that so shocked him that he told Petcherkine: 'There is nothing here but moral dirt and vermin'. (Presumably the scandal was a homosexual relation between monks, since women are strictly excluded from Mount Athos.) Having come so far south, Rasputin decided to go on to the Holy Land, involving a journey of less than a thousand miles across Turkey.

Unfortunately, we possess no details of this first visit to Syria and Jordan. But on a later visit, in 1911, Rasputin made many notes, and from these it is possible to see how deeply he was affected by the pilgrimage. He writes:

How impressive is Golgotha! There in the Temple of the Resurrection where stood the Queen of Heaven, a round hollow has been made, and this marks the place where the Mother of God gazed upon the hill of Golgotha and wept as they nailed Our Lord to the cross. When you look at the place where the Mother of God stood, tears come to your eyes and you see before you the whole scene.

Oh God, what a deed was wrought! And they took down his body and laid it on the ground. Oh, what sadness and weeping at the place where his body was laid.

Oh God, Oh God, why did it all happen? Oh God, we will sin no more, we are saved by Thy own suffering.

These notes were written for his own eyes, and were discovered after his death. They are completely without affectation. They also show that, in spite of his intelligence and immense nervous force, Rasputin was basically an ordinary, superstitious Russian peasant, capable of writing: 'The divine blessing descended on a pillar, and a certain Turk spat upon the pillar and his teeth leapt out and stuck upon the pillar so that all may behold how God punishes unbelievers'.

Rasputin made his way back home via Kazan. In the cathedral there, he was startled to see an image of the Virgin dressed like the vision that had appeared to him before he set out. This must have seemed to him a sign that his pilgrimage had been what heaven was demanding of him. (Later, the Tsarina gave him an ikon of the Virgin of Kazan to commemorate his vision.)

It was more than two years later that Rasputin returned home to Pokrovskoe. He was so changed that his wife failed to recognize him. Typically, Rasputin decided to surprise her, and pretended to be some kind of a travelling merchant. But his eyes and his voice gave him away. The news travelled round the village, and many people came to speak to the pilgrim. His travels in the Holy Land seemed to give him an aura of sanctity; he had walked more than ten thousand miles in two years, and many of the peasants had hardly ever been outside their own village. They found him greatly changed. He had always had an impressive manner, and a gift for making people listen to him. Now his eyes had acquired a penetrating quality that made some of the peasants imagine that he could see straight through them. All who met him have mentioned his eyes, and even photographs show their power. His daughter records that he was able to make the pupils expand or contract at will, giving the impression that he was boring into the mind of whoever he was looking at. Rasputin had discovered that he possessed hypnotic powers as well as second sight. It is a remarkable tribute to his powers that the peasants of his own village were the first to become his followers; after all, he had grown up among them, and most of them knew about his sexual exploits and his period in gaol.

Rasputin was home again, but he did not work on the farm. Instead, he constructed an oratory in the courtyard, and spent hours of every day on his knees. He had not become a monk in every sense; his wife had borne him a son in his absence (who suffered from epileptic seizures), and now she conceived her first daughter, Maria. Two years later, there was another daughter.

Rasputin began to hold prayer meetings in his house after dark. Father Peter heard about these, and his suspicions about the Khlysty revived. The enthusiasm of the peasants for Rasputin struck him as inexplicable. They were mostly women, but there were also men among them. If there had been women alone, he might have believed that Rasputin was using his reputation as a holy man as a weapon of seduction. Since there were men present, it followed that they were all engaging in orgiastic rites. He reported Rasputin to the Bishop of Tobolsk, alleging that he was a member of the Khlysty.

Russian Dissent

In his travels through Russia, Rasputin had encountered some of the heretical sects. These sects are so typically Russian that it is important, at this point, to speak about them in some detail. The Russia of Rasputin and the last of the Tsars cannot be understood without them.

I have already commented that the Russian peasant is not religious by nature; Dostoevsky's talk about the 'God-bearing Russian people' was wishful thinking.

This was wholly true until the seventeenth century, and then one man, the Patriarch Nikon, aroused the dormant fanaticism of the Russian character, and inaugurated the history of Russian dissent. The result was not really a religious movement like the Quakers or Methodists; it could better be compared to the Irish Republican movement, culminating in the years of bloodshed and chaos of the 1920s.

Like Rasputin, Nikon Mordvinov was a peasant who turned to religion when his three children died. He made the acquaintance of the Tsar Alexis on a visit to Moscow in 1645, became a favourite, and was soon the most powerful man in Russia. He was appointed Patriarch in 1652, and while the Tsar was away at the wars, Nikon acted as his regent and governed Russia.

Nikon was a fanatic and a bully, and he decided to reform the church by force. Things were slack in the Russian church; the priest was usually regarded as of small importance, and could be ordered about by the village commune. Nikon treated the priests sternly; he ordered them to demand respect and obedience, and when he thought they were not fulfilling their duties, he had them tortured and imprisoned. He also decided to revise the service and prayer book of the Russian church. Some of these revisions sound absurd. He ordered a slight change in the spelling of 'Jesus', and decreed that believers should cross themselves with three fingers instead of two. He also made many arbitrary changes in the prayer books—for example, changing 'temple' to 'church', and vice versa.

The violent resistance that he met was almost certainly not due to the changes he proposed, but to dislike of being bullied. Those who resisted him called themselves Old Believers. After twelve years, Nikon overreached himself and lost the Tsar's favour; his chief enemy, Avvakum, was recalled from a Siberian exile, and took Nikon's place as the Tsar's favourite. But the Old Believers had not won. The struggle went on with increased bitterness for the rest of the century. Huge numbers of Old Believers committed suicide—sometimes *en masse* by burning themselves on huge pyres. (Mussorgsky's opera *Khovantschina* ends with such a scene.)

Violent passions were aroused, but they were not necessarily religious passions. As in England at the same period, religion and politics were closely entangled. Still, there were many deaths, many mass executions, much cruelty, and the struggle produced convictions where they had not previously existed. As a result, Russia became a country in which religion was an important issue. While the old-fashioned Greek orthodoxy had prevailed, Russia was a country with only one form of Christianity. The schism in Russia produced the same effect as the Reformation in Europe; new sects began to spring up overnight.

Two of these—and perhaps the most interesting—are closely related: the Khlysty and the Skoptzy, the Flagellants and the Mutilants.

It has been suggested that the Khlysty existed as long ago as 1363. This is possible, but it is certain that the great schism gave the sect a new vitality. The Khlysty have a certain amount in common with the ancient sect of the Manichees: they divide the world into spirit and flesh, and believe the spirit to be good, the flesh evil. But their most important characteristic is the belief that Christ keeps returning to earth as a man. The resurrection is understood in this sense. Christ's body remained in the tomb, but his spirit took another body, and has continued to do so throughout the ages. Averzhan was one of these Christs, and was crucified on the battlefield of Kulikovo in 1380 by Dmitri Donskoi. (Kulikovo is the Russian equivalent of the Battle of Hastings, when Dmitri defeated the Mongols.) Another Christ, Yemeljan, suffered under Ivan the Terrible, according to Karl Grass's *Russian Sects*. But the most important of the Christs was Daniel Philipov, who was a contemporary of Nikon. Philipov was a peasant from Kostroma who deserted the army and supported the cause of the Old Believers. The spirit of God descended on him one day when he stood on the hill of Golodina in the Volost of Starodub (in Vladimir), in the form of the god Zebaoth who descended with a host of angels and entered Philipov's body. The Khlysty call this 'the second advent', and give 1645 as its date (which, as Frederick Conybeare points out, conflicts with the tradition that he was an Old Believer). He began preaching in the village of Staraya, which in Khlysty mythology has the same kind of importance as Medina in Mohammedanism, and moved to Kostroma, which is the Khlysty Mecca. He produced a Bible called the Dove Book, and preached that men should not marry, should not drink or swear, and should look out for martyrdom. If one of his converts was married, he should abandon his wife, and his children should be called 'sins'. He was allowed to take a new 'spiritual wife', a member of the Khlysty, who might sleep with him in the same bed as his old wife—but there should be no carnal relation.

It will be seen that this sect resembles equally Manicheeism and Hinduism. Like the Hindus, it believes in the continual incarnation of God, or in Avatars. Like the Manichees, it regards the flesh as evil. (The Manichees regarded it as unlawful to kill or commit suicide, but if one of their members was ill, they thought him lucky and tried to help him out of the world by starvation and neglect.)

The most frequently repeated story about the Khlysty concerns their method of worship. This was always held in the utmost secrecy. The celebrants were dressed in white, and danced around a fire or a tub of water, chanting their hymns. Yussupov's account of their practices declares:

> They attained this heavenly communion by the most bestial practices, a monstrous combination of the Christian religion with pagan rites and primitive superstitions. The faithful used to assemble by night in a hut or forest clearing, lit by hundreds of tapers. The purpose of these *radenyi*, or ceremonies, was to create a religious ecstasy, an erotic frenzy. After invocations and hymns, the faithful formed a ring and began to sway in rhythm, then to whirl round and round, spinning faster and faster. As a state of dizziness was essential to the 'divine flux', the master of ceremonies flogged any dancer whose vigour abated. The *radenyi* ended in a horrible orgy, everyone rolling on the ground in ecstasy or in convulsions. They preached that he who is possessed by the spirit belongs not to himself but to the spirit who controls him and who is responsible for all his actions and for any sins he may commit.

Finally the lights were blown out, and the worshippers coupled freely—the results, according to one writer, frequently being incestuous.

This is an interesting account, but it should not be taken too seriously. No doubt this kind of thing occurred sometimes; but it was not the rule. Conybeare's description is less sensational. The celebrants danced around the tub of water (which, he says, would begin to boil and give off a golden steam *of its own accord*) and flagellated one another, meanwhile chanting their hymns, many of them containing nonsense words that are supposed to be the utterance of the Holy Spirit. Some of them would have hallucinations and declare that a raven or a mother and child were rising from the vapours of the tub. They would finally collapse with exhaustion, and lie asleep for hours. No doubt these rites often led to orgies in the dark. They are reminiscent of the modern snake handling cults of southern America described by William Sargant in *Battle for the Mind*:

> The descent of the Holy Ghost on these meetings, which were reserved for whites, was supposedly shown by the occurrence of wild excitement, bodily jerkings, and the final exhaustion and collapse, in the more susceptible participants. Such hysterical states were induced by means of rhythmic singing and hand-clapping, and the handling of genuinely poisonous snakes . . . brought several visitors unexpectedly to the point of collapse and sudden conversion. But a young male visitor . . . was attending these meetings with the deliberate object of seducing girls who had just been 'saved'. The fact is that . . . protective inhibition causes a breakdown and leaves the mind highly susceptible to new behaviour patterns. . . .

No doubt a great deal of this kind of thing occurred with the Khlysty.

If, in fact, the Khlysty existed as early as the fourteenth century, then it is possible that it was a branch of a strange, anarchic mysticism that developed in Germany in the latter half of the Middle Ages. This mysticism was a revolt against the intellectualism and asceticism of the church, and its adherents called themselves 'Brethren of the Free Spirit'. They preached that every man is God, that every powerful impulse is 'revelation', that a man and woman copulating on an altar are worshipping God as validly as if they were praying or taking the Eucharist. It took Rome two centuries of torture and execution to stamp out this doctrine. By that time, it may well have filtered into Russia. There is a powerful mystical impulse in the Russian temperament.

The Skoptzy were a development of the Khlysty, and should be mentioned here to complete the picture of the background of religious dissent in Russia. The Khlysty judged a man's 'Christhood' by his ability to suffer bodily pain. Daniel Philipov was, according to tradition, crucified twice. Philipov's 'spiritual son' and successor, Ivan Suslov, went one better, and was crucified three times (either at the order of Alexis or Peter the Great). He was also tortured by red-hot irons, and had his skin flayed off him. (On this occasion, a virgin managed to get hold of his skin, and handed it over to him when he rose from his third crucifixion.) Philipov died in 1700, ascending bodily to heaven. Suslov, who had carried his preaching to Moscow, and established his right to remain there by refusing to stay dead, died about three years later.

Seventy years later, an ancient lady called Akulina Ivanovna was known by the Khlysty as 'the mother of God'. It was she who recognized the 'Christhood' of a man called Ivanov, who became reverenced under the name of Kondrati Selivanov, and became the founder of the Skoptzy. Selivanov went further in asceticism than the Khlysty, and declared that men should be castrated, and that women should have their breasts amputated and (if they could bear it) also have their genitals mutilated. In his early fifties, shortly after 'the mother of God' had recognized him as her spiritual son, Selivanov emasculated himself with a red-hot iron. (Later he declared that he had done this at fourteen; even his followers did not accept this estimate.) By this time, Catherine the Great was on the throne; she had murdered (or connived at the murder) of her husband, Peter the Third. This caused her some trouble, for Selivanov claimed to be Peter the Third. Later, a Don cossack, Pugachev, assumed the title and led a rebellion that was very nearly successful. Pugachev was finally caught and taken to Moscow in an iron cage, where he was executed with characteristic barbarity—his hands and feet were cut off and he was quartered alive.[1] Again, in 1768, a Serbian adventurer successfully posed as Peter III and seized the principality of Montenegro in what is now Yugoslavia.

Selivanov's assumption of the title seems to have led to no violent repercussions; he was captured and placed in a mental home in the capital. When Alexander I came to the throne in 1801, he was released. By this time he had many disciples among the wealthy and influential, and he was allowed to conduct his 'religion' openly. He wrote a book called *The Passion* which circulated widely, and he mutilated a hundred adults with his own hand. It was at this time that he actually changed his name from Ivanov to Selivanov. He continued to declare that he was Peter III, and his followers carried a coin with a picture of the sovereign on it (presumably it must have resembled Selivanov) and many kept pictures of the prince as an ikon, and said their prayers in front of it. Selivanov lived until 1830, by which time he was well over a hundred years old. He had been interned in a monastery in Suzdal for the last ten years of his life, but this did not diminish his influence; his followers made it a place of pilgrimage. His followers—there were still many thousands of them at the time of the October revolution—believe that he will reappear in the neighbourhood of Irkutsk when the number of his followers reaches 144,000, and will inaugurate the day of Judgment. The 144,000 will have to be virgins, male and female. Children born into the sect grow up with the know-ledge that they will be mutilated when they reach puberty, any who try to escape are hunted down and assassinated, according to Conybeare. Mutilation is not obligatory among women, but is apparently expected. Sometimes the removal of a nipple is regarded as sufficient.

Sacheverell Sitwell has written of the Skoptzy in his *Roumanian Journey*, and tells of a typical case that took place in 1868 (when Selivanov was generally believed to be still alive, although he had been dead for thirty-eight years). This took place in Tambov, and concerned a rich merchant called Plotitsine from Morshansk.

---

[1] The history of this rebellion was written by Pushkin, who also describes it in a short novel *The Captain's Daughter*. The barbarity of the punishment is, to some extent, justified by the atrocities committed by Pugachev and his followers, who often tortured whole families of landowners to death.

Some of his servants were arrested for failure to pay taxes, and the merchant's frantic efforts to get them released aroused suspicion of the police, who investigated his house. It was discovered to be a colony of about forty Skoptzy, many of them described as 'beautiful young girls'. The men were flabby, with woman-like hips and high-pitched voices; the women who had suffered the operation (not all of them) were almost indistinguishable from the men. All were tried and sent to Siberia.

It might seem that the Skoptzy would at least escape the accusation of sexual orgies so often made against the Khlysty, but this is not so. It is reported that many of the women were mutilated only perfunctorily, and actually became prostitutes who earned money for the communal treasury. Many men performed the operation on themselves, and halted before they emasculated themselves. These Skoptzy were known as the Skoptzy of the Lesser Seal, to distinguish them from the fully mutilated members of the Greater Seal. It is therefore possible that the accusations of sexual orgies made against the Skoptzy may have a foundation in fact.[1]

The Khlysty and the Skoptzy would not be the only strange sects that Rasputin probably encountered on his journeys through Russia. There was a sect of Ticklers, in which the men tickled the women to induce religious ecstasy; sometimes the tickling resulted in a state of exhaustion that ended in death, and those who died were regarded as lucky at having achieved salvation. B. Z. Goldberg mentions various suicide sects which seem to be related to the Skoptzy. In the reign of Alexander the Second, a man named Shodkin founded such a sect, and led his followers into a cave, which they proceeded to seal up. Two women became panic stricken and broke out. Shodkin then called upon his followers to kill one another before the police arrived. The children were murdered first, then the women; when the police arrived, only Shodkin and two of his acolytes were alive.

Such stories as this may seem to contradict the assertion that the Russians are not naturally religious. But this is one of the paradoxes of the Russian character. The peasants portrayed in Chekhov, Gorki, Sologub, seem as incapable of deep conviction as the Normandy peasants portrayed in Maupassant; one would

[1] See B. Z. Goldberg's *The Sacred Fire* (University Books, New York).

imagine all their motivations to be material. On the other hand, this is the reason that they can be convinced by extremist doctrines; their spirituality is a violent reaction to the narrowness of their lives.

Rasputin himself was such a paradox. His religious conviction was total and sincere, yet his spirituality was not of the traditional Russian type. There was no ecstasy of self-abandonment, none of the passionate desire for martyrdom that is the constant theme of the Russian saints from Theodosius onward. He believed wholly in the kingdom of the spirit, but he never wanted to reject the world. This is difficult for a Westerner to understand; the West keeps the world and the spirit in different compartments. On the one hand there is Robert Burns; on the other, St Francis of Assisi; and the Westerner cannot conceive of the two occupying the same body. But understanding of Rasputin must be based on the recognition that he contained elements of both, and had no difficulty in reconciling them.

Note: The following notes from Johannes Nohl's *The Black Death* seems to confirm the supposition that the Khlysty may have derived from the Brethren of the Free Spirit:

'The bas reliefs . . . in French churches . . . represent erotic scenes. In the Cathedral of Alby a fresco even depicts sodomites engaged in sexual intercourse. Homosexuality was also well known in parts of Germany, as is proved by the trials of the Beghards and Beguins in the fourteenth century, particularly in the confessions of the brethren Johannes and Albert of Brünn, which are preserved in the Greifswald manuscript. From these it is evident that the Brethren of the Free Mind did not regard homosexuality as sinful. "And if one brother desires to commit sodomy with a male, he should do so without let or hindrance and without any feeling of sin, as otherwise he would not be a Brother of the Free Mind." '

In a Munich manuscript, we read: 'And when they go to confession and come together and he preaches to them, he takes the one who is the most beautiful among them and does to her all according to his will, and they extinguish the light and fall one upon the other, a man upon a man, and a woman upon a woman, just as it comes about. Everyone must see with his own eyes how his wife or daughter is abused by others, for they assert that no one can commit sin below his girdle. That is their belief.'

Other curious doctrines, 'such as that incest is permissible, even when practised on the altar, that no one has the right to refuse consent, that Christ risen from the dead had intercourse with Magdalena, etc., all indicate the deterioration and confusion of moral ideas caused by the great plagues, particularly that of 1348' (i.e. at about the time when tradition affirms the Khylsty first appeared in Russia).

CHAPTER TWO

THE WANDERER

ONE of the most persistent stories in books about Rasputin is that he preached that sin is necessary to salvation. This is the form it is given in *Rasputin Speaks*, George Sava's book that claims to be a transcript of the words of Rasputin's ghost:

The greatest of these Christs incarnate [of the Khlysty] was Radaev . . . [who admitted]: 'I was well aware that I was breaking the law of man, but my acts proceed from God. Therefore it follows that the women who have sinned with me are more pleasing to Him than those who have resisted me and remained virtuous. For God has appeared in me and taken my flesh; and it is He who has sinned in the flesh, so that sin might be destroyed. It is only the man who debases himself through sin whose penitence is truly acceptable to God. I have debased the women who sacrificed their chastity to me so that they might not be proud and vain of their virtue. What can bring pride lower than abasement and defilement through sin?'

And Rasputin, according to Sava, made the doctrine his own.

Priests and monks, jealous of their authority, said that I staged satanic orgies in the woods under the pretext of divine worship. They asserted that girls—my sisters—submitted to my caresses and that we made huge bonfires of twigs and boughs, round which we danced, singing hymns. So far, they spoke truth. But did I not also say, crying loud above the crackling flames: 'Abase yourselves through sin. Try the flesh and mortify your pride through degradation?'

44

Apparently the spirit of Rasputin had forgotten that he had only one sister, and that she had been drowned.

The gospel that Rasputin preached to his followers in Pokrovskoe was almost certainly less spectacular than this. No reliable source quotes him as advocating salvation through sin. The source of the story about the orgies seems to be Father Peter, the village priest, who sent a complaint to the Bishop of Tololsk, and caused the police to investigate Rasputin's prayer meetings. Rasputin was apparently examined by some representative of the bishop, who found his doctrines unexceptionable, and who was impressed by his piety. The police also made two surprise raids, hoping to interrupt a Khlysty celebration, but were again disappointed—perhaps because the local policeman was one of Rasputin's admirers, and warned him in time.

In any case, Rasputin never remained in Pokrovskoe for more than a few months at a time. Sometimes he stayed throughout the winter; but as soon as the spring came, he packed his bundle and again took to the road. We have no details of any kind about the years between 1894 (when Father Peter probably made his complaint) and 1900, except that a son, Dmitri, was born in 1895, and a daughter, Maria, in 1898. A second daughter, Varvara, was born in 1900. Rasputin continued to wander and preach, and stories of his increasing reputation filtered back to Pokrovskoe. He was reputed to have the gift of prophecy, to possess a second sight that made it impossible to deceive him, and to be capable of healing illnesses by the laying on of hands. (This latter point must be dealt with in a later chapter.) He was also noted for his generosity. Many of his followers made him gifts of money or valuables; he immediately gave them away to the needy. Periodically, he sent money home to his family. Many were prepared to regard him as a saint. But even at this early stage, there were stories that the *staretz* was capable of seducing his female converts. Women who went to him expecting to hear a sermon were sometimes disconcerted when the preacher pressed them to his bosom or suggested that they remove some of their clothes. But Rasputin was unpredictable; his manner could change in a moment— particularly if the women showed signs of nervousness—and he would become the spiritual adviser, apparently incapable of lust. A woman who saw these two faces of Rasputin in St

Petersburg said that she did not know whether he was a saint or a devil.

The obvious answer is: neither. Rasputin's nature differed completely from those of other 'holy men' of his time—men like Bishop Theophan, the monk Illiodor, or Father John of Cronstadt. The Russian saint is usually an ascetic; in this sense, Rasputin was not at all Russian. He was, admittedly, a vegetarian who fasted frequently and who avoided drinking vodka. But in other respects, his nature was closer to that of the American poet Whitman, or even to the Hindu saint, Ramakrishna. The Whitmanesque aspect can be seen in his travel diary; for example, in his description of the sea:

> How shall I tell of that great calm? As soon as I left Odessa on the Black Sea, there was calmness on the sea, and my soul became one with the sea and slept in quietness. Even as the sea, so is the boundless power of the soul.

The pages that follow bring to mind Whitman's *Sea Drift*, or certain pages of *Thus Spoke Zarathustra*. Rasputin is troubled also by human stupidity: 'The waves broke on the sea, and there was alarm in my soul. Man loses the semblance of consciousness, walks as though in a mist. . . . There is more sickness on shore than at sea.' There is a curiously pagan spirit in the pages of the travel diary. The man who writes them is certainly no charlatan. He occasionally descends to platitudes, but this is not a man who has to live in the eyes of other people. He is capable of being alone; in fact, he knows himself best when he is alone. There is a feeling of the true poet about him. It is also obvious that, in spite of the depth of his feeling for Christian imagery and symbolism, he is a pagan—or perhaps simply God-intoxicated, like Ramakrishna. In reading accounts of him, one is reminded frequently of the Hindu saint. His daughter writes: '. . . my father did not separate religion from joy; his transports of exaltation often developed from pleasures of the most temporal kind, and when others thought him clumsy or ridiculous he felt rising in his soul an irresistible buoyancy which he hardly distinguished from the fervour of prayer'. Even Yussupov, a hostile witness, describes the fervour and excitement with which Rasputin talked 'religious platitudes'. Like Ramakrishna, Rasputin had something clumsy and child-like about him, and his attitude to people was usually trusting and affectionate. And, like Ramakrishna, his religious excitement tended to express itself in song and dance. His daughter writes: 'Like so many Russians, he had always adored the dance. . . . He would be driven on in the dance by the surge of feeling that the music awakened in him, and the intoxication of rhythm in his spirit was not very far removed from the religious transports which at other times he was capable of feeling.' He was religious because his vitality expressed itself as love and trust, not because he felt the need to be 'saved'. Both Rasputin and Ramakrishna preached that all religions are of equal worth and constitute different means of reaching God.

Reading about his St Petersburg period, it is difficult to see how it can be maintained that Rasputin was a plausible scoundrel. One witness described how he received a series of suppliants. One rich man wants help with a railway concession, and offers Rasputin a thick bundle of notes. Without even glancing at them, Rasputin thrusts them into his pocket, and promises to help. The next is an old woman who has lost her means of livelihood; Rasputin hands her the bundle of notes, again without looking at them, and turns to the next suppliant.

But where sex is concerned, he is closer to Whitman than Ramakrishna. For him, it is obviously another healthy and vital expression, like dancing. He is not unhealthily obsessed by the sordid aspects of sex, like his contemporary Andreyev (whose play *Anathema* Rasputin had banned). Brothels disgust him; on one occasion, when a rich friend sends a car for him and then has him taken to a brothel, he returns home in a fury and refuses to speak to his friend for some days. But his attitude to sex is pagan, and he does not count it a sin to sleep with some of his admiring converts. This seems to be the simple truth of the matter; sex was Rasputin's weakness—which was a pity, since it provided his enemies with the ammunition they needed. He was not a satyr; it was by no means the deepest need of his nature. But the writers who have described Rasputin's Dionysian orgies with his female converts were probably nearer the psychological truth of the matter than they suspected. Rasputin was closer to Nietzsche's Zarathustra than to most of the Christian saints.

By the year 1900, Rasputin was famous in Siberia. He was approaching his middle thirties, a thin man of middle height with broad shoulders.[1] He has a brown beard that is somewhat thin and straggly, and the outline of his chin can be seen clearly through it. His hands, although coarse and horny, are long and well shaped. The eyes are blue-grey, and very piercing; but the expression on his face is so habitually good-natured that they are not at first noticeable. He has a bald patch above his forehead with a kind of scar; Yussupov says that this came from a blow administered when he was beaten for horse-thieving. He may well be right (although Rasputin's only term in prison was for perjury). The long brown hair is parted down the middle. His manner is cheerful; he overflows with benevolent vitality, and his face becomes childishly pleased when he sees someone he likes. This makes him popular among the peasants, whose hard lives have inhibited such a natural expression of warmth. He has a reputation as a healer, and this is derived partly from his hypnotic powers, and partly from his atmosphere of benevolence. In fact, his benevolence is an important part of his hypnotic powers, since it lulls resistance and produces a feeling of trust. He does not seem in any way to be a dangerous man; he is completely unlike the menacing, powerful figure with glaring eyes portrayed by his early biographers. The only people who instinctively dislike him are those who stand on their pride, or who place great importance on producing an impression. For these, Rasputin's ease of manner is an affront, and his charm is a confidence trick. They feel that Rasputin is something of an actor; they note how well he can modulate his voice, how, in spite of the thick Siberian accent, it can be persuasive or compelling, and yet how he avoids giving an impression of glibness by a trick of hesitating, or even stammering slightly.

After his 'conversion', Rasputin managed to stay out of trouble with the police; but in September 1900 he came close to it. A woman called Lisavera Nicholaevna Bul, itinerant veil dancer, came to the police station in the Verkuta quarter of Tobolsk, and reported that Rasputin had tried to murder her. According to her story, she had been wandering along a road between

He was not tall and heavily built, as most of his biographers affirm.

Fagast and Kazan on August 31, when she came upon Rasputin lying in a field with two small girls, and apparently engaged in committing some sexual offence with them. Rasputin leapt up and chased her, and she ran away over the fields, finally managing to throw off his pursuit under cover of darkness. She was certain that he intended to murder her. It took her three days to find her way to Tobolsk, where she arrived on September 2.

The police were suspicious. The woman explained that she took jobs as a dancer with travelling circuses or theatrical troupes. They probably asked her why she had come all the way to Tobolsk—700 miles from the scene of the alleged offence—instead of going to Kazan, only forty miles away? And how had she managed to travel 700 miles in three days?

At all events, Rasputin could not be found—not surprisingly —and no charge was pressed. Later, when Rasputin was interviewed, the woman herself could not be found—probably by this time she was dancing somewhere at the other side of Siberia. The complaint eventually found its way into the Ohkrana archives. No doubt the police were right to treat the matter with suspicion. No offences against children had been reported; it was her word against Rasputin's. If she had some kind of a grudge against him, then her accusation would be an ingenious way to attack his increasing reputation as a holy man, for even if he was acquitted, people would remember the accusation. If this was her motive, the plot misfired.

For ten years Rasputin was a wanderer who returned home at long intervals. We have no record of what happened to him during this time or where he travelled, although it seems that one of the places where he gained considerable influence was the town of Kazan, the city that had been the capital of the Golden Horde, and that was more oriental than Russian. One biographer begins his book with a colourful description of Kazan, and of Rasputin surrounded by suppliants—mostly sick people who have come to be cured—and has a scene in which Rasputin cures a paralysed man by merely ordering him to stand up and walk.[1] The scene may have some basis in fact; at least it seems certain that Rasputin had a considerable reputation as a healer in Kazan.

[1] Heinz Liepman, *Rasputin, A New Judgement.*

He also made friends with a family called Katkoff, with whom his daughter went to live in 1908.

Maria Rasputin describes her first clear memory of her father. She and her brother Dmitri were playing in the street when a stranger appeared 'carrying a bag at his side, and seeming to walk with effort. He was a tall man with a long brown beard and eyes a little strange, but very gentle, set in a tired face. He looked like one of those pilgrims or singers who often used to arrive at nightfall in Pokrovskoe and spend the night with peasants, who would readily offer them hospitality. . . .' On this occasion also, Rasputin's wife failed to recognize him and asked: 'What do you want, my good man?' The inference is that his absences were for long periods, and his wife did not usually expect to see him.

Maria Rasputin mentions that they then went into their cottage (*isba*). The extant photograph of Rasputin's house in Pokrovskoe shows a building that could certainly not be described as a cottage, so it is to be presumed that at this time (1903) Rasputin's reputation as a healer brought him no material gains. But not long afterwards the family moved into the large house on the main street of Pokrovskoe with a garden and a courtyard. It seems, then, that the year 1903 was a turning point in Rasputin's life. Until this time, his reputation had been mainly among peasants; but in this year he was taken up by the nobility.

It is not certain who was responsible for bringing Rasputin to St Petersburg. Several biographers mention a rich widow from Kazan called Bashmakova, but no one seems to know anything about her.

It seems probable that the credit for 'discovering' Rasputin should go to the Grand Duchess Militsa. Militsa was one of two sisters—the other being called Anastasia—who exercised considerable influence over the Tsarina. They were the daughters of King Nikita of Montenegro (now in Yugoslavia), and were married to two Grand Dukes, Peter Nicholaievitch and Nicholas Nicholaievitch.[1] Like so many women in St Petersburg high society, they regarded themselves as 'mystics'—that is to say that they were interested in religion, magic, spiritualism and

[1] 'Grand Duke' is a title given to brothers and sisters, and to children and grandchildren of the Tsar.

table rapping. They had interested the Tsarina in their seances for a time, but her spiritual advisers told her that it was sinful, so that this particular link between the 'Montenegrins' was broken. Militsa had also been responsible for introducing the Tsarina to a curious charlatan called Philippe Nizier-Vachot, of whom more must be said later.

According to Sir Bernard Pares (who was acquainted with the Grand Duchess), it was Militsa who had discovered Rasputin in Kiev; he was sawing wood in a courtyard—presumably of a monastery. Naturally, she invited him to St Petersburg.[1] And it was from this point, as Maria Rasputin tells us, that her father's fame began to increase, so that his returns to Pokrovskoe became something of an event.

Rasputin's first visit to St Petersburg was almost certainly in 1903. He was fortunate in almost immediately attracting the attention of the Tsarina's spiritual adviser, Father John of Cronstadt.

Father John Sergeieff of Cronstadt—a small fortified town near St Petersburg—was a genuinely saintly man who had a reputation for prophecy. He had been appointed priest of Cronstadt in 1855, and within a decade or so his church had become a place of pilgrimage. Before becoming a favourite of the Tsar Nicholas, he had been the confessor of Alexander III, and had been present at his deathbed. His qualifications for becoming the Tsar's spiritual guide were ideal. Politically he was a complete reactionary who believed in imperial absolutism; even an admirer has described his views on social questions as 'mediaeval'. And yet he was completely unworldly; some of his writings have become classics of Russian spirituality, and his canonization is still expected by many of the devout in Russia. He was famous for the power and urgency of his prayers, and his miraculous cures were effected by continuous prayer by the bedside of the patient. He also established a startling custom of

---

[1] Heinz Liepman offers a completely different account. He claims that Rasputin had been noticed as early as 1902 by the secret police, and that Prince Pirakov, one of the leaders of the Union of True Russians, decided that he might be used to counteract the influence of various charlatans and 'miracle workers' at court. He does not explain how Rasputin came to the attention of Prince Pirakov in Kazan.

public confession. In Russia, confession must be heard immediately before communion; but Father John's church was sometimes packed with hundreds waiting for communion. He therefore suggested that everyone should call their sins aloud in unison, and ask forgiveness. It was an impressive spectacle—hundreds, sometimes thousands of penitents, shouting their sins aloud and sobbing and beating their breasts.

In 1903, Father John was seventy-four, and had five more years to live. He spent as much time as possible in Cronstadt, but also came to celebrate mass in a cathedral in St Petersburg. It was here that Rasputin met him.

The usual account describes how John of Cronstadt had held up the sacraments and repeated the words 'Approach in faith and in the fear of God', when suddenly he cried 'Stop'. He then beckoned to a bearded and ragged pilgrim standing at the back of the church—Rasputin—and told him to approach. He first blessed Rasputin and then, to everyone's surprise, asked to be blessed in return.

The story is substantially true, but it was not—as Fülöp-Miller suggests—a proof of Father John's spiritual insight. Rasputin had been introduced to the priest the day before—in fact, had probably visited Father John and his wife at their home in Cronstadt. The priest's approval may not have been based entirely upon his perception of Rasputin's spirituality. At this time, Rasputin was as violent a reactionary as 'the seer' (as Father John was known to his admirers); their views on the absolute authority of the monarch, the wickedness of liberals and the evil influence of the Jews, corresponded exactly. (Rasputin, however, had more excuse than Father John, since he knew nothing of politics. It is greatly to his credit that, when he had acquired more experience, he became an opponent of anti-Semitism[1] and sympathetic to the liberals. Only his views on the Tsar remained unchanged.)

Rasputin's visit to St Petersburg in 1903 lasted at least five months. We know, from the account of the monk Illiodor, that Rasputin was there in late December. We also know that on his way to St Petersburg in late July, he paid a visit to Sarov, near Nijni Novgorod. At this time, the Tsar had decided to canonize a monk called Seraphin, in the hope that the saint would inter-

[1] He was later responsible for several edicts that benefited the Jews.

cede for the birth of a male heir to the throne. According to the hostile author of *The Fall of the Romanoffs:*

> The ill-famed Rasputin, who later attracted so much public notice, but who at that time was an obscure person unknown to the Sovereigns, was present at the canonization ceremonies, in the guise of a travelling pilgrim or . . . Staretz. He prayed for a long time before the silver shrine containing the relics, his devotional prostration resembling a trance. Subsequently he was heard to prophesy to the assembled crowd that a new miracle was about to take place, and that a year would not elapse before the birth of the long-expected Heir to the Russian Throne would gladden the country.

Rasputin's prophecy proved to be correct; the boy in whose life Rasputin was to play so important a part was born on August 12, 1904, unfortunately he suffered from (hereditary) haemophilia.

The meeting with John of Cronstadt may have led to another contact that was yet another step towards the throne, for it is probable that Father John sent Rasputin to the Archimandrite Theophan, the Inspector of the Theological Academy at St Petersburg. Theophan was another favourite of the Tsarina, a completely unworldly man who was, nevertheless, a political reactionary. Fülöp-Miller has a circumstantial account of Rasputin's meeting with Theophan which is probably pure invention. The scene is the Academy, and the peasant Rasputin—who is staying in the guest house—is listening to a number of theology students engaged in dispute. They draw him into the discussion with the intention of making fun of his answers, but after a while, begin to realize that his simple, direct insight into the scriptures is profounder than their book-learning. They become so interested in his ideas that no one notices the entrance of the rector of the Academy, the Archimandrite Theophan, a 'frail old man' with 'dreamy blue eyes'. He listens for a while, and then begins to ask Rasputin questions, particularly about the meaning of sin. The moukik answers: 'Our saviour and the holy fathers have denounced sin, since it is a work of the evil one. But how can you drive out evil, little father, except by sincere repentance? And how can you sincerely repent if you have not sinned?' Rasputin then proceeds to hypnotize the Archimandrite when he tries to answer: 'only Rasputin's bright, glittering eyes seem to be fixed points'. The old man thinks about it all night, and by the following morning is convinced that Rasputin is right. Accordingly, he proposes that Rasputin should meet Bishop Hermogen of Saratov (whom Maria Rasputin describes as the most popular man in Russia), and together the two Archimandrites propose that Rasputin should become a member of the Union of True Russians, and help them to drive the charlatans out of the court of the Tsars.

Presumably Fülöp-Miller introduces the hypnosis to explain how a man of Theophan's capacity could be convinced by such an absurd piece of illogicality. (Any orthodox churchman would reply: We are in sin all the time; why should we sin more?) But he does not explain why, in that case, Theophan continued to be a dupe of Rasputin when the hypnosis wore off; nor why, in later years, the news of Rasputin's sexual misdemeanours came as such a shock to Theophan.

A less spectacular, but probably more accurate account, is given by Sir Bernard Pares:

> There was at that time at the religious academy of St Petersburg an exceptional young man who was training for the monkhood and came later to be known as the monk Illiodor. He tells us that it was on December 29, 1903, that Rasputin appeared at the academy, a stocky peasant of middle height with ragged and dirty hair falling over his shoulders, tangled beard and steely grey eyes, deep set under their bushy eyebrows, which sometimes almost sank into pinpoints, and a strong body odour. He appeared as a man who had been a great sinner and was now a great penitent, drawing an extraordinary power from the experiences through which he had passed, As such he was received by Theophan. . . .

The monk Illiodor was, in some ways, almost as remarkable a man as Rasputin, and deserves a fuller description. He was some years younger than Rasputin, and was also of peasant origins. His real name was Sergei Trufanov. After his years of study at the Academy under Theophan, he became priest of Tsaritsyn, and immediately established a reputation by the power of his sermons. In fact, he probably modelled himself on Savonarola.

A photograph of him—sitting with Rasputin and Bishop Hermogen—shows a thin, Mongol-type face with high cheek bones, firm, tight lips, and the eyes of a fanatic.

His political position was curious; he was at once left wing and extremely reactionary. He hated Jews and intellectuals, and regarded the power of the Tsar as absolute. At the same time, he also hated the nobility, and preached a kind of peasant communism with the Tsar as supreme ruler. Most of his sermons were on the subject of the corruption of morals—which was real enough—or were denunciations of spiritualism. He also attacked the government and official incompetence. His language was so violent that he was frequently asked to moderate it; but he was in a powerful position, liked by the Tsar, protected by Theophan and Hermogen, admired and almost worshipped by his own congregation. He preached a pan-Slavism that owed much to Dostoevsky; he also believed that the Russian people were 'God-bearing' and should avoid all contact with the corrupt west.

He conceived a project for building a monastery called Mount Tabor, which would be a haven of exceptional purity. His impassioned sermons brought in a great deal of money, but still not enough to build the monastery; so he appealed for labour and materials, and set out to build it himself. The chief feature of Mount Tabor would be a tower built on a hill, from which he could preach to the multitude. He might well have succeeded in his dream if it had not been for the later clash with Rasputin.

Like Theophan, he also believed in Rasputin's purity; the doctrine of 'repentance through sin' would have met with his instant and violent rejection. His puritanism was aggressive; he visited dances, gambling establishments and brothels, and then denounced them from the pulpit, mentioning 'sinners' by name. He refused to appear in front of the Holy Synod to answer for his actions, and popular feeling was so strongly in his favour that there was no attempt on the part of the authorities to take repressive action.

Fülöp-Miller tells an amusing story of the first meeting between Rasputin and Illiodor—for which, however, there seems to be no foundation. According to Fülöp-Miller, Rasputin was taken to see Illiodor by Theophan and Hermogen. The monk was on his knees praying, and the three of them waited respectfully for him to finish. But Illiodor went on praying and kept them waiting. Finally, Rasputin interrupted him, then turned aside his fury by remarking: 'You pray well. But cease persecuting God with your prayers. Even He wants a rest sometimes. Come, these two have something they want to discuss with you.' Illiodor was too astounded to protest and, according to Fülöp-Miller, 'this divided state of mind, a blend of anger, disgust, impotence, fear and admiration, Illiodor never lost'.

But at the time when Rasputin met him, Illiodor was only a gifted student of theology at the Academy; so it is unlikely that this clash of personalities ever occurred.

The truth of the matter is almost certainly that Illiodor began by regarding Rasputin with youthful admiration, and his idea of a monastic community at Tsaritsyn was probably, to some extent, inspired by Rasputin. He was certainly, to begin with, Rasputin's most ardent supporter. Much later, he became his bitterest enemy, and plotted to murder him. Later still, he became a communist, and wrote a book denouncing Rasputin and blackening the Imperial Family.

Theophan and Illiodor introduced Rasputin to a man who possessed more power than either, Bishop Hermogen of Saratov, whom Maria Rasputin describes as 'the most popular man in Russia'. Hermogen was the moving spirit behind the Union of True Russians, a pan-Slavic movement that preached anti-Semitism, anti-Westernism and the absolute authority of the Tsar. It also had strong support at the Imperial court. (Russia, it should be observed, has always had a powerful movement of anti-Semitism; there were pogroms in every reign, and the Tsars have probably been responsible for the death of more Jews than Hitler.)

Rasputin's power and sincerity impressed them. He was a peasant, and seemed to bear out Dostoevsky's prophecy that a renewing vitality would spring from the Russian moujik. He agreed with them about the Jews, about the Tsar, and about the divine mission of the Russian people. None of them were astute enough to see that Rasputin was ambitious, and that his sincerity was combined with a peasant shrewdness. For Rasputin was by no means the person they took him for. From the beginning, he probably had his eye on the throne. (It seems likely that his visit to Sarov—and the prophecy about the male heir—was an early attempt to attract the attention of the royal couple.) He was not ambitious in the ordinary sense; he was not out for money, or even for political power. Rasputin was, in a strange way, a social climber, something of a snob. He wanted to be acknowledged by the great. He was driven by a will to power— to *personal* power. He knew he was stronger than anyone he had ever met, and he wanted everyone in Russia to acknowledge it. He wanted to be close to the sovereign because it was right that his personal power should be combined with the Tsar's political power.

Only this will to power can explain why Rasputin stayed in St Petersburg, even when he knew that the dynasty was collapsing, and that its collapse would involve his own destruction. He felt that he had the power to change history, and never ceased to believe in this power right to the end—even though it had been apparent, from June 29, 1914, that history had no intention of being changed.

In 1903, Rasputin was prepared to plunge into the current of Russian history. For a full understanding of what is to follow, it is now necessary to consider the historical forces that he was about to challenge.

CHAPTER THREE

HISTORY AS NIGHTMARE

As Nicholas II was being crowned, one of his highest decorations, the Order of St Andrew, came loose and fell to the floor, and he interpreted this as an evil omen for his reign. His feelings were strengthened by a disaster that occurred later in the day. Presents were distributed to vast crowds; but for some reason, the Hodynka field, that had been chosen for the distribution, was covered with trenches cut for military exercises. The planks covering some of these trenches gave way under the weight of people, and more than two thousand were trampled to death. The Tsar knew nothing of this, and when a court official asked him if the celebrations should proceed, he waved his hand casually. Later, when told of it, he was horrified and decided to retire to a monastery to pray for his people. His advisers dissuaded him, and he attended a ball given by the French Ambassador instead.

Under the circumstances, it is not surprising that so many historians feel that the reign of Nicholas was predestined to end tragically.

Predestined or not, two people can be held responsible for that tragedy: Rasputin and the Tsarina. If there had been no Rasputin, there could have been no October Revolution. And if it had not been for the Tsarina's temperament, Rasputin could never have become the virtual ruler of Russia.

Still, no historical event can have its causes assigned with such precision. And in the case of the downfall of the Russian monarchy, the causes must be traced back over many centuries—before even the beginning of the Romanov dynasty.

The history of the Romanovs is an Elizabethan tragedy that lasts for three centuries. Its keynote is cruelty, a barbaric, pointless kind of cruelty that has always been common in the East, but that came to Europe only recently, in the time of Hitler. It begins with the reign of Ivan the Terrible, a contemporary of England's Queen Elizabeth. It was Ivan who established the idea of the Tsar (a word derived from Caesar) as the absolute master, whose power over his subjects had no limits whatever.

When Ivan the Fourth came to the throne, the boyars (or nobles) held most of the power, as in the England of King John. Among these, the family of the Shuiskys were most powerful. Most of the boyars were insolent and naturally violent. It was nothing for young noblemen in their early teens to take their dogs hunting and to pursue human game, allowing their animals to tear men into pieces. Ivan's childhood was made bitter by the insults of such young men. His mother had been murdered when he was seven; for the next six years, he had to allow himself to be bullied. Then one day, the Shuiskys set on Ivan's closest friend, Vorontsov, and beat him badly. They would have killed him, but Ivan pleaded for his life. Vorontsov was sent into banishment. Three months later, Ivan struck; his stable boys seized Prince Andrew Shuisky, Ivan's chief enemy, and threw him to·the hunting dogs. From then on, Ivan was the master.

For the next four years, his private life was appalling. He gave free reign to his vengefulness, his cruelty and his sensuality. This was mostly in sport, and his victims were chiefly the merchants—and their wives and daught rs, who were treated as Ivan's private harem. At seventeen, Ivan had himself crowned Tsar—the first Tsar of Russia, since none of his predecessors had dared to assume that title—and found himself a wife, Anastasia Romanov, whom he chose from two thousand girls assembled for his inspection. For the next ten years, Ivan attempted to be the ideal ruler; he surrounded himself with good counsellors—mostly of lowly origin—and instigated various reforms. He also began his career of conquest by throwing the Tatars out of Kazan. (The Tatars, or Mongols, had been the scourge of Russia for many centuries.) Other conquests followed. Then his wife died, and Ivan's character changed. It is charitable to believe that he went insane at about the age of twenty-seven. From then until his death his cruelty was unrestrained. He trusted no one. No one in his court was allowed to express an opinion that was not the Tsar's own; any such inclination was treated as disloyalty and immediately punished. The Tsar's two most reliable advisers were deposed. Many of his supporters fled to other countries, recognizing that no life was safe in the hands of this madman. The desertion of Ivan's childhood friend Kurbsky hurt him most. Ivan transfixed the foot of the messenger to the earth when the news was brought to him, and after the messenger had read aloud Kurbsky's farewell message, he had him tortured.

In his mid-thirties, Ivan decided on a curious action that is somehow typically Russian. He wandered out of the capital (Moscow) with no announced destination, and went to the village of Alexandrov, a hundred miles from Moscow. After several weeks had passed in anxiety and bewilderment for the court, Ivan explained that he had abdicated. A mission was sent from the capital to implore him to return, and Ivan finally consented. It seems that there was genuine fear and alarm when he disappeared. In spite of his cruelty, he was regarded as the indispensable figurehead. As the condition for his return, Ivan specified that all his actions should be condoned by the church and the boyars; everyone agreed to this. Ivan immediately took advantage of his new licence to begin a campaign of robbery and murder. He also divided Russia into two parts: his own personal property (which he called the *Oprichina*, or widow's portion), and the Zemshchina, which belonged to the nobles. He established a political security force to run the *Oprichina*, whose task was to spy on his enemies and destroy them; hence Ivan may be regarded as the inventor of the police state. His black-robed inquisitors toured the country executing the Tsar's vengeance—which, in effect, meant burning and torturing as they felt inclined.

His paranoia reached a kind of climax in the destruction of the city of Novgorod. The Tsar had some insane idea that Novgorod intended treason, so he marched there with an army, burning, raping and looting on the way. He arrived at the city in early 1570, and had a timber wall built round it to prevent any inhabitants from fleeing. Then for five weeks he directed an orgy of torture. Every day several thousand inhabitants of Novgorod were tortured to death in the presence of the Tsar and his depraved son Ivan. All kinds of refinements were invented; husbands and wives were forced to watch one another tortured; mothers saw their babies ill-treated before they themselves were roasted alive or beaten to death. More than sixty thousand people were murdered.

The Tsar then went on to Pskov with the intention of continuing with his orgy of torture, but for some reason altered his mind when he arrived.[1] The inhabitants received him kneeling, and assured him that his mercy was beyond belief.

At about this time, the 'wrath of God' came upon Russia in the form of plagues and famines. The peasants ate the bark from trees and any young children they could catch. Ivan forbade people to travel, and punished disobedience with being burnt alive. Moscow was accidentally burnt to the ground.

The remainder of Ivan's life followed the same curious pattern as the early part. His sexuality was unremitting (and it has been suspected that his insanity was the result of syphilis), his murders and cruelties never ceased. He carried a pointed iron staff, and frequently impaled courtiers who irritated him; one day in a rage, he killed his own son—no great loss to Russia, since the younger Ivan was as evil as his father. But he also talked periodically of becoming a monk, and on one occasion actually placed his crown on the head of a Tatar prince in his retinue and told him that he was now the Tsar; the prince ruled for a year. In the city of Wenden in Livonia, hundreds of citizens who had defied Ivan preferred to blow themselves up in a castle rather than die at his hands. Ivan then tortured to death all the remaining people of the town. His own counsellors and favourites often became his victims. One of the worst and most debauched of these was Prince Ivan Viscovaty. The Tsar had him hung upside down and sliced to death. He and his son then went to Viscovaty's house, and Ivan raped the grief-stricken widow while his son raped the eldest daughter.

Ivan's death, at the age of fifty-four, is somehow typical. He had become sexually incapable, and felt tired and ill. He

[1] Rimsky-Korsakov has written an opera on the subject.

summoned a number of soothsayers to the court, and they forecast his death for March 18, 1584. Characteristically, Ivan told them that they would be burnt alive on that day if he was still alive. Towards midnight on the 17th, Ivan reminded the soothsayers that they were to die the next morning; they pointed out that the day could not be said to have ended until the setting of the sun. The next day he played chess with Boris Godunov, one of his courtiers, but his king kept falling down. Then Ivan fell backwards, and a few minutes later was dead.

The first of the Tsars established a pattern that never changed until the downfall of the dynasty, four centuries later: personal absolutism and oppression.

The greatest of mysteries is that no one assassinated this tyrant in the early years of his reign; it is impossible to imagine Rome putting up with Caligula or Tiberius for forty years. Stranger still, there was universal and genuine mourning for him when he died. And yet these facts throw some light on the Russian character: fatalistic, slothful, anarchic, curiously deficient in idealism, childlike and irresponsible. It was the Russian character that Dostoevsky was writing about in *The Grand Inquisitor* when he makes the Inquisitor declare that people prefer slavery to freedom, because the burden of freedom is too heavy.

If it is true that a happy nation has no history, then Russia must be the unhappiest nation in the world, for its history has always been turbulent; the reign of Ivan the Terrible is typical.

Ivan left Russia exhausted and divided, and his reign was followed by the 'time of troubles', a period that has frequently been compared to the years immediately following the 1917 Revolution. Ivan's feeble-minded son Feodor ruled for a few years, then Boris Godunov seized power. He is generally suspected of murdering the rightful heir to the throne, the young prince Dmitri, but this may be slander, since Boris seems, on the whole, to have been a decent and level-headed man, with a force of character that had even compelled the respect of Ivan the Terrible. But Boris died after five years, and the throne was immediately seized by a man who claimed to be the lost Prince Dmitri. The true identity of this pretender will never be known; probably he was an instrument of the Romanovs, Boris's chief rivals for the throne. He was soon murdered by a mob incited by a Prince Shuisky, who became Tsar. Shuisky was quickly deposed, for the country was in chaos, and everyone was dissatisfied. Two more pretenders arose, both declaring themselves to be the lost Prince Dmitri. One was a runaway slave, Ivan Bolotnikov, who led a peasants revolt, but whose cruelties to landowners and their families were so atrocious that he lost the support of his military friends. No one quite knows what became of Bolotnikov, the first peasant to start a 'class war' and establish the pattern of revolt that later became so familiar in Russia. The other pretender was called The Thief, and he beseiged Shuisky in Moscow in 1608; however, he was murdered by one of his own followers. The throne was now offered to the son of the Polish king, and the outcome of this was that Poles occupied Moscow and many towns of Southern Russia, while Swedes— summoned to help Shuisky against The Thief—had seized Novgorod. There was yet another pretender in Pskov. But finally the Russians gained the upper hand, threw the Poles out of Moscow, and looked around for a Tsar. Their choice fell upon Micheal Romanov, a member of the same family as Ivan's first wife—the one he had chosen from a crowd of two thousand. (So four hundred years of Russian history depended on Ivan's act of choice.) The history of the Romanovs began with an Anastasia, and ended with an Anastasia—the girl who managed to escape the bullets of the revolutionaries in the Ekaterinberg cellar. In between the two Anastasias there were murders and assassinations, endless plots, and many revolts like the one of Bolotnikov. Ivan's long shadow falls down Russian history, and it seems as though cruelty and bloodshed will never cease.

It would be pointless to try to summarize the history of the next three hundred years; but it is a history of oppression of the great mass of the Russian people. And the factor whose importance it would be impossible to over-emphasize is that of serfdom. Since the time of the Mongol domination, 95 per cent. of the Russian people were virtually slaves. Boris Godunov had introduced certain statutes that tied the peasant to his owner's estate, but only as an emergency measure. And there was a time limit—five years—after which the serf was regarded as 'free'. The first two Romanov Tsars, Micheal and Alexis—both weaklings—extended this time limit, and Alexis finally abolished it altogether in 1649. The year that saw the execution of Charles the First in England saw the death of freedom in Russia. (There had, admittedly, been a feeble attempt to establish representative government under Micheal, but it soon died.)

The Romanovs were, on the whole, a dynasty of weaklings—with a few notable exceptions, of whom the most notable was Peter the Great, the son of Alexis. Peter europeanized Russia, built St Petersburg, and introduced many reforms. The one thing he did not do was to grant any more freedom to the serfs. Perhaps he remembered the revolt—of unparalleled cruelty and violence—of Stenka Razin, who came near to overthrowing his father's throne. (Razin—who is one of the heroes of Soviet mythology—was finally betrayed, and hideously tortured to death.) At all events, 'he ruled Russia with a rod of iron', in the words of R. D. Charques. Parts of the legend of Peter the Great are sympathetic to the western mind—his energy and enthusiasm, his interest in technology, his willingness to turn his hand to any manual task. But it must be remembered that he shared many of the oriental characteristics of Ivan the Terrible. He suppressed one military revolt with a ferocity that recalls Ivan; like Ivan, he also murdered his own son Alexis—in this case, not in a sudden rage, but with the preliminary of torture.

Peter the Great should have been succeeded by another Peter, the son of Alexis, but he died of smallpox in his teens, and the throne fell to Anna, Peter the Great's niece, who soon earned herself the nickname of 'Anna the Bloody'. Her cruelty was not sudden and violent, like Ivan's; it had a spider-like quality of patient malevolence.

Another grandson of Peter the Great became Peter the Third. He was boorish, brutish and probably mentally deficient, and he treated his young wife—a German girl called Catherine—like a servant. His wife—who had been originally a pure-minded and idealistic young girl—reacted by taking lovers. The first of these, Saltykov, was probably the father of her son Paul. Hence it is probable that all succeeding Tsars were Romanovs in name only. Another of her lovers, George Orlov, murdered her husband after a *coup d'etat*, so that Catherine became Empress of Russia. Her long reign brought many benefits and reforms to Russia—

but no freedom to the peasants. Any democratic tendencies she may have possessed were stifled by the revolt of Pugachev (already mentioned on page 40), whose cruelties gave her the impression that the Russian peasant was a wild beast who had to be kept chained. The French Revolution strengthened this conviction, and her reign closed in an atmosphere of oppression.

Catherine was succeeded by another madman, Paul, whose four-year reign was a nightmare that made the Russian people think that Ivan the Terrible was back. His madness took the form of military punctiliousness that made him capable of sending an officer to Siberia for wearing his hat at the wrong angle. His mother, Catherine the Great, had never intended that Paul should come to the throne; she intended to pass him over in favour of her grandson Alexander. Alexander finally took matters into his own hands, and had Paul murdered. This was in 1801, and brings us to the beginning of the 'century of reform', the century that was to see the accession of the last of the Romanovs.

The reign of Alexander the First began auspiciously for the Russian peasant. He dreamed of setting up some kind of representative government, and asked the brilliant Speransky—the son of a village priest—to draft a constitution. But the war with Napoleon gave him other things to think about; Speransky fell from favour, and Alexander became as much an autocrat as Peter or Catherine. He repented of the 'liberal delusions' of his youth. He added to the burden of the peasants by starting military colonies in which discipline was maintained by barbarous punishments; at the end of his reign there was more than half a million peasants in such colonies.

Alexander was always talking of abdicating and becoming either a monk or a private citizen in Switzerland. At the age of forty-eight, he seems to have carried out this decision. He went to Taganrog, and there gave it out that he was suffering from malaria. A certain Doctor Lee who was there records that 'His Majesty strenuously refused all medical assistance'. A priest was called to administer the Communion, but he was not summoned again, although Alexander 'died' four days later. Ten doctors made an examination of the corpse, and the royal physician,

Doctor Tarassov, drew up the report. In his memoirs he states that he abstained from signing it; yet the report bears his signature. The conclusion is that either Tarassov forgot he signed it, or that his signature was forged. At all events, the report is suspect, and the condition of the vital organs does not correspond to that of a person who dies of malaria. (For example, there was no hypertrophy of the spleen.) Alexander's body was hurried into its coffin, and the few who saw it said that the Tsar had changed beyond recognition. It is also mentioned that his back and loins were brownish-purple and red, which sounds unusual for a Tsar, whose skin might be expected to be white.

It is generally supposed that Alexander substituted another body for his own, and then disappeared. Eleven years later, a monk called Fedor Kusmich appeared in Siberia. He was regarded as something of a saint, and died in 1864 at the age of eighty-seven—which would have been Alexander's age if he had lived. During the last years of his life there was a widespread rumour that this mysterious man was Alexander I, and the historian Schilder, who wrote of Alexander's reign, accepted it as true. Tolstoy wrote a story about the monk Fedor Kusmich, in which he advances the theory that the idea of 'disappearing' came suddenly to Alexander in Taganrog when he saw a man being flogged to death; the man bore an extraordinary resemblance to himself. (Alexander had instituted this form of punishment— flogging to death by running the gauntlet—in his military colonies.) This would certainly account for the bruised condition of the body, but it does not explain what the Tsar was doing in an out-of-the-way seaport like Taganrog. It seems more probable that the Tsar planned the disappearance in advance.

In 1865, and again in the 1920s, Alexander's coffin was opened, and was found to be empty. The body of the badly bruised man who was suffering from syphilis (a disease from which Alexander was known to be immune) had vanished—probably with the connivance of Doctor Tarassov.

Maurice Paléologue, who wrote a life of Alexander the First, doubts whether Alexander was Fedor Kusmich, and advances the hypothesis that he actually died in a monastery in Palestine. Whatever happened to the 'enigmatic Tsar', it seems reasonably certain that he did not die in Taganrog in 1825.

The story of the end of Alexander the First is somehow typically Russian. (Ivan the Terrible also died as a monk—but the ceremony took place only in the last minutes of his life, when he was in a coma.) Only a Russian could begin his life as a reformer, continue as a reactionary with a streak of cruelty, and end it as an unknown *staretz*. Russians seem incapable of doing anything by halves.

Nicholas, Alexander's younger brother, came to the throne, and his first task was to stamp out a rising of officers, the Decembrist revolt. It is also typical of the Romanov Tsars that Nicholas should himself have undertaken to question the chief conspirators, which he did with such sympathy and warmth that they implicated themselves thoroughly; Nicholas then used the information against them and condemned the five leaders to be hanged. This extraordinary charm of manner characterized many of the Romanov Tsars, including the last of them.

There seems to be an ironic fate working in Russian history; whenever there is hope of reform, some revolutionary upsets it and puts back the clock. This is what happened in the case of Nicholas I. The Decembrist revolt brought a new tyranny to Russia. Behind this façade of total repression lay the usual incompetence and sloth. (It can be found portrayed inimitably in Gogol's *Dead Souls* and *The Government Inspector*.) Liberal hopes smouldered behind the censorship; it may well have been their repression—and consequent strengthening—that made this the golden age of Russian literature. Alexander had been a tyrant, but a wavering, vacillating tyrant; Nicholas was a military idiot of the same type as the murdered Tsar Paul, but less paranoiac. Russia has reason to be grateful for the stupidity that created the condition for the works of Pushkin and Gogol, the plays of Ostrovsky and the operas of Glinka.

His successor, Alexander the Second, was another militarist, but less strong-minded than Nicholas. (The history of the Romanovs is an almost constant succession of strong-minded and weak-minded Tsars.) He seems as much destined for tragedy as his grandson Nicholas. He started his reign with the idea of introducing reforms; and, in fact, took the immense step of abolishing serfdom. But the 'emancipation' was, in fact, only a slightly altered form of slavery. The peasants were allowed to purchase their land, but diehards and reactionaries made sure that the land was over-valued. Instead of the peasant cultivating the whole of the land for his master and taking what he needed to live, the land was divided between peasants and masters, so that in effect, the peasant only had half as much land as before, and had a crippling financial burden as well. It is hardly surprising if the peasants felt that the 'emancipation' was only another way of exploiting them.

Immediately after the manifesto that liberated the serfs (in 1861) came the first attempt on Alexander's life—someone shot into his carriage when he was returning from the Crimea. In the following two years there were two more plots, and in 1866, on the anniversary of Lincoln's assassination, there was an attempt which almost succeeded when a student approached the Tsar on his daily walk and levelled a pistol at him; a passer-by sprang on the assailant. Yet another attempt was made in 1867 when the Tsar was driving in procession in Paris with Napoleon III and the Kings of Prussia and Belgium. After a first shot that struck a horse, the pistol blew up and shattered the assassin's arm.

Having tried bullets, the assassins now tried dynamite. A terrorist called Zhelyabov laid an immense charge of nitroglycerine on a railway line so that its explosion would plunge the train into a ravine. A passing cart cut the wire, and nothing happened when Zhelyabov pressed the plunger. He engineered a second attempt, which involved burrowing eighty yards and laying the explosive under another railway line. This time it exploded and destroyed the train; but it was the Tsar's baggage train; the Tsar had decided to change the order of trains, and had already arrived in Moscow when the explosion occurred. Two months later, in February 1880, a tremendous explosion blew up a section of the Winter Palace. The Tsar would have been dining in the room where it occurred if it had not been for the belated arrival of a guest. A carpenter had smuggled nearly a hundredweight of dynamite into the palace and concealed it in the dining-room chimney. The explosion produced a panic among the people of St Petersburg—not for the Tsar's safety but for their own, and no one would book for the opera unless they were assured that the Tsar would not be there.

Predictably, these attempts on his life intensified the Tsar's conservatism, and the old censorship and police surveillance were intensified. But on the day when he was finally murdered, Alexander was carrying in his pocket a plan of imperial consultation that was to be the first step towards representative government. This was on March 1, 1881, when the Tsar was returning from an inspection of his troops. The day before, Zhelyabov had been arrested, which made the Tsar feel slightly more secure. But by way of precaution, Alexander decided to return to the palace by an unaccustomed route. Zhelyabov's accomplices had also taken the precaution of stationing several bomb throwers along all the possible routes. As the Tsar's carriage passed, one man threw a bomb that shattered the door of the carriage, wounding a Cossack and a boy. The Tsar solicitously got out of the carriage to look at the wounded man, and another bomb exploded behind him. It killed the assassin, but shattered both the Tsar's legs. Twenty other people were killed, and the explosion (the bomb was nitro-glycerine enclosed in thick glass) was so tremendous that it shattered windows for 180 yards. An hour later, the Tsar died in his palace, surrounded by his family.

Not surprisingly, the result of this death-bed scene was to imbue his son, Alexander III, with a hatred of all ideas of reform. Once again the revolutionaries had only succeeded in putting back the clock. The conspirators were hanged, and the chief of police, V. K. von Plehve, was commissioned to wipe out all traces of terrorist organizations in Russia. (He was himself later assassinated by a bomb.) He did this with cold efficiency. Alexander announced his faith in the principles of autocracy, in a manifesto drafted by the religious reactionary Pobedonostsev (who became the new Tsar's Grey Eminence). Censorship was renewed; all hopes of reform were repressed. Alexander III was a strong-willed giant of a man and, in Pares' words, he commanded public thought to stand still. A new atmosphere of claustrophobia descended. The young Tsarevitch Nicholas[1] was only thirteen when his father ascended the throne 'as a soldier mounts a breach', and for the next thirteen years, he saw his father reigning with his 'rod of iron', but always in fear for his life, a prisoner in his own palace. Alexander II had courted death by walking alone in public and being lax about security; his son was determined

[1] Tsarevitch: heir to the throne.

not to be vulnerable in the same way: he lived surrounded by policemen. His policies were stern and repressive. He established 'land captains' in rural districts who were, in effect, police agents with sinister powers, and orders to deal ruthlessly with the least sign of revolt. Inevitably, there were many attempts on his life, but the first serious shock to his system may not have been an assassination attempt. In 1888 the Imperial train was derailed under curious circumstances, and although many historians attribute this to the rottenness of the sleepers, Charles Lowe (in a book on Alexander III) has written:

> His carriage was blown to shreds, his faithful servants lay dead or dying . . . and when he looked around for his children, dreading the terrible possibilities . . . his little daughter . . . threw her hands about his neck and exclaimed . . . 'Oh papa dear, now they will come and murder us all.'

This devastation hardly sounds like the result of a rotten sleeper.

Confined to the palace of the murdered Paul I, afraid to eat a morsel of food that had not been prepared by his French cooks, deprived of exercise yet addicted to heavy meals, it is not surprising that Alexander III died prematurely in 1894, shattered by his attempt to hold back history.

At the time of his death, the peasant Grigory Rasputin was feeling the call to wander about Siberia as a *staretz*. The pale-faced, courteous but vacillating Nicholas II attended his father's funeral with a sad-eyed, beautiful girl whom he would marry later the same year. She was shy, neurotic and religious, and loved her husband with the same almost painful devotion with which he loved her.

The last act of the tragedy was ready to begin. It is fitting that R. D. Charques should call this chapter of his history of Russia 'Reaping the Whirlwind'.

CHAPTER FOUR

'GOD HELP RUSSIA'

THERE was something strange and ghost-like about the St Petersburg to which Rasputin came in 1905. Alexey Tolstoy has caught its essence admirably in his novel *Ordeal*:

Two centuries had passed like a dream: Petersburg standing on the edge of the earth in swamp and wilderness, had day-dreamed of boundless might and glory; palace revolts, assassinations of emperors, triumphs and bloody executions had flitted past like the visions of a delirium; feeble women had wielded semi-divine power; the fate of nations had been decided in hot and tumbled beds; vigorous strapping young fellows with hands black from tilling the soil had walked boldly up the steps of the throne to share the power, the bed and the Byzantine luxury of queens. . . .

Petersburg lived a restless, cold, satiated, semi-nocturnal life. Phosphorescent, crazy, voluptuous summer nights; sleepless winter nights; green tables and the clink of gold; music, whirling couples behind windows, galloping troikas, gypsies, duels at daybreak. . . .

In the last ten years huge enterprises had sprung into being. . . . Fortunes of millions of roubles appeared as if out of thin air. Banks, music halls, skating rinks, gorgeous public houses of concrete and glass were built, and in them people doped themselves with music . . . with naked women, with light, with champagne. . . .

An epidemic of suicides spread through the city. The

71

courts were crowded with hysterical women, listening eagerly to details of bloody and prurient crimes. Everything was accessible, the women no less than the riches. Vice was everywhere. . . .

And to the Palace, up the very steps of the Imperial throne, came an illiterate peasant with insane eyes and tremendous male vigour; jeering and scoffing, he began to play his infamous tricks, with all Russia as his plaything. . . .

There is very little exaggeration here. Peter the Great would have found it difficult to recognize the city he built. One might apply to St Petersburg the witticism that Clemenceau directed at America: that it was the only country that had passed from barbarism to decadence without the intervening stage of civilization.

It was a city of feverish artistic activity. Russian literature and Russian music had both passed their zenith; but their decline was producing strange and remarkable blooms. Most of the major figures were dead: Dostoevsky, Chekhov, Turgeniev, Tchaikovsky, Mussorgsky, Borodin. Only two giants remained: Tolstoy and Rimsky-Korsakov, and both encouraged this mystical and other-worldly tendency of the St Petersburg intelligentsia, Tolstoy by his doctrine of non-resistance, Rimsky-Korsakov by the nature of his later work, particularly his opera *The Invisible City of Kitezh*, which is at once the most mystical and the most Russian of his operas.

A few of the younger generation of writers were social revolutionaries—like Gorki. But most of them regarded themselves as artistic revolutionaries, and delighted in obscure symbolism and in a dreamy pessimism. The most widely discussed musician of the day was Alexander Scriabin, who believed that music would one day unite with all the other arts to produce an artistic experience of such power that men would become gods or supermen merely by listening to it. But his music has little enough of the superman about it. The titles of his major works indicate this: *Poem of Ecstasy*, *Divine Poem*, *Poem of Fire*. It is a music of continual dreamy ecstasy, like a sexual fever that never reaches the point of orgasm, a voluptuous, debilitating music of the nerves and senses. Scriabin himself was a selfish, self-indulgent little man, something of a libertine, who never encountered real adversity, and who died in 1915 of a boil on his lip.

Among the writers, the two most popular were Andreyev and Artsybashev, both sensualists and pessimists. Artsybashev at least began as an optimist in the Nietzschean novel *Sanine*, in which the hero sneers at the unhealthy moral preoccupation of most Russians, and preaches a doctrine of sunlight and frank sensuality. This book, published in 1906, had an enormous impact on Russian youth, who were eager to put its doctrines into practice. Probably no book in world literature has been responsible for the loss of so many maidenheads. But Artsybashev himself then became the typical Russian at whom Sanine had sneered, and his two remaining novels are full of suicide and a joyless sensualism. Artsybashev is a strange figure, who deserves more attention than he has received in English-speaking countries.[1]

Leonid Andreyev was a more total pessimist even than Artsybashev, and an even more 'typical Russian'. Gorki has described Andreyev's brilliant conversation, his obsession with suicide, his long bouts of heavy drinking (usually lasting several days), and the orgies with prostitutes that Andreyev seemed to regard almost as self-punishment. In Andreyev's view, all life is illusion and defeat, a long confidence trick on the part of the universe, and a truly honest and consistent man would kill himself at an early stage to express his disgust with the swindle.

The best of all descriptions of St Petersburg in the Rasputin period is contained in André Biely's novel *St Petersburg* (1913), dealing with the conflict between a bureaucrat father and his Terrorist son; the son is ordered to murder his father, and throughout the book—with its strange under-water atmosphere of greenish nightmare—there ticks the bomb in a sardine tin. Significantly, father and son are descendants of Tartars (Napoleon once remarked, 'Scratch a Russian and you find a Tartar') and the author makes much of this violent, irrational Asiatic element in the Russian character. The bomb also ticked behind the St Petersburg of Rasputin.

[1] See also my *Strength to Dream* and *Origins of the Sexual Impulse*.

Under the circumstances, then, it is hardly surprising that the Petersburg of Nicholas II was a city of moral disintegration, of feverish sexuality. It is true that there was a great deal of religious mysticism in the atmosphere; but this only precipitated the disintegration. There is an element in mysticism that makes for immorality. For example, the most penetrating religious thinker of the period, V. V. Rozanov, was also a political journalist; but he regarded politics as so unimportant that he would write an article for a conservative paper under his own name, then write a revolutionary article under a pseudonym. *Sub specie aeternitatis*, morality becomes unimportant.

In half a century St Petersburg had changed from the city of militarism and bureaucracy to the city of art and decadence. Rich men with artistic taste abounded. There was the millionaire Belaieff, who financed Scriabin; the 'Maecenas' of the opera, Mamontov, who launched Feodor Chaliapine, the greatest basso of modern times. There was Sergei Diaghileff, who began by editing an expensive art magazine, and whose Russian ballet was responsible for bringing Russia a new artistic prestige. Diaghileff discovered the talent of Rimsky Korsakov's pupil Stravinsky, and later gave much encouragement to Sergei Prokofief. He was also responsible for introducing Vaslav Nijinsky, the great male dancer, to the world outside Russia.

There is a story concerning Nijinsky that catches the essence of St Petersburg in the first decade of the century. Nijinsky came of a poor family, but had obtained a scholarship to the Imperial School of Dancing, and found himself, in his late teens, chaotically involved in the feverish social life of the capital. One night, Nijinsky and his friend Anatole Bourman visited the palace of Prince Yussupov (the father of the man who was later to murder Rasputin), which the prince had turned into a gambling casino and a club for 'artists'. (Typically, the government approved of such establishments; it was felt that providing the means for making an easy fortune would help to allay popular unrest!) Bourman and Nijinsky won 500 roubles, and Nijinsky insisted that they should spend it by treating several prostitutes to supper. They picked up six wretched drabs on the Nevsky Prospect, and drove to a poor restaurant where the guests would not feel out of place. Nijinsky then ordered an expensive supper (which had to be fetched from outside). The women grabbed the food and ate like animals; the spectacle was so nauseating that Nijinsky and Bourman were incapable of eating. The women then made advances, and when Bourman repulsed one of them, she tried to hit him with a bottle, which Nijinsky snatched away. They distributed the remainder of the money and fled. Afterwards, Bourman asked Nijinsky what had made him do this. He explained that he wanted to share his new prosperity with the miserable creatures whom he had often pitied on his way to the theatre. 'But it is too terrible. I won't do it again.'

There was a strange lack of communication between the upper and lower classes, unbridgeable even by good will. It was this, more than anything else, that finally brought about the revolution. The Russians might love and worship their Tsar, but the Tsar could never be popular in the sense that certain English kings have been popular.

Unfortunately, Nicholas II was loved by no one but his own family. He was the gentlest, most pleasant and most charming of men; but even these virtues turned against him. His father had been an autocrat with the temper of a bull; but at least his ministers knew where they stood with him. Nicholas was neither strong nor weak; he was yielding, but with a streak of stubbornness. Pares writes:

> When receiving (his ministers), he almost invariably gave them the impression that he was particularly pleased with them, which the peculiar charm of his person turned into a conviction. While they were with him, he seemed constitutionally incapable of saying anything to them which might cause them unpleasantness, and more usually than not, their dismissal arrived as a complete surprise by post afterwards.

There is a typical story concerning the Tsar's vacillations. At the time when Russia was trying to organize a French loan, a French banker called Netzlin visited the Tsar and urged upon him the necessity of making some concessions to his people to avert a revolution. Netzlin was delighted with his reception; the Tsar was so charming that Netzlin was convinced that he had succeeded where others had failed. He was startled when, instead of the expected concessions, the Tsar issued a manifesto reasserting his absolute authority. The Tsar's ministers were not surprised; this was what they had come to expect.

When still a child, Nicholas had fallen in love with Princess Alice of Hesse, a grand-daughter of Queen Victoria, a gentle, sad, shy girl. Against a great deal of family opposition, they married, and Princess Alice—who had been brought up as an English-woman—became the Tsarina Alexandra. She was completely unsuited to court life, being even less sure of herself than her husband was. She was something of a neurotic, and her shyness could sometimes develop into hysteria. She hated pointless conversations, and gave her visitors the impression that she was longing for them to go. Her awkwardness was maliciously noted by all the ladies of the court. The head of the Imperial Chancery, Taneyev, was surprised when he one day dropped some papers in the Tsarina's presence and she immediately bent to pick them up—and then caught herself doing it and blushed.

The Tsar's mother had originally been opposed to the marriage, and had finally given way beside her husband's deathbed. But she never liked her daughter-in-law, and set up a rival court, where criticism of the Tsarina was frequently the chief subject of conversation. Alexandra herself made as few social appearances as possible, so there were few to defend her. The court ceased to be the centre of social life in St Petersburg, and minor political salons took its place. Inevitably, this intensified the atmosphere of malice and intrigue. Nicholas and his consort felt themselves surrounded by enemies, and spent most of their time at Tsarskoe Selo; there, immersed in one another, they felt completely happy.

From their own point of view, the marriage was totally successful; they never ceased to adore one another. From Russia's point of view, it was a disaster. The Tsar was a vague and irresponsible man—intelligent enough, but with no sense of reality. This can be seen in the episode of the disaster of Hodynka Field that occurred at his coronation. A more sensitive man would have called off the remaining celebrations. He seemed to have no capacity for deep feeling, except where his own family was concerned. When he received the news of the destruction of the Russian fleet at Tsuchima, he commented: 'What a terrible disaster', then went on playing tennis. He lived in a dream world.

If Nicholas had been married to a different type of woman, this would not have mattered. But the Tsarina was even more subjective than he; she constantly demanded protection and attention; in the early years of their marriage, when the Tsar was too busy to consider her moods, she complained continually about her loneliness, and finally succeeded in giving her husband a guilt complex about her. Instead of turning his energies outward towards Russia, he turned them in towards his family. And since Nicholas was her whole life, she was jealous for his position, and resented any suggestion that he should become a constitutional king. He was *her* Nicholas, and he had to be supreme. A healthy, extroverted woman would have recognized the dangers of the situation; Alexandra was like a hen sitting on her eggs.

The trouble was that Nicholas had the ideal temperament for a constitutional monarch—as Sir Bernard Pares pointed out. He had the intelligence to size up a situation and make a decision, but he would alter his mind five minutes later. With a strong Prime Minister—a man like his father's friend Witte—he might have been an admirable Tsar. As it was, he was at the mercy of his own vacillations.

The inevitable consequence was that the first half of his reign was a chaos of incompetence. He began by squashing all liberal hopes of a constitution, declaring: 'I shall maintain the principle of autocracy just as firmly and unflinchingly as it was preserved by my unforgettable father'. In the same address, he referred to the hopes for a constitution as 'senseless dreams'.

One of the chief objections to his marriage with Princess Alice was that she was a Catholic. However, the Tsarina embraced the Orthodox faith, and in a short time had become a fanatic about it. Possibly the disappointments of the first years of marriage intensified this tendency to mysticism. (But religious fervour ran in her family; her sister Elizabeth, married to the brutal and half insane Grand Duke Sergius, founded a religious order after her husband's assassination and became the abbess.) Soon, her interest extended to spiritualism and table-rapping, encouraged by her friends, the Grand Duchesses Militsa and

Anastasia. This passion was not of long duration—she considered it sinful—but her interest in the occult side of mysticism intensified.

By 1901, the Tsarina had produced four daughters, but still no male heir. It was a subject that continually occupied the mind of the royal couple, and the Tsarina suspected—rightly—that her enemies used it as a jibe. At this point, the Grand Duchess Militsa introduced a French 'miracle worker' called Philippe Nizier-Vachot, who was the son of a butcher from a village near Lyons. Militsa had met 'Doctor Philippe' in Compiègne. She was impressed by his undeniable hypnotic powers, and persuaded him to come to Russia. In due course, he was introduced to the Tsar and Tsarina as a 'truly holy man'. Philippe was not a real doctor, but Militsa persuaded the Tsar to grant him the title of Military Doctor and State Counsellor, so that his practice in Russia became legal. The Tsarina explained to Philippe that she wanted a boy, and he told her that he could guarantee this by exercising his magical powers on her behalf. His powers of suggestion were so strong that the Tsarina started a phantom pregnancy; her stomach swelled and she wore maternity gowns. But no baby appeared, and the court doctor finally examined her and told her that she was not pregnant. This fiasco did not increase the Tsarina's credit in Russia, and it offered her enemies justification for declaring that she was a hysteric. Philippe was finally sent back to Lyons, loaded with presents—the royal couple were too gentle to hold the humiliation against him—and he died shortly afterwards.

There were other miracle workers and prophets at court. There was an idiot woman called Daria Ossipova, whose gibberings were believed to be inspired by God. There was also another 'holy fool' called Mitya Koliabin, a strange cripple with stumps for arms and a deformed palate. He came from the district of the monastery of Optima Pustyn (described in *The Brothers Karamazov*), and the monks were the first to discover that his ravings, when in an epileptic fit, were inspired prophecies. A sexton called Egorov claimed to be able to interpret them, so he became Koliabin's companion. Like the others, Koliabin was introduced at court by Militsa and her sister, and was asked to prophesy whether the Tsarina would produce an heir to the throne. He went into an ecstasy, and his shrieks caused the Tsarina to have hysterics; but Egorov explained that it was still too early to foresee the future on this particular question. Even so, the Tsarina continued to see Koliabin, and had an interview with him as late as 1906.

The Bishops Hermogen and Theophan were becoming alarmed about this deluge of charlatanism, and decided that it was time to attempt to bring the Tsarina back to her old devotion for the Orthodox Church. They decided that a new Russian saint was required to perform a miracle, and suggested a certain Seraphim of Sarov. In the early nineteenth century, Seraphim had made certain prophecies that were agreeable to the Romanovs. It was suggested that Seraphim should be canonized. In the face of much opposition from the Church, the hermit Seraphim became St Seraphim of Sarov. Almost immediately, the Tsarina conceived, and in due course was delivered of a boy. The saint was justified, and the Tsar became his lifelong devotee. (During the Japanese war, he sent medallions of the saint to the army, causing some wit to remark: 'The Japanese have shells; our soldiers have ikons'.)

It will be seen from the foregoing that the Tsar lacked the realistic talents that make a good leader. Witte tells a story that makes this very clear. An idiotic Russian ambassador in Constantinople suggested that Russia should seize the Bosphorus, after he had engineered certain 'incidents' as an excuse. News of these incidents would be sent, not to the Tsar or the government, but to Russia's financial representatives in London, who would then distort them somewhat and send telegrams to Odessa and Sevastopol; flotillas would be immediately dispatched to seize the Bosphorus. It cost Witte a great deal of energy and patience to make the Tsar see that the result would inevitably be a European war. When Witte told Pobedonostsev, the old reactionary's comment was 'God help Russia'.

The muddle and incompetence went on for the first ten years of Nicholas's reign without serious consequences. But the revolutionary ferment slowly increased. It was given a sudden violent impetus by a scandal that occurred in 1897, the year after the Tsar was crowned. The police, headed by Plehve, were, as usual, arresting all kinds of people suspected of revolutionary sympathies—most of them idealistic young students. One of them was a beautiful girl of eighteen called Marie Vietroff, in whose room a few 'forbidden' books had been found. This was not a particularly serious offence, and its usual consequence would have been temporary banishment from the confines of St Petersburg, and suspension from the university. But for some reason, Marie Vietroff was interned in the Peter and Paul fortress for two months. No one knows exactly what took place during that time, although the guesses by commentators have included rape and torture. Applications by friends finally secured the order for her release; but a few days before this was due, she committed suicide by deliberately incinerating herself. She soaked her mattress in paraffin from a lamp, lit it and lay on it. She lived for two days after, but her parents were not informed of the accident until she finally died, on 12 February 1897.

Inevitably, the revolutionaries made the fullest capital out of it, and the circumstances were so appalling that they needed little exaggeration. The girl had taken two days to die in the most horrible pain, and yet her parents were not informed. Why? In case she told them what had been happening to her? And what had driven a beautiful and gifted girl to commit suicide shortly before she was about to be released? The revolutionaries produced a pamphlet that accused the authorities of torture, and it circulated in thousands; all the efforts of the police were unable to suppress it. Count Paul Vassili called it 'the beginning of the storm that later nearly drove the Romanovs from their throne'. (He was writing before the 1917 Revolution.)

Small groups of terrorists began assassinating policemen and other officials with disconcerting regularity. Then came the Russo-Japanese war of 1904.

Russia had been drifting into war with Japan for some years. Sergius Witte, one of Nicholas's most intelligent statesmen, did his best to warn the Tsar, but without effect. The quarrel was over Korea and Manchuria. After the Boxer rebellion of 1900, several countries had taken advantage of China's weakness; Russia had become conscious of the need for control in the Far East after the construction of the Trans-Siberian railway, and occupied Manchuria. There was some disagreement with the Japanese about North Korea. Russia was in the wrong, but refused to budge. The great Japanese statesman Ito came to St Petersburg to try to settle things peaceably, but was snubbed and insulted. So the Japanese advanced into North Korea, and the Russians declared war. The Russian generals were incompetent, and surrendered Port Arthur, then Mukden. The Russian fleet was ordered to destroy the Japanese fleet, and hurried halfway round the world. On the way, they almost caused a war with England by opening fire on the English fishing fleet in the Dogger Bank, under the impression that it was the Japanese navy. Finally, the Russian fleet arrived in Japanese waters, and was annihilated by the Japanese at Tsushima.[1] Witte was sent to try to patch up an armistice, and he succeeded beyond everyone's expectations; even so, Russia lost its foothold in the Far East.

One of the men partly responsible for the war was Plehve, the police chief who had suppressed the revolutionaries in the reign of Alexander III, and probably the most hated man in Russia. Plehve thought the Tsar would gain popularity through a 'successful little war'; he developed considerable resentment against Witte, who opposed the war, and forged documents to prove that Witte was a revolutionary. On his way to see the Tsar with these forgeries, Plehve met a real revolutionary outside the Warsaw station, who tossed a bomb under his carriage. It took three days to gather up the pieces, none of which was much larger than a tennis ball. This was in July 1904.

Immediately, the revolutionary ferment became stronger. The authorities were anxious to take violent action, something that would startle the world and cow the revolutionaries all over Russia. But they needed an excuse. They therefore plotted with an *agent provocateur*, a priest named Gapon, who was known as a spokesman of the workers. Gapon agreed to lead a deputation of workers to the Winter Palace, where they would present a petition to the Tsar. Accordingly, on January 22, 1905, Gapon

[1] An interesting sidelight on discipline in the Russian navy is provided by Edgar Wallace, who was sent by the *Daily Mail* to investigate the Dogger Bank incident. At Vigo in Spain he found two Russian petty officers who had been present, and who explained how the confusion had taken place in the fog. Wallace wired the story home, and was told to proceed to Tangier, the next port of call of the Russian navy, and try to get further information. There he discovered that his informants had been executed and buried at sea.

led columns of workers into the city. They were joined by more workers, and by women and children. As they stood outside the Winter Palace, calling on their 'little father' (the Tsar), troops suddenly opened fire on them. The crowd scattered, trampling children underfoot, and the troops fired again and again. Mounted Cossacks charged after unarmed civilians and cut them down with swords or struck them with rifle butts. Then a cannon opened fire down the Nevsky, cutting down others who fled. Nijinsky, then a schoolboy of fifteen, was on his way to dancing school when he was caught up in the moving crowds; suddenly, he realized they were being charged by Cossacks on horseback. He was knocked unconscious by a blow from a knout. Later Nijinsky helped one of his schoolfellows search through the morgues for the body of his sister, but they were unable to find her. One hundred and fifty people were killed on 'Bloody Sunday' and 200 wounded. The Tsar, when told the news, asked anxiously: 'Are you sure you've killed enough people?' He had always been inclined to approve of force. When he heard that the Phanagoritsy regiment had shot down unarmed workers, he commented: 'Fine fellows'. (This seems to have been a stock exclamation, for on a later occasion, when a governor of the Baltic States complained about an officer who was executing innocent people without a trial, the Tsar wrote on the report: 'Ah, what a fine fellow!')

Inevitably, the disorders increased. In August, the crew of the battleship *Potemkin* mutinied and murdered its officers. Eisenstein has caught something of the brutality of the police regime in his film about the mutiny, particularly in the sequence in which civilians are shot down on the Odessa steps for helping the mutineers with food. It is necessary to remember that scenes like this were taking place every day, all over Russia. Artsybashev has also captured this violence in his early volume *Tales of the Revolution*. One of the most powerful of these, *The Revolutionary*, tells how a timid and peaceable young schoolmaster is driven to insane rage by the cruelties of the soldiery who have been sent on a 'reprisal' expedition, and organizes the villagers to massacre them, allowing himself to be killed afterwards without resistance. History books are too impersonal to tell the truth of such things. Unfortunately, the Tsar, living in the peace of Tsarskoe Selo, was also impervious to their truth; only this can explain the unconscious cruelty of a man who was not cruel by nature.

There were now risings all over Russia, and many of them followed the pattern of Stenka Razin and Pugachev: the peasants would murder landowners and their families; the military would move in, and exact horrible reprisals. If the Tsar had witnessed any one of these incidents with his own eyes, it would probably have changed Russian history, for he would have recognized the price paid in human suffering for the maintenance of his out-dated ideals. But Nicholas stayed in his palace, and invited some of the leaders of the workers round for tea, and gave them a grave little lecture. The answer of the revolutionaries was to murder the Tsar's brother-in-law, the brutal Grand Duke Sergius. His wife Elizabeth—the Tsarina's sister—had been staying close to her husband for many weeks, convinced that her presence would deter any assassin. It did, for the terrorist Kaliayev later admitted that he had been about to throw a bomb into the carriage when he saw that Elizabeth was there. But one day, Sergius walked out of the front door alone. Kaliayev threw his bomb, and there was a tremendous explosion. When Elizabeth rushed out, she discovered the headless body of her husband on the pavement. Parts of his body were later collected from neigh-bouring rooftops, and a finger was found on the roof of the Arsenal. Elizabeth, who seems to have been a rather saintly woman, went to see Kaliayev in prison, and offered to plead for his life if he would express contrition for his act. Kaliayev refused, saying that his death would help the cause of revolution more than his life could. He later went to his death bravely. The court regarded Elizabeth's act with a certain amount of cynicism; Sergius was universally hated, and his ill-treatment of his wife was a common subject of gossip.

Faced with the prospect of revolution, the Tsar asked Witte's advice. This Sergius Witte was a remarkable man who had risen from the people to become one of Alexander III's most trusted ministers; he had enormous ability, but was a self-seeker with a broad streak of malice in his personality. It is to Witte's credit that he did not play for popularity with his sovereign, but told Nicholas frankly that there were only two alternatives: either to establish a military dictatorship, or to give the people some kind of a constitution. Nicholas toyed with the idea of a dictatorship, and thought of offering it to the Grand Duke Nicholas; but the latter did not fancy being blown up by a bomb, and threatened to shoot himself if Nicholas tried to force him to become dictator. So, with considerable unwillingness, Nicholas agreed to grant some kind of a constitution. His manifesto of October, 1905, declared that he was willing to grant the people freedom of speech, conscience, meetings and associations, and that they could elect their own representatives for a parliamentary assembly, which was to be called the Imperial Duma.

The first effect of this concession was universal peace and rejoicing. This did not last for long. To begin with, the Duma was by no means a true parliament. The government remained, and did everything possible to thwart the Duma. Inevitably there were squabbles. Some of the progressives were more-or-less satisfied; others were not; so the progressives split into two parties. Witte, who had been made Prime Minister (the first in Russian history), did his best to satisfy all parties, but ended by angering the Tsar, who felt that he was losing his power. So Witte was dismissed, and later Nicholas dissolved the Duma in a fit of pique. The new Prime Minister, Goremykin, was a nonentity who flattered the Tsar by insisting that he was still the absolute autocrat.

At this point, there appears on the scene one of the most remarkable men of the time, Peter Stolypin, the Governor of Saratov. Stolypin was a conservative and a royalist, and yet he stood for progress. He was an astonishing character, of great courage and intelligence. Towards the end of the 1905 Revolution, he had travelled about, restoring order by his extraordinary personality. On one occasion, he came to a village where the villagers opened fire, afraid of reprisals. Stolypin walked into the bullets and begged them not to force him to use his powers against them. One revolutionary seized the sleeve of his coat; but Stolypin, with great presence of mind, asked the man to hold his coat—which he did—and walked on. The villagers laid down their arms and were treated mercifully.

Stolypin was to occupy an increasingly important position over the next few years, and he might have brought about all the reforms demanded by the Bolsheviks. But again, the revolutionaries failed to recognize that this man was basically on their side, and made a number of attempts to assassinate him. On one occasion, his house was blown up, his daughter crippled for life and his son injured; Stolypin was unharmed, although forty people were killed or wounded. This blow did not turn Stolypin into a vindictive reactionary; he continued to work for progress. His most important measure was a bill for allowing peasants to claim their share of the village holding. The reactionaries objected that the peasants were too stupid to take advantage of the offer; but Stolypin proved right in the long run. The more intelligent peasants set about persuading the others, and established the rudiments of political consciousness; the result was that a quiet revolution occurred, and villages began to apply themselves to the task of self-administration with a new spirit of purpose. Pares describes the results:

> By 1914 there was already a yeoman population of 8,700,000 households, with a strong sense of property, and consequently with a strong instinct of public order. On the new farms, the men were full of a new and businesslike energy. The cattle took on an altogether healthier appearance . . . the principle of co-operation flourished everywhere. . . .

This sounds like a description by a Soviet propagandist of a Collective Farm. But it was actually a completely new aspect of Tsarist Russia. The New Russia had arrived long before the 1917 Revolution, and if the Tsar and the revolutionaries had recognized Stolypin's amazing qualities, the revolution would not have been necessary.

Unfortunately, the Tsar felt some mistrust of Stolypin—who was, by this time, Prime Minister—and the revolutionaries were convinced that any Prime Minister must be an enemy of progress. One day, a revolutionary named Bogrov managed to worm his way into the confidence of the Kiev police by pretending to betray a plot, and the police granted him a ticket for a gala performance of Rimsky-Korsakov's *Tsar Saltan* that would be attended by the Tsar and Stolypin. The Tsar was heavily guarded; Stolypin was unprotected, and Bogrov had no difficulty in shooting him through the chest.

This was in the year 1911, by which time Rasputin was in power—Stolypin earned the hatred of the Tsarina by ordering the *staretz* out of St Petersburg. And a forty-one-year-old revolutionary leader, Vladimir Ulianov (whose brother had been executed for complicity in the murder of Alexander II) heaved a sigh of relief. Stolypin's land reforms were stealing a weapon from the hands of the Bolsheviks and delaying the revolution. Ulianov had by then adopted his party-name: Lenin.

But all this is to leap ahead of the story. For it was soon after the manifesto of 1905 that the Tsar wrote in his diary: 'Met a man of God, Grigory, from the Tobolsk province'. A new force had entered Russian politics; but it would be another three years before anyone recognized it.

CHAPTER FIVE

CITY OF DREAMS

RASPUTIN came to a capital riddled with spiritualism, with symbolism, with mediaevalism. An observer of the time has written:

> There is, perhaps, no country where spiritualism has so great a vogue. Several Russian princely houses have their familiar spirits; in some, the piano is always played by invisible hands whenever a member of the family, no matter where he or she may be, is dying.[1]

The same writer goes on to quote a rumour that the Tsar was persuaded to embark on the Russo-Japanese war by mediums. It is not surprising that certain young revolutionaries—like Maxim Gorki—should feel that Russia was ruled by madmen.

Rasputin came to St Petersburg early in 1905, and moved into the flat of a journalist called George Petrovitch Sassonoff—which he shared with several other people. He became a regular visitor at the houses of Militsa and Anastasia, 'the Montenegrins'. Possibly he hoped they would introduce him at court, since Militsa had been a favourite of the Tsarina since she nursed her through an illness. But since her last visit to St Petersburg, Militsa was no longer the Tsarina's trusted confidant. They had divided on the issue of spiritualism. Perhaps the disastrous Japanese war had destroyed the Tsar's faith in mediums; perhaps he no longer felt the same need for the advice of his father, whose spirit he had invoked several times in the earlier part of his

[1] Brayley Hodgetts: *The Court of Russia in the Nineteenth Century.*

reign. At all events, the Montenegrins continued to be enthusiastic table-rappers, and their company was no longer so welcome at the palace.

Rasputin was welcomed with particular enthusiasm by Anastasia's husband, the Grand Duke Nicholas, for whom he cured a dog. Their liking for the *staretz* was so great that when Rasputin's wife fell ill with an internal complaint, the Grand Duke paid for her to come to St Petersburg and have an operation.

In a short time, Rasputin had established a reputation as a miracle worker in the capital. An Ohkrana spy reported, on April 12, 1905: 'Crowds assemble at Rasputin's, and people wait two or three days before being able to approach the monk. Everyone acknowledges his remarkable prophetic faculties and his thaumaturgical gifts.' The report goes on to mention some of the miracles that his followers attributed to Rasputin: causing a handful of earth to turn into a rose, and curing a woman whose legs had been paralysed by simply telling her to get up and walk.

It was probably at about this time that Rasputin diverted some of the gifts he received to Pokrovskoe, and enabled his wife to buy the large house on the main street that is mentioned by his daughter. He gave away most of the money that his admirers brought him, but he still possessed strong family feelings. Besides, he was not above the desire to impress his neighbours in Pokrovskoe.

To begin with, he lived quietly in the capital. He knew that he was under surveillance from the police, and it was an uncomfortable sensation until he got used to it. He was not to know, at this early stage, that the police watched him simply because he was a member of the Union of True Russians, and the chiefs of police were capable of making use of the information in their own political manoeuvres. The Ohkrana was simply interested in everything that went on; it was their job to be everywhere and know everything. But on occasion, it was also their job not to know too much. (For example, the head of the French branch of the Russian secret police, Rachkovsky, had been asked for a report on the bogus 'Doctor' Philippe, and had revealed him to be a charlatan who had been twice prosecuted for practising medicine without a licence. Rachkovsky was dismissed.) Later, Rasputin became so accustomed to being watched all the time that he even made friends with the police spies and used them to run his errands.

And finally, on November 1, 1905, came the moment for which he had been waiting; it was on that date that the Tsar wrote in his diary: 'We have got to know a man of God—Grigory—from the Tobolsk province'. The meeting took place in Militsa's house.

It is not known who was responsible for first mentioning Rasputin to the Tsar; it was probably the Grand Duchess Anastasia. Most books on Rasputin declare that it was the Tsarina's closest friend, Anna Vyrubov; but according to Pares, she did not meet Rasputin until two years later.

The usual story of Rasputin's introduction at court is spectacular, and exists in several different versions. The version given by Liepman is typical. Rasputin was in the habit of visiting the gypsy encampment at Novaya Derevnya, on the banks of the river, where he joined in the dancing and singing. On the evening of July 19, 1907 (i.e., two years after the entry in the Tsar's diary), Rasputin was drinking heavily at the gypsy camp. But at the palace, the Tsarevitch was seriously ill; he had bruised himself, and had been in a fever for three days. The Imperial doctors were able to do nothing, and had given up hope. At this point, Anna Vyrubov whispered Rasputin's name in the Tsarina's ear, and a messenger was instantly dispatched to fetch him. He found him eventually at Novaya Derevnya. 'In the name of the Tsar', called the messenger, 'is there a certain Grigory Rasputin here?' Rasputin identified himself. The messenger told him to take his horse, and go to 'a certain residence'; Rasputin drunkenly refused, and shouted 'More dancing!'. But the leader of the gypsies had recognized the Tsar's messenger, and begged Rasputin to go. Rasputin stood silent for a while. 'Those who saw him', writes Liepman, '. . . in the light of the gypsy fires are unanimous in declaring that on receipt of that message from the Court there was a change in him. His glowing eyes looked straight ahead . . .' Rasputin fell on his knees and prayed, and 'a superstitious shudder went through the silent crowd'. Then Rasputin told the messenger: 'I have prayed for him. The crisis is already past. He will recover.' With that, he leapt on the horse and cantered off to Tsarskoe Selo. And '. . . whilst he was still with the gypsies, though no longer drinking and dancing, but on his knees in prayer, the improvement set in, as he had publicly said that it would, and as he told the Tsarina as soon as he set eyes on her'. Rasputin entered the sickroom, and fell on his knees beside the bed of the Tsarevitch. 'His eyes were closed, but there was such an expression of intensity on his rugged, powerful face that they (the Tsar and Tsarina) remained there, not daring to speak.' Finally, Rasputin stands up with the words: 'Your son, little mother, is now sleeping peacefully. . . .' And later that night, the Tsar wrote in his diary: 'Made the acquaintance of a Man of God, Grigory, from the Tobolsk province. Alexei was saved from certain death by his prayers.'

Fülöp-Miller's version is slightly less dramatic. According to him, it was the Grand Duchess Anastasia who mentioned Rasputin's name to the Tsarina, and who went on to describe how, only that morning in church, John of Cronstadt had beckoned to Rasputin and asked for his blessing. (This incident, it will be remembered, actually took place several years earlier, in 1903.) Rasputin was sent for (it is not specified where he was found), and came to the palace twenty-four hours later. (The long delay is not explained.) His entry into the sickroom is less dramatic than in Liepman: 'Grigory Efimovitch went up to the Imperial couple with a beaming smile and, without ceremony, embraced the all-powerful ruler of all the Russians and his consort, and gave them a smacking kiss'. He talks cheerfully to the sick boy, telling him stories about Siberia, and then fairy tales. The child is so enthusiastic that he sits up. Finally, Rasputin leaves, after promising to return the following day; the Tsarina 'impetuously seized the hands of the peasant and kissed them'.

But, as Alan Moorehead points out, 'it cannot have been only because of the illness of the Tsarevitch that Rasputin was first accepted at court; the child was only fifteen months old at the time'. Moreover, there is no sign that Rasputin made any deep impression on the Imperial couple for at least two years after his first introduction. The whole story, as told by Liepman and Fülöp-Miller, would seem to be only another example of Rasputin's power to inspire myths. The sentence quoted by Liepman: 'Alexei was saved from certain death by his prayers' does not occur in the entry describing the Tsar's first meeting with 'the man of God from the Tobolsk province'. Liepman has also, of course, altered the date of the entry by two years.

The years 1905 to 1907 were a time of continual crisis for the Tsar and for Russia. The first Duma was formed, and promptly passed a vote of censure on the government. But the government refused to resign, and the Tsar, worried about this threat to his absolute sovereignty, dissolved the Duma after less than three months (July 1906). In December, there had been a revolution in Moscow, with heavy street fighting, barricades, and much bloodshed. The troops remained loyal, and revolution was averted. But when certain members of the first Duma fled over the border to Finland and tried to rouse Russia by means of a manifesto, they met with no response; the country was already tired of revolution. In 1907, the second Duma was formed, and again dissolved. Then, in the autumn of 1907, the third Duma was formed, and succeeded in existing for five years. And it was during the time of the third Duma that Rasputin rose to become the most powerful man in Russia.

And yet as early as 1906, Rasputin was already famous as a healer. When a bomb destroyed Stolypin's house and injured his children, the Tsarina offered him Rasputin's services. Stolypin refused; he did not meet Rasputin until the year of his assassination in Kiev. Stolypin's description of this meeting is worth quoting:

> He ran his pale eyes over me, mumbled mysterious and inarticulate words from the Scriptures, made strange movements with his hands, and I began to feel an indescribable loathing for the vermin sitting opposite me. Still, I did realize that the man possessed great hypnotic power, which was beginning to produce a fairly strong moral impression on me, though certainly one of repulsion.

Rodzianko, who quotes this, goes on to add that if Rasputin could produce such an impression on the iron will of Stolypin, how much greater would be his power over a weak nature like that of the Tsarina.

And yet the truth is that Rasputin probably had no need to use his hypnotic powers with the Tsarina. She was only too anxious to believe him. Rasputin represented for her the strength and honesty of the Russian peasant. From the beginning, he treated the royal couple familiarly; but he also gave them the impression of liking them as human beings, and this was of enormous importance to both of them—particularly to the Tsarina, who felt herself surrounded by hostility. The anonymous author of *The Fall of the Romanoffs* says:

> At this time (1905–6) the strange conduct of the Empress Alexandra became noticeable. Her Majesty never appeared in public, private audiences were unwillingly granted and only in the most urgent cases, Court receptions were abolished. On these occasions, when a Court pageant or banquet could not be avoided, it was the Dowager Empress Marie who, at her son's side, came forward to greet the assembled guests. No one, except the restricted court circle, saw the Empress, and all kinds of rumours were spread about regarding her peculiarities. Some said that, fearing to grow stout, she had followed the system of a German . . . cure to dissolve the increasing fat against the advice of her doctor, and the result was a complete breakdown of the nervous system. Others stated that she suffered from nervous eczema, which at times covered her face and hands, and prevented her showing herself in public. . . . Others believed she was simply mad.

This pathologically shy woman felt herself to be a stranger in a hostile country. Then Rasputin appeared, a personification of the Russian peasantry, and assured her that she was loved by all simple Russians, that it was only at court that she was disliked and criticized. He became a second father to her. And it was at this point—sometime in 1907—that the Tsarevitch Alexei had the fall that led to his first serious illness. Nothing is known of the scene; no one who was present has described it. But it may well have been, to some extent, as Liepman and Fülöp-Miller describe it. Rasputin radiated strength and certainty and benevolence. In his healthy presence, all their fatalistic misgivings disappeared; they believed again in man's power to control his own destiny. It was impossible to be a fatalist in the presence of this power.

Rasputin's 'Powers'

At this point, we must raise the question that is of central importance in the story of Rasputin: that of his healing powers. It happens to be a question to which no one has given the attention it deserves. If Rasputin really possessed such powers, and if he was (as seems probable) a member of the Khlysty, then nothing is more likely than that he believed himself to be another of the Khlysty 'Christs', and this would be an important key to his strange personality. His enemies, on the other hand, have stated that he performed his 'miracles' with the help of a certain Doctor Badmaev, a Mongolian who claimed to have studied medicine in Tibet, and who certainly seemed able to produce remarkable cures with his herbal concoctions. One writer believes that Rasputin paid Badmaev to administer small doses of poison to the Tsarevitch, and to leave off the doses when Rasputin prayed for the child's life. No one with any knowledge of the home life of the Royal Family can take this story seriously; it is worth mentioning only because it illustrates a certain attitude towards Rasputin: the assumption that he was quite simply a clever scoundrel with an impressive manner.

But, even assuming that Rasputin was not the saint the Tsarina believed him to be, is it possible that he possessed genuine thaumaturgic powers? There was an incident concerning the Tsarevitch that took place in 1912 that even his enemies found difficult to explain away. This was at a time when Rasputin had been banished from the court by the machinations of the Prime Minister Kokovtsev. The Royal Family were taking a holiday at Belovetchkaya, near Grodno, in September, 1912, and the Tsarevitch slipped as he was leaping out of a boat, and hurt his knee, causing an internal hæmorrhage. Blood poisoning soon set in, and the boy fell into a fever. After several days, the doctors despaired of his life. Fedorov, the Tsar's chief physician, believed that only a drastic remedy could save the boy's life, but was not sure whether to risk it without first consulting the Tsarina. In the meantime, the Tsarina asked her friend Anna Vyrubov to send Rasputin a telegram at Pokrovskoe, asking him to pray for the boy. Immediately, she received back a telegram: 'The illness is not as dangerous as it seems. Don't let the doctors worry him.' As soon as the telegram arrived, the boy began to recover.

There are three possible explanations for this incident. The first is that Fedorov applied the 'drastic remedy' he believed necessary; but when asked, he made a non-committal answer and walked out of the room. Is it likely that he would refuse to take the credit if he had actually saved the Tsarevitch's life? Another explanation is that the Tsarina's faith in Rasputin communicated itself to the boy, who had until then been surrounded by despair. This is also possible; but Mosolov, the head of the chancery, mentions that the boy was delirious; in which case it is unlikely that he knew about the telegram until his recovery.

Rasputin, then, either took a chance on the boy's recovery—and risked all possibility of his return to favour at court—or actually believed that he was somehow capable of curing the boy at a distance of nearly two thousand miles.

The evidence is all in favour of the latter assumption. Rasputin did not confuse his thaumaturgic power with his hypnotic power, even though, at the beginning, he might well have done so. In 1891, he had cured the wife of an innkeeper of asthma by praying beside her bed and laying his hand on her forehead; he stayed in the inn for a month, and when he left, the woman was cured. Asthma is, of course, a nervous ailment, and might be susceptible to hypnotic suggestion. But in later life, Rasputin several times denied that he used hypnotism at all; his healing power came from another source. The case of his cure of the Tsarevitch by telegram seems to prove this assertion.

The argument that Rasputin was demonstrably no saint, and that therefore he could not possess thaumaturgic powers, reveals ignorance of the principles of healing. At the time when Rasputin was wandering over Siberia, Mary Baker Eddy was teaching her disciples in America that anyone can become a healer provided he followed her instructions. She had learned the technique of healing from a remarkable man called Phineas Quimby who had learned its elements from a French hypnotist called Poyen. Quimby had made the discovery that it was the patient's faith in the remedy that brought about the cure rather than any intrinsic merit in the remedy. He took this one stage further, and decided that no medicine was necessary; a certain 'buoyant' attitude of mind and emotion would cure the patient without medicine. Quimby was delighted by his discovery. When a Swedenborgian clergyman was cured by him and declared that he was 'reproducing the wonders of the Gospels', Quimby strongly disclaimed that he was calling on supernatural agencies or was performing miracles. His cures he insisted, were natural and scientific, and the method could be taught to anyone who would take the trouble to learn it, whether he possessed hypnotic powers or not. Quimby proved his point by teaching his method to several followers who possessed no hypnotic powers. (Quimby's own were considerable.) So that although Quimby began as a disciple of a hypnotist, he ended by disclaiming the importance of hypnotism (which in those days was called mesmerism or animal magnetism).

The meeting between Quimby and Mrs Eddy was dramatized by Ernst Toller in his play *Mary Baker Eddy*. I quote part of it here because it is an admirable summary of the method and ideas employed by Mrs Eddy's disciples, and probably by Rasputin.

Mrs Eddy was forty-one when she met Quimby in 1862. She was a hysterical hypochondriac who suffered from spinal weakness, paralysis of the arms and legs and periodic attacks of catalepsy.

QUIMBY: Give me your hands.

MARY: I can't. They are paralysed.

QUIMBY: (Taking her hands) Look me in the eyes.

MARY: Yes.

QUIMBY: How do you feel now? I will tell you. You are in great pain.

MARY: Yes.

QUIMBY: The pain is in your limbs.

MARY: Yes.

QUIMBY: You cannot sleep. You suffer from cramp. You have suffered from cramp for many years.

MARY: Yes, yes.

QUIMBY: They have told you you're paralysed. They have told you you're paralysed. They have told you your whole body is poisoned and that you are incurable. You have believed these false doctors, false doctors who know nothing of men and women. What is the good of the surgeon's knife if it only cuts into the body? Sickness is not a thing of the body. It is the sickness of the mind affecting the body. And only he who purifies the mind can heal the body. The mind can make sick people well. The mind is a healer.

MARY: The mind is a healer . . .

QUIMBY: You are sitting opposite me. You look at me. You see only me. Only me! Forget the world. Forget everything. Forget the false doctors, forget your family, your advisers, your prejudices, the stupid pills and the ridiculous medicines. I am sitting in front of you and I am healing you.

MARY: You . . . are . . . healing . . . me.

QUIMBY: (Dipping his hands in water and sprinkling it over her) I dip my hand in pure water and pass it over your brow. I feel your pain passing into my own hands. You have no more pain.

MARY: No . . . more . . . pain.

QUIMBY: No! . . . Lift up your right hand.

MARY: I cannot.

QUIMBY: Lift up your right hand!

MARY: (Raising it) My God!

QUIMBY: Lift up your left hand!

(Mary raises her hand and begins to sob)

Now stand up!

(Mary tries to rise and sinks back again)

QUIMBY: Stand up! You want to stand up! You *can* stand up!

(Mary stands up)

(Quickly) Now walk! Walk! Faster! Here! Now over there!

(Softly, to himself) She really can walk.

PATIENTS: A miracle. . . .

QUIMBY: A miracle, you say? We must seek, we must strive to understand. People talk of miracles because they understand so little of the power of the mind. There are no miracles; everything follows natural laws. We must meditate and seek.

Mrs Eddy learned Quimby's method, and later taught it to her own followers (although she was soon denying that Quimby had ever taught her anything). What is of interest is that while

Mrs Eddy was still subject to recurring attacks of her illness, Quimby was able to treat her from a distance, *telepathically*, and still secure the same results that he could produce when present.[1]

Quimby himself was a totally honest man, obsessed by his work; accounts of him indicate that he had something of the saint in his composition. Mrs Eddy had nothing of the saint about her; she was a hysteric, intensely suspicious, capable of vindictiveness, a free and fluent liar, and by no means dead to the 'appetites of the flesh', even in her sixties. Like Rasputin, she believed that her power to heal (which she undoubtedly possessed) came directly from God, and from her insight into the scriptures. Quimby, her teacher, seems to have thought otherwise. He recognized that he had stumbled on a discovery—supported by the researches of J. B. Rhine into parapsychology in our own century—that the human mind possesses powers that earlier centuries would have labelled supernatural.

'People talk of miracles because they understand so little of the power of the mind.' It is difficult, at the moment, to offer any logical explanation of the phenomena of parapsychology—'second sight', telepathy, prevision, thaumaturgy and so on—but perhaps it is worth making the attempt.

At the beginning of the twentieth century, a philòsopher called Edmund Husserl stumbled on an important insight: that simple 'perception' is something that almost never occurs. If you place this book on your knee and look around the room, it may seem that you are simply 'seeing' and hearing whatever presents itself to your senses. In fact, your mind is continuously selecting, filtering, interpreting, colouring—and sometimes distorting and misinforming. We have all heard of cases of hysterical women who believe they have been raped, or of religious fanatics who believe they have seen Christ and the angels marching through the sky. But in such cases, the question of illusion or reality is not as straightforward as it sounds. *We are all doing something similar during every minute of our waking lives.* (The only perceptions we might call 'pure' are the sounds that filter through to us on the edge of sleep, or the things we see when the mind becomes a blank.)

[1] See *Mrs Eddy*, by Edwin F. Dakin (Universal Library), page 48.

Under ordinary circumstances, it is very difficult to catch the mind at its work of distorting and selecting. There are optical illusions that can be produced by patterns of lines—when two straight lines will appear to be curved because certain transversal lines have been drawn across, or when two lines curved inwards appear to be shorter than two lines curved outwards—and these show how much the mind relies on a kind of shorthand, on 'taking things for granted'. But the distorting power can be much better studied through the psychology of sex or religion, since the mind's strongest forces are here in question.[1]

Husserl invented techniques for studying the mind's 'distorting' powers, and called his method 'phenomenology'. It is undoubtedly the most important philosophical method of the twentieth century.

The first step towards understanding Rasputin, then, is to recognize that there are forces that lie below the threshold of consciousness, and that they constantly interfere with the way in which we see the world. Our position might be compared to that of a nation that believes it has a wholly free press, when, in fact, there are hidden inquisitors who censor everything that appears in print. Seeing things without distortion or prejudice is not simply a matter of opening our eyes and looking; it is a matter of a long and rigorous philosophical training. Husserl called the assumption of 'simple perception' 'the natural standpoint'. Everything that has been written on Rasputin has been written from the natural standpoint, without an attempt to take into account the sub-threshold forces of the mind. (These should not be confused with the Freudian subconscious, although obviously there are certain areas of overlap.)

Simple perception, then, is a fallacy. Besides the conscious prejudices that we are aware of imposing on the world, there are a thousand subconscious prejudices that we assume to be actuality.

But there is an even more basic 'colouring' that the mind 'adds' to the world; this can be called the question of affirmation or negation. Reality can be seen with the ecstatic intensity of a mystic, or with the nausea of a paranoiac. It can also be seen in a hundred ways between these two extremes; the common

[1] See, for example, my *Origins of the Sexual Impulse*.

experience is somewhere about midway, a shade on the side of negation.

This matter of affirmation or negation is also difficult to pinpoint, since we accept our moods as inevitable in the way that we accept slight indigestion or a cold sore on the lip. But the mind's capacity for colouring its experience can sometimes be caught out. Consider, for example, the following passage from Schredin's *Golovlyov Family*, one of the gloomiest novels in Russian:

> She spent the greater part of the day dozing. She would sit down in her armchair in front of the table on which her grimy cards were spread out, and doze. Then she would wake up with a start, glance at the window, and without any conscious thought in her mind, gaze for a long while at the wide expanse of fields stretching into the distance as far as the eye could see. Pogorelka was a sad looking place. It was situated awkwardly; it had no garden, no shade, no claims to comfort whatever. . . . The few outbuildings behind it also showed signs of decay; and all around it lay fields, endless fields, with not a tree to be seen on the horizon.

Here, it might seem, the novelist is imposing no distortion, attempting no Graham Greene-like interjections ('the view was as blank as the smile of an idiot'). The scenery really is flat and dreary. And yet the description goes on:

> She looked intently into the distance, gazing at the villages soaked with rain that showed like black specks on the horizon, at the white churches in the village graveyards, at the coloured patches of shadow cast on the plain by the clouds.

For the reader whose mind has accepted the dreariness and is slightly depressed by it, the mention of 'villages soaked with rain that showed like black specks' brings a curious flash of life, the smell of rain on wet roads, and evokes for a moment all the smells and sights of a village on a wet day. For a moment, the artificial walls erected by the novelist's sensibility vanish, and the smell of real life blows in. We realize that a kind of confidence trick has been played on us, a confidence trick that is abetted by our own mental habit of noticing only certain aspects of our experience, and allowing these to form our moods. We realize that the flat, dreary, treeless plain is only one aspect of the truth. A Van Gogh might see it distorted with the force of life, or glittering like a diamond. But it would be unphilosophical to object that it is the mystic's view that is distorted and unrealistic. What happens when the mention of 'rain soaked villages' causes a ripple in the mind is that *the senses open* and admit more actuality than we normally perceive; the village, instead of being claustrophobically confined within invisible walls, is related to a greater actuality. The mind *has* to build invisible walls, to select and isolate what it sees, for the same reason that a horse has to be blinkered in the traffic; a broader vision would impair our efficiency and ability to survive, and therefore endanger the future possibility of a broader consciousness. But, as Blake points out, although man is 'caverned' in his five senses, he can 'pass out what time he will', open 'the doors of perception' and become aware of the strangeness, the *otherness*, of external reality. It is not quite true to say that he can pass out whenever he will; it requires a strong mental discipline, or the use of certain drugs (mescalin, for example); still, it can be done by someone who recognizes that the 'natural standpoint' is only a convention, not an ultimate reality.

Now one of the bases of our natural standpoint as social creatures is an attitude of mistrust towards the world. It may not be the extreme mistrust of Van Gogh's darker moods, when he wrote 'Misery will never end', but it is equally far from the life-affirmation of his paintings, or of certain pages of Nietzsche's prose.

The 'possibilitarian' makes the discovery that perhaps our mistrust of the world is exaggerated. H. G. Wells writes:

> But when a man has once broken through the paper walls of everyday circumstance, those unsubstantial walls that hold so many of us securely prisoned from the cradle to the grave, he has made a discovery. If the world does not please you, *you can change it*.

The first step in this instinctive rejection of the natural standpoint is the decision to turn away from security. Traditionally, such men become wanderers and, in the first stage, world-rejectors.

It is true that the 'ideal' cannot be found in the outer world, and many of the romantics of the nineteenth century wrote despairing works in which the wanderer ends by committing suicide or dying of exhaustion. But few—if any—of them tried the effect of actually becoming a wanderer; if they had, they might have discovered that their mere act of wandering in pursuit of the 'ideal' brings about certain changes, a degree of freedom from the prison of the old personality. First of all, the act of rejecting security brings a healthy feeling of a new beginning, and a feeling of superiority to those who still wear their mistrust of life as a convict's ball and chain. The whole being receives a new impetus.

But the change is seldom deep or permanent unless it is also involved with religion. For there is nothing to stop the formation of a new personality based upon the feeling of material insecurity, and this new personality must, inevitably, be inferior to the old one in certain respects. For example, the 'wanderer' soon discovers that he pays for the first hours of excitement and freedom with a hundred minor anxieties—where to sleep, how to find the next meal—and with a feeling of aimlessness. The external world demands more attention than ever. This increase in attention to externals must be compensated by a corresponding increase in subjectivity; the aimlessness must be counterbalanced by a return to the mainsprings of purpose in the depths of consciousness. This can only be done through prayer or meditation. The act of prayer is a rejection of one's conscious personality. The prayer of the superstitious is directed outward, as if to an authority; the prayer of the naturally religious is directed inward, to the source of the purpose that rises like sap through consciousness. In this way, the new personality cannot harden into a shell, and the original impulse of freedom is preserved.

But the most important result of this new attitude towards the world is that it develops the 'mystical impulse'; things begin to *look different*, simply because more vitality goes into the perception. The senses 'open', having more energy at their disposal; mistrust makes for a miserly storing-up of energy to meet possible emergencies, and this is all released. The mind is sustained by purpose, yet is relaxed, and the result of this co-ordination of brain, nerves and body is a new degree of health. All doctors recognize the importance of the mental attitude of the patient towards illness; a patient who believes he is bound to die has already lost half the battle. The converse is also true. No doubt this explains Rasputin's invariable rude health, which was so strong that his presence could bring strength to a sick person.

It is not surprising that Rasputin's wife found him greatly altered on his return from his first visit to Palestine. Most of us experience only one great personality change in our lives, in passing from adolescence to adulthood; after that, the personality remains static. Rasputin had achieved a 'second adulthood', and had also discovered what seemed to be an infallible formula for fresh development: prayer and the rejection of worldly goods. For the rest of his life, Rasputin found strength in prayer, and was indifferent to possessions.

It can now be seen why he gained such an ascendency over the Tsar and Tsarina, hag-ridden as they were by fears of evil fatality and the end of the dynasty. They took it for granted that fate would pursue them with ill-luck; and, like most people with this attitude, they drew ill-luck to themselves. The ' natural standpoint' had them by the throat. But Rasputin's whole being was a denial of fatality and of man's ultimate defeat. They were neurotic; he was splendidly anti-neurotic. They took their limitations for granted; he was a guarantee that man's limitations are only an unconscious convention, a habit that can be broken like any other habit—perhaps even the habit of death. In his presence, they became capable of affirmation; his vitality recharged them. Their minds were half-asleep, and confused their uneasy dreams with reality; his was fully awake.

Gurdjieff

It is unfortunate that we possess no documents written by Rasputin in the early years of his wanderings, and that he talked about them to no one. But we do possess fairly full documentation of a career that presents many parallels to Rasputin's—that of his contemporary, George Ivanovitch Gurdjieff—which provides indirect support for many of the conjectures made above. It is instructive to compare their careers.

Gurdjieff was born at about the same time as Rasputin, at Alexandropol in Armenia, and spent most of his childhood and youth in Kars, which was then in Russia. (It is now in Turkish territory.) He was always interested in magic and the unknown powers of the mind; as a child he had seen dervishes performing feats of magic, and a Yezidi boy who was unable to walk out of a circle that had been drawn round him. Gurdjieff was educated by the dean of the Military Academy at Kars, who thought his mind interesting enough to deserve developing. Eventually, Gurdjieff decided that he would wander about the world and search for the answer to the questions that troubled him—of the human personality, and its limitations and possibilities. In his book *Meetings with Remarkable Men* he tells about some of these journeys. They included trips to Australia and Tibet (where he was tutor to the young Dalai Lama) and an expedition into the Gobi desert looking for a buried city. This period of wandering lasted about the same time as Rasputin's—throughout the second half of the 1890s—and some time during the first decade of the new century, he appeared in Moscow and began to give talks to small bands of selected followers. P. D. Ouspensky, who became his chief disciple, met him there in 1914, and until the revolution, Gurdjieff divided his time between St Petersburg and Moscow.

All who met Gurdjieff have recorded impressions that recall descriptions of Rasputin. Llewelyn Powys said that 'there was something about his presence that affected the nerves in a strange way', and described his pupils as 'hypnotized rabbits'.

Rom Landau was one of the first to compare Gurdjieff to Rasputin. Describing a meeting with Gurdjieff, he writes:

I had been specially careful not to look at Gurdjieff and not to allow him to look into my eyes for at least two minutes. I had turned all the time towards the young man. . . . And yet the feeling of physical weakness pervaded me more and more.

I was intensely awake, and conscious of what was going on

within me, and I was observing this fascinating new experience with the keenest awareness. The feeling inside my stomach was one of acute nervousness, amounting almost to physical pain and fear. This weakness did not affect me above the navel; it was limited to the stomach and legs. My legs were suffering from a sensation similar to that which people experience before a trial at court. . . . I was sure that if I tried to get up my legs would sag under me and I would fall to the floor.

Though I had not the slightest doubt that my queer state had been produced by Gurdjieff's influence, I was perfectly composed, and determined to get out of it. I concentrated more and more on my conversation with the young man, and slowly the feeling inside seemed to melt away and I began to feel normal again. . . .

There are several explanations of my queer experience. It might have been a form of hypnosis or even autohypnosis which, for certain reasons, could affect only the lower half of my body. . . . It may have been a form of electric emanation such as Rasputin is said to have possessed in a high degree. This form of radiation seems to act even if its owner is hardly conscious of it, and it belongs to him almost in the same way that certain odours belong to certain coloured races.

There may have been another reason for my strange experience. According to clairvoyant people . . . a clairvoyant examination may produce (similar) effects. . . . Rudolph Steiner examined people occasionally in this way, the object . . . being to see the person's spiritual instead of his merely physical picture. . . .[1]

I have quoted the last paragraph because it hints at the same power that Rasputin is said to have possessed—of being capable of 'seeing inside' people.

Now compare Landau's account of Gurdjieff with Yussupov's description of a similar encounter with Rasputin:[2]

The *staretz* told me to lie down on the couch. He stood in

[1] Rom Landau: *God is My Adventure* (Faber & Faber, 1941).
[2] Prince Yussupov: *Rasputin, His malignant influence and his assassination*, page 113.

front of me, looked me intently in the eyes, and began to
stroke my chest, neck and head. Then he suddenly knelt down
and—so it seems to me—began to pray, placing his hand on
my forehead. He bent his head so low that I could no longer
see his face.

He remained in this position for a considerable time. Then
he suddenly jumped to his feet and began to make passes. He
was evidently familiar with certain of the processes employed
by hypnotists.

His hypnotic power was immense. I felt it subduing me
and diffusing warmth throughout the whole of my being. I
grew numb; my body seemed paralysed. I tried to speak, but
my tongue would not obey me, and I seemed to be falling
asleep, as if under the influence of a strong narcotic. Yet
Rasputin's eyes shone before me like a kind of phosphorescent
light. From them came two rays that flowed into each other
and merged into a glowing circle. This circle now moved
away from me, now came nearer and nearer. When it
approached me it seemed as if I began to distinguish his eyes;
but at that very moment, they would vanish into the circle
which then moved further away.

I was conscious that the *staretz* was speaking but I could
not make out his words.

Such was my condition as I lay motionless, unable to call
out or stir. Yet my mind was still free, and I realized that I
was gradually falling into the power of this mysterious man.

But soon I felt that my own inner force was awaking and
was of its own accord resisting the hypnosis.

This force grew stronger in me. . . . Into my consciousness
floated a vague idea that an intense struggle was taking place
between Rasputin and myself, and that my own personality,
in battling with it, made it impossible for him to dominate
me completely.

I tried to move my hand, and it obeyed me. But I did not
alter my position; I waited until Rasputin himself should tell
me to do so.

By now I could clearly distinguish his figure, face and eyes.
That terrible circle had completely disappeared. . . .

'Well, my dear, that'll be enough for the first time,' he said.

In both cases, we may wonder how far auto-hypnosis played a part—or, to put it more bluntly, how far it was the result of imagination. And yet there are too many other recorded examples of the power of both Rasputin and Gurdjieff for this to be wholly true. Gurdjieff's disciple Ouspensky possessed a thoroughly scientific temperament, and had known Gurdjieff for a considerable time when he had experience of Gurdjieff's telepathic power. In his book *In Search of the Miraculous* he describes this experience at some length, and adds: 'I can say with complete assurance that Gurdjieff did not use any kind of external methods, that is, he gave me no narcotics, nor did he hypnotize me by any of the known methods'. Later, in his own room, Ouspensky heard Gurdjieff's voice 'inside his chest', and replied mentally to questions that Gurdjieff put to him. Gurdjieff, at this time, was sitting outside on the veranda with several other people.

Like Rasputin, Gurdjieff was not averse to taking advantage of his female disciples, and there are many stories of his sexual power. Rom Landau records an anecdote of an American lady, 'one of our great novelists', who was sitting at a table near Gurdjieff when she suddenly turned pale and seemed on the point of fainting. She admitted to her companion that Gurdjieff had looked at her and 'I suddenly felt as though I had been struck right through my sexual centre'.

According to some of the accounts quoted in Fülöp-Miller, Rasputin's methods were not dissimilar, although the narrative of one Vera Shukovskaya indicates a less subtle approach:

> He pulled me into the bedroom and tore off my dress as we went. . . . And the next moment he was nothing but savage animal desire. . . . The last thing I remember is his tearing off my underclothing, then I lost consciousness. . . . I awoke and found myself lying on the ground, torn and defiled.

But this was the lady's second visit, and she also speaks of the hypnotic power that drew her back to him.

The more one studies Gurdjieff and Rasputin, the more striking appear the parallels. Admittedly, Gurdjieff had a far better mind than Rasputin, and his battle against the 'sleep of the mind' was conducted on a wholly conscious level. But like Rasputin—and unlike his disciple Ouspensky—Gurdjieff appears to have been genuinely religious, and phrases like 'with the help of God' occur many times in *Meetings with Remarkable Men*. It seems likely that if it had been Gurdjieff, and not Rasputin, who was introduced to the Tsar in 1905, Gurdjieff might easily have become the most powerful—and most hated—man in Russia. Luckily for Gurdjieff, he never became involved in politics; so he outlived Rasputin by more than thirty years, dying in Paris from overeating after the Second World War.

The comparison of Gurdjieff and Rasputin makes us aware of the central problem of Rasputin's personality, the problem that has hardly been touched by most of his biographers, and that is implied in the title 'Saint or Devil?' These men were not simply clever scoundrels; they possessed real power. In that case, what were they? Not saints, certainly; equally obviously, they were not supermen, if by superman we mean an altogether higher type of human being. How can such spiritual hybrids be defined?

Aldous Huxley explores a similar problem in his *Grey Eminence*, a study of Father Joseph of Paris. How, he asks, could the same man be a saint and a power politician—and, moreover, be the man who was most responsible for the Thirty Years War? Father Joseph practised the ascetic principle of detachment from the world and absorption in God; at the same time, he acted as Richelieu's ambassador and adviser, and pushed Europe towards war. And, like most politicians, he did not see clearly the consequences of his acts in terms of human suffering. Indirectly, Father Joseph was responsible for the deaths of about eight million people in Germany alone. And yet his writings prove him to have been well on the road to sainthood.

> Not merely intellectually, but by actual direct acquaintance, he knew something of the other world, the world of eternity.[1]

Perhaps this is the reason that sainthood is so inadequate. The saint cares about God more than about man's possible evolution; there is something sterile and onanistic about his goodness. Reading Ramakrishna, one is struck by the same feeling; there is an element of childishness about his God-devotion, something selfish and ultimately rather silly.

[1] Page 15.

With Rasputin and Gurdjieff, the problem is even more difficult. Gurdjieff, for example, was thoroughly materialistic, although after a serious motor accident in 1935, one of his followers admitted that he had become 'more altruistic, less materially minded'. A whole chapter of *Remarkable Men* is devoted to an account of his methods of making money; some of them are barely legal, and it is evident that he takes pleasure in describing his rascalities. Rasputin was not interested in money, but he loved wielding power, and could be childishly boastful about his influence.

Ramakrishna has an interesting remark that throws some light on the problem. He commented that people are drawn towards holy men as wasps are drawn to a honey pot, because in the slow process of making direct acquaintance with God, the saint generates a power that emanates from him without an effort on his part.

This power is something that we can observe in everyday life. One has only to go to Speakers Corner at Hyde Park to notice that some speakers can be brilliant and passionate, and yet lose influence over their audience the moment they stop speaking. They lack this power of which Ramakrishna speaks; it can only be acquired by a long, slow discipline, and the nature of the discipline assures that, once it has been achieved, the power cannot be misused.

Unfortunately, there are exceptions to this law. Certain men seem to be born already in touch with the 'inner power-house', in the way that certain babies are born with two heads. Since they possess power without moral discipline, they can be the most dangerous type of human being. Napoleon was such a freak; so was Hitler. This is the kind of power that the anarchists mean when they say that power corrupts. Hitler's power seems to have been in many ways similar to Rasputin's; the word 'hypnotic' is frequently used of his effect on audiences. (Significantly, it was no longer apparent in direct personal intercourse; the power only worked in the presence of a large audience.) Kurt Ludeckke writes of Hitler's oratory:

Again his power was inescapable, gripping me and swaying me as it did everyone within those walls. Again I had the sensation of surrendering my will to his leadership. . . . I had given him my soul.

This sounds as if a female disciple of Rasputin is speaking.

Rasputin and Gurdjieff were also such freaks—although to a lesser extent than Hitler. They had spent years developing their power. Still, it came easily, and their moral development did not keep pace with it. To some extent, therefore, they were corrupted by their power. This seems to be the answer to some of the contradictions in Rasputin's character that have confused so many of his biographers. Of these it will be necessary to speak in more detail later.

To summarize: the evidence of friends, enemies and 'un-prejudiced observers' indicates that Rasputin undoubtedly possessed remarkable powers. These were of two different kinds, which should not be confused together (although they interacted to some extent): thaumaturgic and hypnotic. The hypnotic powers had something to do with the force of his personality, developed by years of wandering. But the thaumaturgic powers were the outcome of his basic attitude towards the world. Most human beings find it difficult to relax from a certain defensive attitude towards the world, with the consequence that they remain within the limits of their personality, which surrounds them with a defensive stockade. From childhood on, Rasputin took his freedom, and the benevolence of the universe, for granted. His attitude to the universe was relaxed and expansive—the attitude, in fact, prescribed by Phineas Quimby and by Mrs Eddy. (Mrs Eddy not only believed that physical sickness is a reflection of the sick mind; she also taught that misfortunes and accidents of chance are a form of sickness, and can be averted by the recognition of universal benevolence.) He was a spiritual explorer because he was not afraid to trust, to venture outside the stockade of his personal limitations. The returns taught him that his attitude was not a miscalculation. It is doubtful whether, on this level, he had anything of the charlatan about him. He radiated confidence in life.

But this confidence was not the child-like trust of a St Francis or Ramakrishna. Perhaps because he was a peasant, born in a country where peasants had been treated as animals for centuries, he maintained a strong class consciousness, and he never got over the wonder of dominating his social superiors. He was not quite disinterested enough to be a true saint, although compared to most of his contemporaries, he was a paragon of disinterestedness. This aggressive class consciousness was the flaw in his personality that eventually destroyed him.

CHAPTER SIX

THE RISE TO POWER

WHEREVER he went, Rasputin made enemies; but he never made so many as in St Petersburg between 1907 and his death. The reason is not far to seek: St Petersburg was a city of decadence; that is to say, it was full of life-devaluers.

It is true that, in a sense, all human beings are life-devaluers—all, that is, except a few poets and mystics. Perhaps only a man about to be executed grasps for a moment the full value of life. It is reported of the American gangster Charley Birger that his last words on the scaffold were: 'It *is* a beautiful world'; but it took the prospect of immediate death to make him recognize it; his life is a long record of brutality and stupidity.[1] In the face of death, 'something drops from eyes long blind'; the imagination and the senses work in conjunction, and human boredom seems the ultimate absurdity.

St Petersburg had reached a certain ultimate of life-devaluation, with such writers as Andreyev, Artsybashev, Biely and Briussov. Under the surface, there was still the sloth and indifference that is portrayed in the novels of Gogol or Goncharov; on the surface, there was a feverish and despairing glitter. Money changed hands quickly; women changed their sleeping partners easily. And Count Vassili, who had known four Tsars, wrote in a disgruntled frame of mind:

Salons . . . have disappeared. Those incomparable hostesses,

[1] Birger was executed in Williamson County, Illinois, in April 1928; he was a bootlegger and multiple murderer. See Paul Angle's *Resort to Violence*.

whose judgements made or marred a social reputation . . . have been replaced by women who have pushed themselves to the front, either through their money or their audacity; who gather round them people to play bridge or to discuss the most trivial and commonplace subjects. . . . As for flirting, this art, which was carried to perfection in those old times of which I am thinking, is also extinct. Why should one give oneself that trouble when it is so easy to obtain all that one wants without practising it?

As to the reason for this fever and boredom, Vassili goes straight to its root:

Whatever the faults of the Romanovs . . . whatever cruelties they have been responsible for, no one can deny that they have been strong men. . . . The present Tsar is the first representative of their race in whom weakness and indecision find themselves allied, the first whose existence counts for practically nothing in the eyes of his many subjects, whom they neither respect, fear nor hate.

And he ends his book with words that have the tone of authentic prophecy:

Never, believe me, in the whole history of Russia did a sovereign more need the protection of the Almighty than his majesty Nicholas II . . . in this nineteenth year of his sad and unfortunate reign.

This was written in 1913.

Vassili was right. The Russians were used to being ruled by strong Tsars, and now they had a weakling. In most ways, the people were better off under Nicholas than under his father; they certainly had more freedom. But freedom is an inner condition, and it cannot co-exist with boredom and the devaluation of life. In this sense, the inhabitants of St Petersburg were less free than at any time since Ivan the Terrible.

Into this hot-house came a peasant who knew something of the meaning of freedom, who was certainly no life-devaluer, who was not a martyr to neurasthenia and who did not believe that life is a long-drawn-out defeat. His mere existence was an offence to the spiritually sick. And inevitably, he was unable to suppress his own reaction of disgust. The smell of pampered bodies and sweaty minds revolted him, and his reaction was to be rude. His situation was not unlike that of Handel in the London of the 1720s—with one important difference: Handel could afford to assert his independence of fashionable society (even though it almost cost him his life and reason) because he was a creative genius; their hatred could not penetrate the room where he was writing. But Rasputin's material was human beings; he had to move among them constantly. It was impossible for him not to be constantly aware of envy and hatred. His reaction, inevitably, was to become still more aggressive with the people he disliked. He also began to feel the need for friends—or at least for people he could trust. This craving for friends contributed to his downfall.

Rasputin chose his friends oddly. One of them was a little Jew called Aaron Simanovich, a jeweller whom Rasputin had first met in Kiev and whose son he cured of St Vitus Dance. It was this Simanovich who later wrote a sensational life of Rasputin that is thoroughly unreliable. Simanovich moved to St Petersburg in 1902, and soon became the Tsarina's jeweller. Among her other curious shortcomings, the Tsarina was something of a miser—a strange fault for a member of Russia's royal house. Simanovich used to sell her jewels on extended credit—a kind of hire-purchase system!—and at a low price. Probably he regained what he lost with the Tsarina from other members of the court, for he records that the Russian nobles had 'an extraordinary ignorance of business'. Unlike Rasputin, Simanovich was perfectly at home in the steamy atmosphere of St Petersburg intrigue; he plunged into it with delight, seeing endless opportunities for money-making, and was soon organizing night-clubs, cabarets, gambling dens and probably brothels. Simanovich's career might seem to justify the anti-Semitic views held by the Union of True Russians; but against this, it must be remembered that the Jews in Russia have never had any rights—and this in spite of the fact that Russia's Jewish population was equal to that of all the rest of the world. Pares writes: 'It was not so much a question of what rights the Jews did not possess, but whether they had the right to exist at all'. Jews were confined to settlements on the edge of towns, were forbidden to have Christian servants and usually not allowed to send their children to school. The police were permitted to treat Jewish subjects with complete arbitrariness, and there was almost no legal redress; they were also allowed to run 'protection rackets' to an extent that would have made Al Capone raise his eyebrows. So it is hardly a matter for surprise if a Jew like Simanovich felt no compunction in taking advantage of a decadent society.

Simanovich, by his own account, became Rasputin's political tutor. Like most men who devote their lives to intrigue, he considered idealism futile and unprofitable; consequently, his admiration for Rasputin was somewhat mixed with contempt. He tells how he sometimes scolded Rasputin like a child, and gives the impression that he was the Svengali behind the Svengali. He may well be telling the truth. Rasputin knew nothing about politics, and the story of his career shows that he learned very little, in spite of Simanovich.

Simanovich often acted as intermediary between Rasputin and another lady of the court who was one of Rasputin's warmest supporters, Anna Vyrubov, the daughter of Alexander Taneyev, chief of the Imperial Chancery, and a distinguished composer.[1] Taneyev became one of the Tsarina's favourites through her love of music, and he was able to insinuate his plump and somewhat plain daughter into royal favour. The Tsarina liked her for her honestly affectionate nature and her intense religious devotion. (As a child, she had been cured of a serious illness by John of Cronstadt, who had prayed by her bedside, then sprinkled her with holy water.) Anna was also rather stupid, delighted in gossip, and was a middle-class prig—which was no doubt another reason for the Tsarina's attachment to her. Soon, the royal couple began to make plans for providing the ugly duckling with a husband. A naval lieutenant called Vyrubov was found, and Anna was propelled into the marriage—with many misgivings. The officer had been shell-shocked at Tsuchima, and his manner was sometimes alarmingly tense. Anna decided to consult her friend the

---

[1] Not to be confused with his nephew Sergei Taneyev, a far better composer, whose operatic trilogy *Oresteia* is a masterpiece. Sergei Taneyev is known outside Russia because Tolstoy's wife fell in love with him, and cherished her unhappy passion for many years. One result was Tolstoy's *The Kreutzer Sonata*.

Grand Duchess Militsa, and Militsa told her that she had better meet a man who apparently knew everything: Rasputin. So in April 1907 Anna Vyrubov came to the house of Militsa and met the strange and impressive peasant, who stared at her for a while, then told her that the marriage would be unsuccessful. He added a few more details, which later turned out to be curiously accurate. Anna was shaken, and expressed her misgivings to the Tsarina. However, she was reminded that the marriage had been arranged; so on May 13, 1907, she became the somewhat reluctant bride of Lieutenant Vyrubov. Things went badly. Anna found the marriage less unpleasant than she had expected; but she was somewhat bewildered by the attitude of the Tsarina, who now showed distinct signs of jealousy. Naturally, she did her best to soothe her friend; but this only excited the hostility of her husband, who began to feel that he was an unnecessary third. Finally—probably through the machinations of the Tsarina— Vyrubov was appointed to a ship that was making a world cruise, and he set out for Cronstadt. On his arrival, he discovered that the ship would be delayed a few days by engine trouble, so he immediately went back to see his wife at their villa at Peterhof (the Tsar's summer residence). To his surprise, he found the place surrounded by guards, and was told that he could not enter his own house because his wife was alone with the Tsarina. He waited until the Tsarina had left, then returned—still to be denied entrance. At this he lost his temper and forced his way into the villa. Some time later, his wife rushed out screaming, and went to the summer palace to take refuge with the Tsarina. What her husband had accused her of is not known—it can be guessed—but it incensed the Tsarina enough to order that divorce proceedings should be started immediately. So Madame Vyrubov's marriage came to an end after only a few months, and she became even more firmly entrenched in the Tsarina's favour. Rasputin's prophecies about the marriage had come true.

It seems likely, then, that it was Anna Vyrubov who mentioned the name of Rasputin a month later, when the Tsarevitch had his first serious illness. Although Rasputin had met the Tsar two years earlier, he had only been to Tsarskoe Selo once or twice in the meantime; we can infer this from the fact that he had not met Anna Vyrubov until 1907, although Anna had been the Tsarina's best friend since February 1905. What took place in the Tsarevitch's sickroom has already been described in the last chapter—or inferred from the accounts of Fülöp-Miller and Liepman. From this time onward, Rasputin became the Tsarina's spiritual adviser, and a close friend of Anna Vyrubov. It was generally assumed by the St Petersburg gossips that he was also Anna's lover. From what we know of Anna, this is completely improbable. From this time onward, Anna Vyrubov became Rasputin's chief means of contact with the Royal Family and the court circle. When Rasputin was attacked by indignant ministers, or denounced for his debaucheries by church dignitaries, Anna Vyrubov was always there to assure the Tsarina that it was all deliberate malice, and that their 'Friend' was as holy a man as any saint in the Russian calendar, incapable of an impure thought.

As Rasputin's influence at the court increased, there were new accomplices and helpers. There was, for example, the strange physician Peter Alexandrovitch Badmaev, a herbalist. Badmaev was some twenty years Rasputin's senior; he had studied Chinese and Mongolian at university and later became a lecturer and a civil servant. Like his celebrated fellow countrywoman Madame Blavatsky, Badmaev hinted at secret masters in Tibet who had taught him their medical secrets. But unlike Rasputin, he possessed real political shrewdness, which he sometimes placed at the disposal of the Tsar when advice was needed on Mongolian affairs. (During the Japanese war, he persuaded Mongolian chiefs to enter on the side of Russia, and won the Tsar's gratitude.) Badmaev instantly recognized that Rasputin was worth having as an ally, and the two became friends. They were a formidable alliance, for Badmaev enjoyed political intrigue, and often used his influence with the Tsar to secure appointments for his friends —who were often his ex-patients. It was this Badmaev who was later accused of engineering the Tsarevitch's illnesses so that Rasputin could conveniently 'cure' them.

But after Simanovich, Rasputin's most important accomplice was a sinister adventurer called Maniulov, a little Jew who worked for the Ministry of the Interior and was always dressed with faultless elegance. Like Simanovich, Manasevitch-Maniulov was a born intriguer. He had started on the road to power by

becoming the protégé of an old prince with homosexual inclina-
tions, Meshchersky, the friend of Dostoevsky. 'The spider-like
Meshchersky' (to quote Pares' description) accustomed his
favourite pathic to luxury, then sent him to St Petersburg as a
police spy. He was so successful there that he was sent to Paris
to work under Rachkovsky—the man who was dismissed for
being too frank about 'Dr Philippe. He may well have been the
cause of Rachkovsky's dismissal, for Rachkovsky accused him
of spying on himself, and Maniulov was transferred to Rome to
bribe the priests. He worked for Plehve for two years, and
intrigued against Plehve's enemy Witte. However, he also
worked for Witte, and was used by Witte as an intermediary
with the priest Gapon, who led the march to the Winter Palace
in 1905. His machinations were so complicated that it is impossible to describe them briefly. He betrayed Plehve to Witte
and Witte to Plehve. He posed as a revolutionary and betrayed
the revolutionaries to the police; but he also betrayed police
secrets to the revolutionaries—particularly to the famous Burtsev,
to whom he said frankly: 'I am a vicious man; I love money and
I love life'. (And later he helped Burtsev to escape from prison
and from Russia.) By these complicated betrayals he made a great
deal of money, which he spent quickly. During the Japanese war,
he stole the Japanese cipher, and was awarded the order of
Vladimir by the Tsar.

This musical comedy villain quickly saw how useful Rasputin
could be, and took care to make himself indispensable. There
seems to have been something likeable about his blackguardism,
for he soon became one of Rasputin's favourites. He was to be
seen at Rasputin's house almost every day, and, as soon as he
appeared, Rasputin would cut short any interview and hurry to
embrace him. They would then lock themselves into a room
alone and talk in low voices—sometimes for hours.

It seems unfortunate that most of the people who cultivated
Rasputin as soon as he became a royal favourite were the very
worst types, intriguers, self-seekers and reactionaries. It seems
almost as if fate was determined that his powers should be
turned to the worst possible account. It is possible to like and
approve of Rasputin, but completely impossible to approve of
most of his associates, with the possible exception of Badmaev,

who seems to have been an honest and good man. (After the Revolution, Badmaev, Maniulov and Anna Vyrubov were arrested as they tried to escape from Russia; but Badmaev's courtesy and honesty soon made his gaolers his friends.) Anna Vyrubov was phenomenally stupid, and something of a liar. (She declares in her memoirs that Rasputin never had anything to do with politics!) Maniulov was a swindler, blackmailer, thief and even a betrayer of his own people—he instigated pogroms when it suited his purpose. Simanovich was a crook with a taste for malicious gossip (which forms a considerable part of his book on Rasputin). Stürmer, whom Rasputin was instrumental in making Prime Minister, will be described at length later; but he was perhaps the most disastrous of the lot.

When Rasputin came to St Petersburg, he knew little of politics, and disliked intrigue. Within five years, without fully intending it, he was at the centre of all the intrigue in St Petersburg. It is not surprising if his enemies—such men as Stolypin—assumed that he was tarred with the same brush as Maniulov and Simanovich, while sincere men like Yussupov and Rodzianko saw him as a kind of super-Tartuffe.

But how did Rasputin come to be involved in so much intrigue if he was not interested in politics? The answer would seem to be: because men like Simanovich and Maniulov lost no time in persuading him to use his influence at court and because he was the sort of man who always had a crowd of suppliants waiting at his front door. When he saved the life of the Tsarevitch in 1907, he was already a man of power and influence in St Petersburg—but not on the political level. People came to see him because he was a healer, and because he had the reputation of being able to foretell the future. Rasputin seldom refused to see the people who came to him. When it became known that he was beginning to pay visits to Tsarskoe Selo—entering by a back entrance, so as not to cause gossip—it was natural that the suppliants should ask him to use his influence to get their sons made *aides de camp* or their nephews into the civil service. A man like John of Cronstadt, or even the monk Illiodor, would have refused, explaining that they had no power to grant such favours. Unfortunately, in this particular respect, Rasputin was a weaker man. If his 'secret' visits were suddenly the talk of St Petersburg, it is unfortunately probable that this was partly the result of his own indiscretions. He was a naïve, open soul, and he could probably see no reason for keeping his visits secret. And as soon as he became aware that he had enough influence to secure minor appointments—without having to speak to the Tsar or Tsarina —he used it as casually and as generously as he gave away his money.

Now, although Rasputin did not at first know it, his new position as the intimate of the Tsar and Tsarina made him one of the most envied men in St Petersburg; not simply because he was an acquaintance of royalty, but because he was in a unique position for obtaining all kinds of secret information. Since the Tsar and Tsarina no longer held open court, the number of people who saw them regularly was small. About three-quarters of this number were ministers, church functionaries and so on. Most of these were never sure what the Tsar was thinking—he was too changeable, too easily influenced by the person he was talking to, and, above all, too liable to change his mind. On the other hand, there were a small number of courtiers with whom the Tsar ceased to guard his tongue: the Groom of Chamber, the Governor of the Palace, Anna Vyrubov, Admiral Nilov and General Zablin and perhaps half a dozen more. These were in a position of real power; their tit-bits of information were worth a great deal of money to many officials, bankers and financiers.

Information was a commodity, and certain adventurers quickly cornered the supplies, and sold it at a profit. The chief of these was the sinister Prince Andronikov, a dubious homosexual who described himself as '*aide de camp* to the Almighty'. Andronikov moved in a self-created atmosphere of mystery, carried a large portfolio (which actually contained old newspapers) and spent his days slipping in and out of various ministries, exchanging gossip and picking up what information he could. His chief source was almost certainly the Tsar's Groom of Chamber, about whose relationship with Andronikov there were the inevitable rumours. Andronikov received a monthly stipend from the Ministry of the Interior, whom he kept supplied with information, and on this he ran his own small salon, which was frequented by anyone who had anything to gain from the Tsar. Other similar salons were run by Burdukov, the Master of the Horse, and Baroness Rosen. Both had their source of information at court, and both enjoyed the sensation of power that it brought them. There were perhaps two or three other salons that specialized in information, but none compared with these three.

In one stride, without really intending it, Rasputin outdistanced all rivals in the information market. Andronikov and Burdukov could obtain accurate information quickly, and both had a certain slight influence at court through their sources of information. (Burdukov relied mainly on Admiral Nilov and General Zablin.) But Rasputin was not only able to supply any information about the Tsar's decisions; he was in a unique position for directly influencing them. It is not surprising that his rivals felt bilious with envy, and rationalized their jealousy as concern for the future of Russia.

But for some months after he came to the palace, Rasputin remained an unknown force and gossip about him was restricted to the immediate circle of the Tsarina. Beletsky, the Chief of Police (who lost his post through Rasputin's intervention, and later gained it back through him) dates the beginning of Rasputin's power from 1908. But by this time Rasputin had been a daily visitor at the palace for six months. During these early months he did little but consolidate his position with the Tsarina and the rest of the Royal Family, particularly the Tsarevitch.

And yet, even in these early months of his influence, Rasputin must have felt a certain boredom and irritation. He liked the Tsarina, but it cannot have escaped his notice that she was a domineering and yet hysterical woman. Early photographs show the sad and mournful beauty; some later photographs have little trace of this beauty, but the sadness seems to have turned the face into a kind of wax candle, dripping with self-pity. She was Rasputin's patroness, and he liked her; but if she had only been a St Petersburg society hostess, it is doubtful if he would have felt much tolerance.

As to the Tsar himself, Rasputin's attitude was a curious mixture of respect and contempt. He described him graphically as 'a man without insides', by which one presumes he meant a man without any true will of his own, too easily influenced by other people. The Tsar's attitude to Rasputin was always ambivalent. He had no doubt whatever of Rasputin's extraordinary powers; he witnessed them too many times. But, unlike the Tsarina, he was under no illusions about the sanctity of the *staretz*. When, on later occasions, various ministers denounced Rasputin, he listened sympathetically, and asked them to provide further evidence. Possibly he was somewhat jealous of the adoration that his wife offered Rasputin; he could have no doubt of its depth and strength after he read some of her letters that were stolen from Rasputin a few years later—and which an indiscreet minister handed to the Tsar instead of to his wife. Nicholas's attitude to Rasputin was a curious mixture of dislike, fear and respect, and on several occasions he was on the verge of withdrawing his favour. As will be seen, it was on these occasions that Rasputin quelled the mutiny by performing another of his 'miracles'.

Rasputin's relations with the young Tsarevitch are somewhat problematical. Most writers portray the relationship as a sentimental idyll, with the boy as a hero worshipper. This is unlikely, and the boy's tutor Gilliard states flatly that Alexey disliked Rasputin. This is possible, and it is even more possible that Rasputin found the boy an irritating brat. Brought up in a family of women by an adoring mother who felt guilty about his affliction, Alexey would have had to be a saint not to become spoilt and unmanageable. Added to this, Nicholas was in reaction against the sternness of his own father, and would give the boy anything he asked for. According to Gilliard's account, the Tsarevitch had a naturally kind nature, which showed itself on one occasion when he pleaded for a cook who was in disgrace. Gilliard also mentions that the boy was confused when, on an outing with his tutor, some peasants threw themselves on their knees in front of him. If so, this stage soon passed by, and the child began to enjoy feeling his authority. Prince Paul Vassili writes irritably:

A lot of rubbish has been written about his illness. . . . The reality is sad enough without exaggeration making it worse. . . . From morning to night, the Tsarevitch is told that his existence is so precious to his parents that no caprice of his is allowed to pass without being at once gratified. He is constantly impressed with his own importance, and already knows very well his rights, though he ignores his duties. Arrogant by nature, this arrogance is fostered instead of being corrected. No one is allowed to rebuke him, or even contradict him. The Tsarevitch beats his sisters, tyrannizes over his servants, and whenever anyone attempts to correct him he instantly threatens the unfortunate person with all kinds of punishments.

Prince Vassili is very obviously prejudiced; nevertheless, his views are worth citing, if only as a corrective to the usual view of the ethereal, angelic child whose life was so brutally cut short by the bullets of revolutionaries. He repeats an interesting story in which the Minister of Foreign Affairs, Izvolsky, was waiting to be received by the Tsar. Izvolsky was talking to someone, and the Tsarevitch ran through the room—the child was then five or six—without Izvolsky noticing him. The child walked up to the seated adults and declared imperiously that 'when the Heir to the Throne crosses the room, Ministers ought to stand up'. Izvolsky was too confused—or perhaps overcome by a desire to box his ears—to reply. Later, after his audience with the Tsar, Nicholas asked cheerfully what the misunderstanding had been about, and as Izvolsky had some difficulty in finding words, the Tsar remarked smiling: 'Yes, later on you'll find it harder to deal with my son than with me'. Prince Vassili comments severely that a less infatuated father would have rebuked the child for insolence to a man entitled to respect.

Another story of Prince Vassili seems to contradict Gilliard's story about the peasants. The child liked being saluted by troops whenever he met them, and by regiments at reviews. But if his father was present, the troops naturally saluted the Tsar and ignored the Tsarevitch. So when the boy was taken with his father to watch parades, he used to run ahead so as to arrive first and be saluted. This caused some annoyance among army commanders, and the Grand Duke Nicholas complained to the Tsar that the troops became so confused that they didn't know whom to salute. The Tsarevitch was ordered to stay by his father's side in future.

It can be seen that if only half the malicious gossip about the boy's temperament were true, Russia was likely to gain another Tsar in the true tradition of previous absolute despots.[1]

Gilliard undoubtedly recognized the danger of all this molly-coddling and spoiling and begged the Tsar to give the child more freedom. They were sensible enough to agree to this, although within a month the child had fallen off a table and hurt his knee, which produced a crisis. (Presumably it was this crisis that enabled Rasputin to gain the royal favour; this seems likely when we consider that the Tsarevitch was about three at the time Rasputin saved his life—the age when a child begins to climb on furniture.) Pares notes that, in spite of this crisis, which almost proved fatal, neither parent reproached the tutor, nor suggested revoking the decision to allow the child more freedom.

Prince Vassili alleges that the Tsarevitch beat his sisters; this is almost certainly untrue. But it is true that the life led by these four highly attractive girls was not as enviable as the outside world might suppose. Since there was no court life, there were no balls, no opportunities to meet elegible young officers. They spent most of their time at Tsarskoe Seloe or at the Winter Palace, four 'princesses in a tower'. Maria Rasputin comments that she saw more faces in a day than the princesses saw in a week.

The eldest, Olga, was serious and studious, and usually had an English book under her arm. (English was the family language; the Tsarina had been brought up in England, and spoke Russian badly.) Inevitably, her reading was strictly censored. Tatiana, the prettiest, was something of a coquette, but had her father's quiet charm and good nature. Marie was shy, but also sweet tempered and quiet. The youngest, Anastasia, born in 1901, was the most lively and vital of all; she enjoyed practical jokes and teasing her sisters.

Not surprisingly, Rasputin liked the girls without reservations, and immediately became a favourite with them. Probably his interest—at least in Olga and Tatiana—was not entirely platonic, although it is unlikely that he had any actual designs on them.

---

[1] On the other hand, Vassili was not as well informed as he pretends: for example, he states that the Tsarevitch never had a tutor, and had to rely on his mother and sisters for occasional instruction; he was apparently unaware of Gilliard's existence.

He made a habit of going into their bedroom to kiss them good-night—sometimes without the ceremony of knocking—and their governess, Madame Tyutchev, was scandalized and reported this to the Tsarina. The Tsarina was equally scandalized that anyone should suspect her holy Grigory of having a sinful thought, even towards pretty teenagers in their night dresses, and promptly dismissed her. Rasputin immediately took advantage of her dismissal to seduce the nurse of the princesses. The woman later spoke of this to her confessor—mentioning that the seduction had taken place at the baths.[1] The confessor told her to go to the Tsarina and warn her against the influence of the 'devil'. But again the Tsarina's faith proved unshakable; she decided that the nurse was suffering from a nervous disorder, and had her sent to a mental home in the Caucasus. She later defended Rasputin to the Tsar, pointing out that if Rasputin was free with his kisses and hugs, he was only following the example of the Apostles, who were always embracing people. But the dismissed governess took care that the story of Rasputin's evil influence in the palace spread all over St Petersburg. Gossip later suggested that the Tsarina and her two eldest daughters were all Rasputin's mistresses; but this was a failure in psychological perception. Rasputin's influence over the Tsarina depended on her idea that he was a saint, and he took the greatest care to stay on his best behaviour in the palace. Even before Anna Vyrubov, he took care never to appear drunk. Yet as late as 1912, Damansky, the Assistant Procurator of the Synod, repeated to Rodzianko the rumour that the Tsarina was Rasputin's mistress, and the Russian soldiers during the war took it for granted.

1908 and 1909 were years of consolidation. Rasputin was a rising man in St Petersburg, but he took care to do nothing that would unite his enemies against him. As the rumours of his influence on the Imperial household grew, every hostess in St Petersburg wanted him at her parties. And even his bitter enemy Rodzianko had to admit: '. . . the speed with which he acquired

1 Rodzianko later told the Tsar that the baths was one of Rasputin's favourite places for taking advantage of his female followers, and that, since communal bathing was a Khlysty custom, this proved him to be a member of the sect.

followers and disciples was amazing, especially in society . . . particularly among the women. They clung to him like flies to a honey pot.'

These were years of triumph, when Rasputin seemed to attract success. Ever since 1903—the year of his meeting with John of Cronstadt—his star had been in the ascendant. Now everything was on his side. He was physically powerful and had what is called a 'magnetic personality'. His reputation as a seducer was sufficiently sinister to make every bored society woman in St Petersburg want to give herself to him. He still kept his appearance picturesquely casual, but he took care not to be physically offensive. The Tsarina and her daughters presented him with embroidered blouses and shirts, and other admirers gave him velvet trousers and patent leather boots. He became something of a dandy, not even disdaining the occasional use of scent. He still gave away money as fast as it came into his hands, but was happy to accept presents of clothes and sweet wine. The Grand Duchess Militsa even bought him a new house in Pokrovskoe, this time of two stories—the only two-storied house in the town.

And yet Rasputin's manners became steadily worse. Pares says that 'he made a point of humiliating the high and mighty of both sexes', and Simanovich speaks of his 'incredible insolence'. Another indignant observer mentions that Rasputin shouted orders at his female disciples, and addressed one society lady as 'fat cow'.

It seems regrettably true that Rasputin enjoyed imposing his will on 'society'; but this need not be taken as evidence of some neurosis of inverted snobbery. St Petersburg society was totally corrupt; its favourite occupations were moneymaking, adultery and gossip. The men were intriguers and the women hysterics. Even if Rasputin had been a eunuch, he would have aroused hatred and envy wherever he went. As it was, this Dionysian monk with his enormous vitality, his insatiable sexual appetite, his gargantuan capacity for wine—united with a curious ability to become sober at a moment's notice—affronted their febrile appetites. 'Nihilism' was a fashionable word, not simply in its political significance, but as a denial of all absolute values. The intellectual leaders, the fashionable artists and writers, provided the excuses for this purposeless drifting. On the one hand there was the savage nihilism of Andreyev and Artsybashev; on the other, the nostalgic mysticism of various neo-religious movements. (The finest novel to come out of this school was Briussov's *Fiery Angel*, a long backward-look at the Middle Ages when the devil was still a terrifying reality.) Rasputin had nothing in common with any of these people. The life flowed in him too strongly for him to have any sympathy with the futility-and-despair school of Andreyev, whose chief motive impulse was alcoholic remorse. (Rasputin never suffered from hangovers; he could throw off the effects of excessive drinking in a few hours.) As to mysticism and the Christian ethic of self-sacrifice and self-torment, he was completely out of sympathy. His religion was sincere, but vital and primitive, closer to the ecstatic Dionysianism described by Nietzsche in *The Birth of Tragedy*. It was an instinctive worship of the power in the universe, and it was logical that sex should play a part in it.

This man knew something about the irony of 'success'. Success meant living among these nonentities, accepting their adoration and flattery and seeing through their transparent designs to use him. It meant living in a constant atmosphere of envy and hatred, and occasionally having to suffer open insult from men who prided themselves on being too 'honest' to flatter the peasant. And yet all the time, he was aware that the whole thing was a misunderstanding. Admittedly, he had a genuine gift of second sight and of healing. Yet his power was based on the Tsarina's idea that he was a saint and the Tsar's belief that he was a 'very Christ'. (The Tsar made this remark—which Rasputin lost no time in reporting to the monk Illiodor—before Stolypin began his work of undermining Rasputin's reputation.) And although he was a man of extreme intelligence and foresight—as even hostile biographers admit—he was no intellectual, able to reconcile his instincts with his professed beliefs. Therefore he had no defence against the accusation that he was a hypocrite, an insincere rogue; he had never heard of Nietzsche, and it is doubtful if he would have understood him if he had. His only defence in this atmosphere of intrigue and misunderstanding was contempt. It is not surprising that he chose his intimates from such openly professed scoundrels as Maniulov and Simanovich, and treated his female disciples as a submissive harem.

While Rasputin was consolidating his position in the palace and becoming the most-talked-of man in St Petersburg, the Tsar had other things to think about. The internal situation was irritating enough, even though Nicholas felt he had nothing to fear from the third Duma. Policemen and politicians continued to be assassinated; the Bolsheviks agitated openly; newspapers ignored the possibility of heavy fines, and frequently rushed into print with opinions that embarrassed or angered the Tsar. But the foreign situation was also developing awkwardly. As early as 1908, the first rumbles of the Great War were sounding. Admittedly, Nicholas and Kaiser Wilhelm were supposed to be on the warmest of terms. The Kaiser lost no opportunity to assure Nicholas that Russia wanted and needed an absolute autocrat. He had urged Nicholas into the Japanese war, assuring him that Korea was destined to be Russian, and then hastily reversed his advice when the disasters multiplied. The Kaiser also took care to flatter Nicholas's most competent statesman, Witte, and invited him for a visit at the end of the Japanese war. Witte's fall from power may have had something to do with Nicholas's increasing resentment against the Kaiser. Besides, Wilhelm had bullied and cajoled Nicholas into signing a treaty of alliance that excluded France at a time when Russia's Foreign Minister was working hard for a Russo-French alliance, and Nicholas's irritated ministers (including Witte) had forced him to repudiate it. (Typically, Nicholas had signed the treaty without informing his government, and had ordered his Naval minister to countersign it while the Tsar held a hand over its contents!)

There was another embarrassing matter that blew up in 1908, a legacy from the days of Bismarck and Alexander II. Before the Russo-Turkish war of 1877, Alexander II had entered an agreement with Austria according to which, in exchange for Austrian co-operation in the war, Austria would have the right to occupy the Slav states of Bosnia and Herzegovina. Austria failed to co-operate, so the agreement should have been void. But in October 1908, Austria suddenly announced that the two Slav states were the property of Austria. This caused an international uproar. Nicholas discovered, to his rage, that his Foreign Minister, Izvolsky, was to blame, having been cleverly duped by the Austrian minister. England and France were outraged, for

Russia had entered an alliance with them the year before, and they now discovered that Izvolsky had been secretly dealing with Austria. Kaiser Wilhelm was also rather irritated by the indiscretion of his Austrian allies, but after some grumbling, he decided to stand by them. Patriotism flared, and the Duma was as patriotic as the blackest reactionaries. For a while, it looked like war.

And it was at this point that Rasputin intervened. No one knows exactly what happened, for at this time Rasputin was not regarded as a man of political influence, and no one took the trouble to spy on him. But Rasputin stated on several later occasions that he averted a war with Austria by telling the Tsar firmly that such a war would be the end of Russia. In the light of his reaction to the prospect of war in 1914, this sounds more than plausible. Rasputin may not have been a particularly good Christian, but he believed in universal peace and brotherhood; moreover, as a peasant, he knew what the war would mean in suffering to the Russian people. In October 1908, his credit with the Tsar was still high, and the Tsar believed in his prophetic powers. So Izvolsky was sent to London to soothe Britain, then on to Berlin; treaties and alliances were discussed—and finally dropped—and Russia allowed Austria to keep Bosnia and Herzegovina. As Rasputin remarked on several occasions: the Balkans were not worth the life of a single Russian soldier.

CHAPTER SEVEN

THE ENEMIES MULTIPLY

THE Union of True Russians had been largely responsible for Rasputin's introduction to St Petersburg society; now he had become an influence with the Royal Family, they began to question their wisdom. With the Bishops Theophan and Hermogen, Rasputin remained humble and respectful, and until early 1910, they both continued to believe in his sincerity and sanctity. With the monk-priest Illiodor, he took less trouble to conceal his feelings. Rasputin liked Illiodor—naturally, since the younger man admired him—but he considered him something of a prig. He could understand why Theophan and Hermogen should be celibate—they were old men—but Illiodor was young, and by no means unattractive. Rasputin genuinely felt that a man who rules sex out of his life is robbing himself without knowing it. Possibly there is something to be said for his point of view; Christian asceticism often has a curiously negative character. For example, William James describes the life of Saint Louis of Gonzaga, who vowed himself to virginity at the age of ten and who, to guard himself from temptation, never raised his eyes from the ground. (He refused to be alone in a room even with his own mother.) James adds: 'I can find no other sorts of fruit than these of Louis's saintship', and one can see his point. A man whose mind is wholly occupied by some intellectual or spiritual pursuit has a valid excuse for ignoring sex; but a man who regards it as evil is probably stunting his own development as a human being. Rasputin's view of sainthood was that it is an attribute of humanity, not a denial of it. Consequently, he often

chaffed Illiodor about his celibacy. At this time, Rasputin undoubtedly hoped that Illiodor would become a close friend and
ally; but how could this come about while this barrier on the
question of sex existed between them? Illiodor, for his part, was
not as shocked as he pretended to be. But he was aware that he
had a difficult choice to make. It was all very well for Rasputin
to misbehave himself in St Petersburg; but Bishop Hermogen
was Illiodor's near neighbour, and any looseness of behaviour at
Tsaritsyn would probably reach his ears very quickly. Apart from
this, the friendship of Hermogen and Theophan was important
to him, and he assumed—wrongly, as it turned out—that their
power would be greater than Rasputin's if it ever came to a clash.

During 1908 and 1909, Rasputin met Illiodor more frequently
than Theophan or Hermogen, and they had many talks on the
question of how Russia could be restored to its old strength and
sovereignty. Both of them felt that the answer was: a strong Tsar
backed by a strong church. But Rasputin was becoming aware of
his own power, and his attitude sometimes shocked Illiodor. He
spoke casually about the Imperial family, referring to the Tsarina
as 'Mama', and said of Nicholas, 'he cannot breathe without me'.
Undoubtedly, Rasputin took a certain malicious pleasure in
boasting to Illiodor. He told of how the Tsar had called him 'a
very Christ', and added that he was often obliged to speak sharply
to him. He even—although this sounds like Illiodor's exaggeration—described kissing the Tsarina in her daughters'
room.

In December 1909, Illiodor invited Rasputin to Tsaritsyn to
show him the 'spiritual fortress' that was still being built. They
spent some time visiting Illiodor's followers in their homes, and
Rasputin produced his usual powerful impression on the simple
peasants. But Illiodor could not help being irritated at the way
Rasputin seized his most attractive parishioners and kissed them.
According to Fülöp-Miller, Illiodor had other reasons for feeling
annoyed with his remarkable guest. Shortly after they arrived at
Tsaritsyn, a young carter, a disciple of Illiodor, came to beg for
help; his wife had been 'attacked by a devil', and was rolling on
the floor in convulsions, screaming obscenities. Illiodor took
Rasputin and a bottle of holy water; he threw the water over the
writhing woman, and intoned exorcisms. The woman showed

no sign of stopping. At this point, Rasputin asked to be left alone with the woman. Unwillingly, Illiodor obeyed. A long time passed, then Rasputin came out, saying: 'I have driven out the devil'. The woman had apparently returned to normal.

A few days later, the same scene was repeated. This time, the devil had attacked the niece of a certain Madame Lebedev. The girl was in a coma following her convulsions. Again Illiodor failed to produce any impression, and Rasputin was left with the unconscious girl. This time, he was alone with her for hours, and Illiodor became restless—no doubt remembering some of Rasputin's chaff about seizing opportunities. Finally, Rasputin emerged, and announced his triumph—the girl was sleeping peacefully. Rasputin's reputation as a healer spread throughout the surrounding villages.

After this, Rasputin invited Illiodor back to Pokrovskoe—where he was still spending a great deal of his time. On the way, he talked openly to the monk about his past, declaring that he had been a drunkard up to the age of thirty, and sparing no details of his adulteries. He seemed to take a pleasure in shocking the younger man—or perhaps he divined that Illiodor was more interested in power than in religion, and wanted to find how deep the crust of asceticism went. Once in Pokrovskoe, Rasputin seemed to lose all restraint. If the kisses he distributed to Illiodor's prettiest parishioners shocked the monk, the fervour with which he embraced his own 'parishioners' made Illiodor wonder if Pokrovskoe was Rasputin's private harem. Rasputin's wife, according to Illiodor, seemed indifferent to her husband's open infidelities, and he quotes her as saying: 'He has enough for all'. Illiodor says that he kept wondering: 'Is he a saint or a devil?' —presumably because Rasputin was tempting him to sexual uncleanness—and he later called his book *The Holy Devil*—the first of the sensational biographies of Rasputin.

The proof that Illiodor's attitude to Rasputin verged on discipleship is that he did not denounce Rasputin to Hermogen and Theophan. He kept his own counsel, and continued to be friendly to Rasputin. And when disturbing rumours of Rasputin's 'debauches' reached Hermogen's ears, some time in 1910 (the St Petersburg newspapers were starting to launch attacks on him already), Illiodor defended him. It is this that gives one reason to suspect that Illiodor's account of Rasputin's behaviour at Pokrovskoe is exaggerated.

The Prime Minister, Stolypin, was becoming alarmed at rumours of Rasputin's influence with the Tsar. Finally, he decided to speak openly to the Tsar about it. Nicholas, as usual, listened politely, and Stolypin was encouraged to suggest that he should draw up a report on Rasputin, which would be shown to the Tsarina. Nicholas agreed, and Stolypin left the palace convinced that he had found the way to break Rasputin's influence. Lukianov, the Procurator of the Holy Synod, proceeded to 'dig'. It did not take a lot of investigation to convince him that the contradiction between Rasputin's religious convictions and his sexual behaviour could be easily explained: Rasputin was a member of the Khlysty, and sexual orgies were a part of the Khlysty rites. (It must be realized that very few people in Russia knew much about the Khlysty, for the brotherhood went to some trouble not to advertise their activities.) On the basis of various documents—of dubious authenticity—Stolypin drew up his report, and presented it to the Tsar. Nicholas glanced at it and dropped it into a drawer. He told Stolypin that he had better go and meet Rasputin for himself, and make up his own mind whether the *staretz* was a hypocritical debauchee.

Stolypin's account of this interview—his first with Rasputin —has already been quoted. He believed that Rasputin made an attempt to hypnotize him.

> I pulled myself together and, addressing him roughly, told him that on the strength of the evidence in my possession, I could annihilate him by prosecuting him as a sectarian (i.e. a Khlyst). I then ordered him to leave St Petersburg immediately. . . .

Stolypin had somewhat exceeded his instructions in telling Rasputin to get out of St Petersburg. But it happened that Rasputin himself was becoming alarmed at the amount of hostility he was arousing. His family told him that strangers had been to the village and asked questions. Father Peter, who still hated Rasputin, had given them a great deal of 'information'. The investigators had also been to Verkhoture, trying to find out whether there was any evidence that Rasputin had definitely been initiated into the Khlysty. St Petersburg newspapers were beginning to make guarded attacks on him—in spite of the heaviness of the fines that the Tsar could arbitrarily impose on any newspaper that offended him. Things were getting too warm for comfort. A long visit to Pokrovskoe would have met Stolypin's requirements; but he knew he would be under constant observation there. He decided to make another pilgrimage to the Holy Land. This would serve many purposes. It would reinforce his reputation for piety with the Tsarina, and would allow him a holiday from police spies. It would also give him an opportunity to renew some old acquaintances. But, most important, it would be a break with the life of intrigue and malice that was beginning to turn him into an intriguer himself.

Rasputin began his penitential journey in March 1911. During this time, he was in constant communication with the Tsarina. Various letters and notes were later gathered together by his daughter and printed as Rasputin's *Journal of a Pilgrimage*, a work of about 16,000 words. It reveals that he was sincerely glad to escape the atmosphere of St Petersburg, and that the monasteries and sanctuaries of the Holy Land once again made a deep impression on him. The Tsarina studied his letters—which were often scrawled on worn scraps of paper—and carefully preserved them. Some of her own replies were in a vein of almost mystical adoration that proves the extent of Rasputin's hold over her. She also fumed about Stolypin, and asked the Tsar to dismiss him. Nicholas was too sensible to do this—competent ministers were rare—but his manner towards Stolypin became colder.

The penitential journey lasted several months, and when Rasputin returned, he went straight to Pokrovskoe. But the Tsarina had not forgotten him, even though she apparently recognized that it would not be tactful for him to return to St Petersburg. She sent Anna Vyrubov and her friend Mme Orlov to visit him at Pokrovskoe. In her memoirs, Anna Vyrubov reveals that 'although the Tsarina had the fullest confidence in Rasputin's integrity she thought it worth while to make some enquiries into his private life in Siberia'. Perhaps Bishop Theophan had been spreading rumours at court, and she was curious to learn whether Rasputin's life at Pokrovskoe was really one long debauch. (Pares states that Theophan had also visited Rasputin at Pokrovskoe, and had received the confession of a woman whom Rasputin had seduced; unfortunately, he gives no date.) The two women took the train as far as Tioumen, and were met there by Rasputin with a horse and cart. Rather to their dismay, they were told that they had to travel in this vehicle for about sixty miles over bumpy roads. For Rasputin, this was no distance at all; for the two court ladies with their maids, it must have been an uncomfortable journey to Pokrovskoe.

She describes Rasputin's house as 'almost biblical in its simplicity'. The upper floor contained the sleeping chambers; these were unfurnished except for straw mattresses laid on the rough wooden floor, although tapers burned before ikons on the wall. The household, according to Anna Vyrubov, consisted of Rasputin's 'old wife' and three children—including the idiot boy—and two spinsters who helped in the house and on the farm. Meals were eaten in the simple dining-room, all sitting round the same bare table, and in the evening, four friends of Rasputin—who called themselves 'the brethren'—usually came to read the Bible and sing psalms.

Life was not as dull as it sounds; much time was spent out of doors, especially by the river. Rasputin and the 'brethren' went fishing most days, and they often cooked the fish over camp fires by the river. The religious atmosphere and the simplicity impressed Anna Vyrubov, who enjoyed her visit so much that she returned on a later occasion—probably in Lent, 1912, when Rasputin was again exiled from the Imperial Family. On her return to the Tsarina, she reported favourably on Rasputin's home life in Pokrovskoe—observing that the clergy of the town seemed to dislike him. She had also been taken by Rasputin on a visit to Verkhoture—presumably in the same bumpy cart— and observed that the hermit Makáry 'held Rasputin in higher respect than the village clergy'.

This visit took place in late August 1911. In early September, the Imperial Family paid a ceremonial visit to Kiev, taking with them the Prime Minister Stolypin, and the Minister of Finance, a quiet and efficient little man called Kokovtsev. Rasputin decided that he would accompany Anna Vyrubov to Kiev. They arrived on September 18, and one of the first things they saw was the Imperial carriage driving past with the Tsar and

Tsarina. This was followed by another carriage with Stolypin. As Stolypin's carriage passed, Rasputin unexpectedly began to call out: 'Death is after him. Death is driving behind him.' It was another example of his strange gift of second sight. For the following day, the Tsar wrote to his mother:

> During the second interval [of Rimsky-Korsakov's opera *Tsar Saltan*] . . . we heard two sounds, as if something had been dropped. I thought an opera glass might have been dropped on somebody's head . . . Directly in front of me in the stalls, Stolypin was standing; he slowly turned his face towards us and . . . made the sign of the cross . . . Only then did I notice . . . that his right hand and uniform were blood stained. He slowly sank into his chair and began to unbutton his tunic.

Later, the Tsar tried to visit Stolypin in hospital, but was not allowed to see him. Possibly Stolypin refused to see Nicholas. Earlier in the day, observing that the Tsar was surrounded by police, while he and Kokovtsev were left unguarded, he remarked bitterly: 'We are superfluous'. So died Peter Stolypin, the most efficient man ever to work for Nicholas II, and the only man who might have averted the revolution.

There was nothing now to keep Rasputin out of St Petersburg, so he returned—after first following the Royal Family to Livadia in the Crimea, from which he was expelled by a police chief who wanted to demonstrate that he was not afraid of the Imperial favourite.

But in St Petersburg, things had not improved. Anticipating his return, the anti-Rasputin movement had been gathering force. The Bishop of St Petersburg, Monsignor Anthony, went to see the Tsar to protest about Rasputin, but was irritably told to mind his own business.[1] The Bishop died soon after this.

Illiodor, seeing Rasputin's disgrace, had by this time decided that it would be safer to combine his forces with Theophan and Hermogen. Theophan—the gentle Bishop who had been largely responsible for Rasputin's introduction to society—was already violently anti-Rasputin, although it is not known exactly what

[1] Rodzianko gives early 1911 as the date for this interview, but most of the dates given in these pages of his book seem to be inaccurate. He mentions that Mgr Anthony's visit took place on Rasputin's return to St Petersburg.

led to this change of heart. Hermogen was further from St Petersburg—at Saratov—and was unwilling to condemn Rasputin without definite evidence. Presumably Illiodor supplied this by giving details of his visit to Pokrovskoe in the previous year. Illiodor's excuse for his own change of heart was that he had since received the confession of a nun, Xenia, whom Rasputin had raped.

Rasputin's version of what brought about the crisis of his relations with Hermogen is quite different, and is given in his daughter's book. It is at least as plausible as Illiodor's account. According to Rasputin, Illiodor was so influenced by his chaffing on the subject of sex that he broke away from his ascetic practices. One day, the wife of a St Petersburg officer, a Madame Olga Loktin,[1] went to confess to Illiodor. She was somewhat neurasthenic, and Illiodor may have believed her admiration to be a different sort of passion. At all events, he tried to rape her, and the horrified woman began to scream. When Illiodor's followers rushed in, Illiodor declared that the mad woman had pleaded with him to have sexual intercourse with her, and that he had hurled her from him. Madame Loktin was dragged out into the courtyard, beaten and stripped, and tied to the back of a cart which then drove off through the snow. As a result of this, she suffered from a complete nervous breakdown and became a little insane. (Fülöp-Miller says that she then transferred her attentions to Rasputin, and became one of his most passionate admirers; but her insane outbursts enraged Rasputin, who could never summon up patience to treat her kindly.)

Illiodor decided to anticipate Rasputin's denunciations by denouncing him to Hermogen. So on December 29, 1911, Hermogen asked Rasputin to come and see him. When Rasputin arrived—presumably in the monastery at Saratov—he discovered that it was not to be a private interview. Illiodor was there, and the idiot Mitya Koliaba, the 'prophet' whom Rasputin had displaced at court. There were also two witnesses—a Cossack and a lay brother—and a journalist.

Again, there are two versions of this interview. Illiodor's account states that Hermogen asked Rasputin whether the stories about his sexual debauches were true, and Rasputin,

[1] Whom Pares credits with teaching Rasputin to read and write.

completely cowed, answered: 'It's true, it's all true'. The indignant Hermogen then began hitting Rasputin with an enormous cross, and ordered him not to touch women any more, and to stay away from the palace. Afraid for his life, Rasputin agreed.

One of the witnesses, the Cossack Rodionov, states that Hermogen began with a violent denunciation of Rasputin, to which Rasputin replied insolently, threatening to 'make short work' of the Bishop. The Bishop anathematized him, and Rasputin hurled himself on him and proceeded to beat him, until the others dragged him off. Rodionov's story certainly sounds more plausible—and true to Rasputin's character—than Illiodor's.

Rasputin was himself roughly handled by Mitia Koliaba— who had old debts to pay off—and the lay brother, but managed to break away. He lost no time in going to see the Tsar and presenting his own version of what had happened—beginning with the attempted rape of Madame Loktin. The Tsar immediately issued an order banishing Hermogen and Illiodor to different monasteries. Hermogen had the right to be tried by twelve other bishops, but the Tsar overruled this. Hermogen accepted his banishment quietly; after an illness, he went to the Zhirovetsky monastery.

Illiodor, on the other hand, declined to accept his banishment. He left St Petersburg and travelled about the country, denouncing Rasputin wherever he went. He had stolen certain letters from the Tsarina and her daughters to Rasputin (on the visit to Pokrovskoe in 1910), and he now had these copied and circulated. Eventually, he was caught and imprisoned in the monastery of Florishchevo. The decline in his fortunes seems to have driven him to a frenzy. He started to write a book denouncing Rasputin, and declaring that the Tsarina was his mistress. He was unfrocked, and managed finally to escape to Norway disguised as a woman. There, he continued his memoirs—which became steadily more scurrilous and inventive—and wrote to the Tsarina, offering to sell them to her for an immense sum. She ignored his letter. Later still—during the war—Illiodor sold his pamphlet on Rasputin, together with the Tsarina's letters, to an American magazine.

The affair created a considerable scandal. Hermogen's assault on Rasputin was not the sole reason for his banishment. The Bishop of Tobolsk had died—the same man who had ordered an investigation into Rasputin a dozen years earlier—and Rasputin proposed his own candidate for the post, his old friend and drinking companion Barnaby—who was working as a gardener. Rodzianko declares that Rasputin's aim was to be made a priest, but this sounds unlikely. Rasputin's patron, the Procurator Sabler, pressed Barnaby's appointment on the Synod, and finally bullied them into it by hinting that it was the Tsar's wish. At this, Hermogen made a furious denunciatory speech, and strode out of the assembly. The reason the Tsar gave for banishing him to a distant monastery was that he was deliberately disrespectful to the Tsar.

But the anti-Rasputin faction gained in strength every day. A certain Professor Novoselov, a lecturer at the Moscow Theological Academy, published a pamphlet proving that Rasputin was a member of the Khlysty, and denounced the church for tolerating such abuses. Probably he had been put up to it by Theophan and Lukianov. The pamphlet was promptly suppressed. The paper *Golos Moskvy*, owned by the President of the Duma, Guchkov, immediately published an article by the same author, with extracts from the pamphlet. This was also suppressed, and issues of the pamphlet and the newspaper passed from hand to hand. Other newspapers, encouraged by Guchkov's example, began writing articles about Rasputin in which he was denounced as a 'fornicator of human souls and bodies'. The Tsarina's comment on all this was 'He is hated because we love him'. But the Tsar was irritated into issuing an order forbidding any newspaper to write about Rasputin. In doing so, he broke his own undertaking about freedom of the press given in the famous manifesto of 1905.

Guchkov—a remarkable and adventurous man, who had fought in the Boxer rebellion and the Boer war—now proposed a full-scale debate on Rasputin in the Duma, impairing his own popularity with the sovereign even further. He was soon succeeded as President of the Duma by Micheal Rodzianko—a gigantic man with a deep voice, who was totally honest, but by no means free from vanity and stupidity.

Rasputin now had a range of formidable enemies working for his downfall. Quite suddenly—in the course of a single year—

he had become one of the most discussed, and hated, men in Russia. He had proved his strength in the clash with Hermogen and Illiodor; but now his enemies were men of even greater power. Guchkov was something of an adventurer, but a man of tremendous boldness, and leader of the Octobrists, the party of patriotic reform, whose ideal was the parliamentary system of England. Rodzianko had an honest and impressive manner that carried weight even with the Tsar. He had also spoken to the Tsar's mother—the Dowager Empress—about Rasputin, and discovered that she also regarded him as evil and dangerous. The Dowager Empress was naturally opposed to anyone whom her daughter-in-law liked. But the most powerful opponent— for the present—was the man who had taken over the job of Prime Minister from Stolypin, Kokovtsev. Kokovtsev had been chosen for one good reason: he was the only man in Russia who was strong enough and reliable enough to take over. He was not much liked by anyone—a small man, perfectly dressed, who never looked one in the eye and who spoke with a precision and dryness which—says Prince Vassili—reminded one of a schoolboy reciting something learned by heart. 'In a word, one felt that he was too neat, too well groomed, too polite, too civil.' Compared to most Russian officials, he was honest— although people noticed that enterprises in which he owned shares always prospered mysteriously, as if someone in a high position were making use of secret information. . . . Compared with Stolypin or Witte, he was a nonentity; still, he was efficient and businesslike—qualities that do not usually distinguish Russians. And since, as the Minister of Finance, he had occasionally plotted to thwart the Duma, the Tsar liked and trusted him.

But at least, Kokovtsev and Rodzianko made no secret of despising Rasputin. Far more dangerous, in their way, were the men who pretended to be Rasputin supporters and secretly plotted against him. One of the most unpleasant of these—and a man who will appear later in this narrative—was an adventurer called Alexis Hvostov, who was Governor of Nijny Novgorod. A story concerning Hvostov demonstrates Rasputin's increasing political power in 1911. Immediately after Stolypin's murder, a new Minister of the Interior was needed—for Stolypin had occupied this post himself. The Tsar sent Rasputin to Novgorod to see if he thought that Hvostov would be a suitable candidate. Hvostov had never heard of Rasputin, and was irritated when this unkempt peasant with the broad accent arrived at his house. He treated him haughtily and did not even offer him a meal. Rasputin did not take offence openly—but as he left Hvostov, he dropped a hint that the Tsar would receive an unfavourable report. Hvostov found it hard to believe that the peasant had any influence, but he was curious enough to send to the tele-graph office to see the copy of the telegram that Rasputin had sent to Tsarkoe Seloe. It was to Anna Vyrubov, and to Hvostov's stupefaction, it read: 'Tell mama that the grace of God is in Hvostov, but there is still something lacking in him.' Hvostov had a sudden suspicion that he had made a fool of himself, and rushed off to St Petersburg for an audience with the Tsar. But the Tsar received him coldly, told him that the sewage repairs in Novgorod were not important business—Hvostov had used them as an excuse—and dismissed him. Rasputin soon had the great satisfaction of seeing Hvostov trying to lick his boots. Rasputin bore no grudge, and Hvostov eventually secured the coveted appointment—but not until four years had passed. And while Hvostov flattered Rasputin to his face, he plotted behind his back. He told Rodzianko that his reason for being friendly with Rasputin was that he hoped to get him thoroughly drunk in a public place so as to compromise him with the Tsarina.

Two more of Rasputin's enemies should be mentioned here for completeness: Vladimir Purishkevich, a brilliant conservative and member of the Duma—whose influence, however, was negligible—and Prince Felix Yussupov, who had met Rasputin in 1909. But Yussupov was not to see Rasputin again until 1914—he was abroad, studying.

These were the enemies who were ranging themselves against Rasputin in 1911. And they lost little time in going into action. Rodzianko demanded an audience with the Tsar, and received it on March 10, 1912. He knew he was handling gunpowder; both Stolypin and Bishop Anthony had already been snubbed when they tried to talk to the Tsar about Rasputin. But Rodzianko was an impressive man, and he hoped to carry the meeting by force of personality. He also decided to try a little tact. Having broached the subject of Rasputin, he added quickly: 'Will it be your Majesty's pleasure to hear me to the end? If not, say but one word, and I'll be silent.' In a low voice—probably thinking what would be his wife's reaction if she could hear this interview—the Tsar murmured: 'Speak'. Rodzianko launched into the usual denunciation of Rasputin, and offered to provide documentary proofs that Rasputin had been using his reputation as the Tsar's favourite to seduce and rape every girl who came into contact with him. Rodzianko should have known better; the Tsar had already received a fat report on this subject from Stolypin, and had not bothered to read it. However, the Tsar probably saw that this was an easy way to terminate the interview, so he told Rodzianko to go ahead. Rodzianko went off feeling very pleased with himself.

He had reckoned without Nicholas's guilt feelings towards his wife. Alexandra was the only person in the world that Nicholas cared much for; he needed to have someone whom he could trust completely, to whom he could confide everything. But if he started doing things behind her back, it formed barriers between them, even if Alexandra was unaware of them. So on this occasion, he had no sooner authorized Rodzianko to start digging into Rasputin's career than he felt obliged to tell his wife what had happened. She was furious. She quickly discovered that Rodzianko had bullied Damansky—a Rasputin supporter in the Synod—into handing over Lukianov's old report—the one that proved Rasputin to be a Khlyst. She told Damansky to go and get the report back, and Damansky—harried and rather frightened—hastened to see Rodzianko, and hinted that 'a very exalted person' wanted the papers back. 'Sabler?' asked Rodzianko (naming Damansky's superior). 'No, the Tsarina, Alexandra Federovna.' And here, Rodzianko made Damansky's hair stand on end by snapping: 'Will you kindly inform Her Majesty that she is as much a subject of the Tsar as I am myself, and it is the duty of us both to obey him. I am not in a position to obey her wishes.'

But angering the Tsarina was the last way to get what he wanted. When Rodzianko completed his indictment of Rasputin,

he asked for another interview with the Tsar. It was refused.
Instead, he was told to submit his report in writing—and he
knew what that meant. Once again, Rasputin had triumphed.
Rodzianko went to see Kokovtsev in a fury, and asked him to
do something. But he knew he had been checkmated.

Kokovtsev did his best, but it was no use. The Tsar simply
told him to go and talk to Rasputin himself! Kokovtsev took
this advice seriously, and went to see the *staretz*. His description
of the interview reads very much like Stolypin's. Rasputin
stared at him and tried to hypnotize him—or at least, Kokovtsev
thought so. Finally, perhaps touched by Kokovtsev's pleas, he
said: 'All right, I'll leave'. He then went on to make some remarks
that seem to prove once again his amazing prophetic foresight.
He talked to Kokovtsev about the food situation, and advised
him to pay special attention to the railways. (He repeated this
advice again later.) Even Sir Bernard Pares speculates whether
this was political shrewdness or sheer inspiration—for it was the
blockage of the food supplies through the railways that finally
toppled Nicholas off his throne.

Kokovtsev's victory—such as it was—cost him dear. The
Tsar became markedly cold towards him, and the Prime Minister
could have no doubt that Nicholas was wondering whom he
could get to replace him.

Still, Rodzianko was cheerful. He was even more cheerful
when he heard a story that began circulating in St Petersburg a
few weeks later. The Imperial Family had left for Livadia for
their usual summer holiday, and Anna Vyrubov smuggled
Rasputin on to the train. The Tsar got to hear about it, and lost
his temper—he was tired of being compromised by this plausible
peasant—and ordered the train to be stopped. Rasputin was put
down at a station called Tosno—between St Petersburg and
Moscow—and a police agent saw to it that he went back to
Pokrovskoe.

It looked like victory for the anti-Rasputinites, even if the cost
was the Tsar's disfavour for Kokovtsev and Rodzianko. But the
next news they received dampened their high spirits. The
Tsarevitch had had another accident when leaping out of a boat,
and his life had been despaired of. The Tsarina dispatched a
telegram to Rasputin—as recounted in Chapter 5—and received

a reply telling her that her son would live. The Tsar at once repented of his harshness to Rasputin; plainly, the man was a saint and a miracle worker, even if he could be an embarrassment. By the end of 1912, Rasputin was established at court more firmly than ever.

And it was at about this time that the chief of police remarked to Rodzianko: 'I am utterly sick of him. Every time he gets off the train, he goes straight to the baths with two ladies.' Rasputin was indefatigable. Amidst all the political upheavals, in constant danger of assassination, his mind never strayed far from his favourite subject: sex.

CHAPTER EIGHT

THE STORM GATHERS

WHAT was happening to Rasputin? Reading about this period, it seems that anyone but an idiot would have realized that he was sitting on a powder barrel.

It is difficult to avoid the conclusion that some serious deterioration began to set in at about this time. Rasputin was surrounded by enemies and intrigue. It hardly required second sight to know that he would be assassinated sooner or later. And yet this man —who had had the strength to be a homeless wanderer for ten years—seemed unable to tear himself away from this unhealthy atmosphere. One of the reasons, undoubtedly, was sex. The police reports of the period are full of entries like this: 'On the night of January 17, Maria Gill, wife of a captain in the 145th Regiment, slept at Rasputin's'; 'On the night of November 25, Varvarova, the actress, slept at Rasputin's'; 'Rasputin came home in the motor-car . . . with the prostitute Gregubova. He was blind drunk, kissed Gregubova passionately and stroked her cheeks'; 'Rasputin, accompanied by the twenty-eight-year-old wife of the . . . Burgess Yazininski, left in a car. . . . The pair, in a very tipsy state, then proceeded to Madame Yazininskaia's flat, from which Rasputin did not return home until midday.' The reports usually state that Rasputin was 'dead drunk'; but it is noteworthy that if he was summoned to the palace, his drunkenness would vanish immediately.

And yet even this life of endless promiscuity and drinking does not explain why Rasputin stayed in St Petersburg; it only adds another problem: why was Rasputin living like this?

According to his detractors—which means almost everyone who has written about him—there was no problem at all. Rasputin was a drunken peasant who had lied and cheated his way into royal favour, and went on to make the best of a good thing.

But this view does not fit the facts. Rasputin was no saint, but he was a very remarkable man; apart from Gurdjieff, he was probably the most remarkable man in Russia at that time. And, being a Russian, there was something of the eastern tendency to world-rejection in him. Like the Arabs described by T. E. Lawrence, he was no ascetic; yet he had the same love of the 'cold eddyless wind of the desert', of the open steppe; this love of freedom breathes through his descriptions of the sea or the night sky in his journal. Before he had met the Tsar, he had been free. He had had his admirers and followers, but he did not belong to them; he wandered constantly. And yet now he was living in an atmosphere of intrigue, danger and insult. The police spies report that Rasputin was seen to flee from the house of a man called Belkovsky, pursued by two other men; he leapt into a passing cab, and stood all the way to the Liteiny to see if he was being followed. This may have been one of the many plots against his life. The police spies also report that he was assaulted by an army officer at the station. On another occasion, the police spies held back two furious husbands at his front door while their wives escaped down the back staircase. His life was turning into a low comedy—but a comedy with constant undertones of danger. Why did Rasputin stay at the centre of the storm, when he could so easily have disappeared to Palestine for a year or so until it had blown over? Even without his remarkable intuition, his common sense must have told him that his chances of survival were low.

There is only one plausible answer: he knew that his disappearance would mean the collapse of the throne. This is not as improbable as it sounds. An atmosphere of fatality seemed to hang over the Romanovs. Memoirs of the time—like Vassili's—sound as if they have precise fore-knowledge of the 1917 catastrophe. And in 1912, Rasputin's prophecy to the Tsar was being repeated all over Russia: 'While I live, your throne is secure. If I die, you will lose your throne and your life.' Rasputin was tied to St Petersburg because he felt the coming catastrophe, and believed that he was the only man who could avert it. His belief was not entirely without foundation. He had averted a war in 1909. Again, in 1912, when tension between Bulgaria, Serbia, Turkey and Austria threatened to blow into a war, it was Rasputin whose influence was decisive in preventing it, as even Pares admits. When the 1914 war led directly to revolution, Rasputin's attitude was justified. There may be some truth in the notion that Rasputin was the man most responsible for the 1917 revolution; but what is just as certain is that his intervention prevented the revolution from occurring sooner.

Whether this is regarded as a good thing depends on one's attitude towards the communist revolution. There are experts on Russia who argue that most of the changes that have occurred in Russia—particularly the industrialization—would have occurred anyway. Politically speaking, it was undoubtedly only a matter of time before Russia was 'constitutionalized'. On the other hand, it is difficult to read the history of the Romanovs without feeling that Russia was due for a thorough spring cleaning, and that even the Duma was a half-measure. And on this account, it is difficult for history to excuse Rasputin. His political influence was wholly pernicious, since he encouraged a weak Tsar—who for his own protection should have been 'constitutionalized'—in his delusions of grandeur. The main thing that can be said on behalf of Rasputin's monarchism is that, unlike that of most of the Tsar's flatterers, it was completely sincere. Rasputin was no reactionary. He was a peasant who stood for the peasants and for minority groups—like the Jews and the Finns—and did his best to bring about reforms. He disliked the extreme left-wing revolutionaries, not because they stood for reform, but because they stood for a narrow-minded form of materialism. The portrait of revolutionaries in Dostoevsky's *Devils* is by no means unfair or exaggerated. For most of them, materialism was almost a mystical creed; it had little in common with the common sense and deeply moral attitude of the rationalist sects like the Dukhobortsy and Molokanye.[1] They preached atheism and the dissolution of the family, and regarded 'spirit' and 'free will' as meaningless—the product

[1] Who preached that the only thing necessary to salvation was love of one's fellow man.

of biological and chemical processes. A man like Rasputin—who took his thaumaturgic powers and second-sight for granted—could never feel the slightest kinship with these ideas.

So, for better or for worse, Rasputin found himself ranged against every powerful faction in Russia. The Bolsheviks hated him as a mystical fraud; the liberals hated him for encouraging the Tsar's absolutist tendencies; the conservatives hated him for encouraging the Tsarina to meddle in politics. The Tsarina's own brother, in conversation with the Foreign Minister in 1912, referred to her as a 'danger', and said: 'The Tsar is a saint and an angel, but he doesn't know how to deal with *her*'.

Under these circumstances, Rasputin's steady deterioration becomes understandable. All men, even the strongest, see themselves largely through the eyes of their fellow creatures; it is impossible not to be distorted through living in an atmosphere of hatred. In 1905, Rasputin had hardly an enemy in the world, and was universally admired and regarded as a holy man—by men such as John of Cronstadt and Bishop Hermogen, as well as by thousands of ordinary people with whom he had come into contact. Under such circumstances, it is not difficult to live like a holy man. By 1912, he was the most hated man in Russia. Even the peasants disliked the idea of an upstart from their own class imposing on the Tsar and Tsarina. He began to show definite signs of a need for forgetfulness, and when this was not possible, there were explosions of anger and contempt. 'Through all Rasputin's conversation ran the strain of humiliating the great of the earth', writes Pares. As to the 'great of the earth', many of them had darker designs on Rasputin than mere humiliation.

In 1912, Rasputin changed his address to 64 Gorokhovoy—probably with the idea of greater privacy. This was a five-room apartment on the third floor, with a convenient back staircase that could be reached through a courtyard. The area was something of a slum. The courtyard was usually draped with wet washing, and the house smelt of cooking.

There is some confusion about Rasputin's addresses before he moved to the Gorokhovoy. Füllöp-Miller mentions three of them: on the Nevsky Prospect (a flat rented by the rich widow, Bashmakova), the Kirochnaia and the English Prospect. Since we know that his first residence in St Petersburg was with the journalist Sassonoff, he would seem to have had at least four addresses in St Petersburg. Yet Rodzianko mentions that Rasputin was still living with Sassonoff as late as 1911. On the whole, it seems probable that he moved directly from Sassonoff to the Gorokhovoy, and that the Nevsky Prospect flat—and the rich widow who rented it—is an invention of the journalist Charles Omessa.

Rasputin's two daughters also came to live with him at 64 Gorokhovoy—so the lurid stories of non-stop rapes and orgies recounted by Fülöp-Miller are probably also an exaggeration.

This new flat was under constant surveillance by the police and various other spies. Most of the records for this period have little value except as gossip. Presents were received every day—cases of madeira, parcels with caviare and cheese, baskets of fish—even furniture and carpets. The Tsar contributed a bureau. Visitors came in and out constantly, but most of them were disappointed. Rasputin flatly declined to intercede directly with the Tsar or Tsarina—he knew they were sick of petitions. The Tsar had told him: 'We are glad to see you every day, but do not send any more petitioners'. Pretty women were usually luckier, particularly if they were willing to let Rasputin see that they were dominated by him. Stories that he tried to rape all attractive petitioners are obviously untrue; to begin with, the police records show that most of them only stayed for ten minutes or so. But he liked to feel his power. Rodzianko tells an absurd story that illustrates how the women themselves were largely to blame for the lurid rumours that began to circulate. A woman from the provinces wanted to get her husband promoted, and went to see Rasputin. He addressed her familiarly, told her he would think about it, but told her to come back the next day in a low-cut dress with bare shoulders—presumably finding her dress too modest for his taste. The woman went away offended, determined not to return. But on her return home, says Rodzianko, she was 'seized with an unaccountable yearning', and kept recalling how Rasputin's eyes had 'seemed to pierce her through and through'. The next day she 'procured' a low-cut dress and presented herself at Rasputin's. No rape occurred—but her husband received his promotion.

Rodzianko tells the story to illustrate Rasputin's hypnotic

powers, but it is clear that it illustrates only the hysteria of the lady in question. Rasputin behaved familiarly with women, but it seems that his usual objective was simply to 'take the starch out of them'. Many of the police reports show this. 'Rasputin asked her to kiss him; she refused, however, and left. . . .' 'The wife of Colonel Tatarinov visited Rasputin and afterwards told detectives that the *staretz* embraced and kissed a young girl in her presence; she found the incident so painful that she decided never to visit Rasputin again.' A female petitioner told the concierge: 'He told me to take off my coat. . . . He hardly listened to my request, but kept on touching my face and breast, and asking me to kiss him. Then he wrote a note, but did not give it to me, saying that he was displeased with me and telling me to come back the next day.' It can be seen that many of Rasputin's visitors seem to have been a little prudish. These incidents may indicate that Rasputin had taken a glass of wine too many with his lunch, but they hardly show him to be a satyr who tried to strip every female petitioner.

The value of Rasputin's notes is doubtful. They were usually very brief—for Rasputin still had considerable difficulty in writing—and one priest was afterwards overheard by the spies jeering at Rasputin's clumsy writing. These notes usually read: 'My dear friend. Please do what you can for the bearer. Grigory.' When they were taken to Rasputin's few friends or admirers— like Stürmer or Bishop Barnaby—they might be honoured; but ministers who disliked Rasputin usually threw them in the waste-paper basket.

Anna Vyrubov was often sent by the Tsarina to deliver notes to Rasputin, and she records her intense dislike of these errands, which involved pushing up the stairs through crowds of petitioners. She recalls that one poor student begged her to help him get an overcoat, and she had one sent to him. It would seem, then, that most of Rasputin's petitioners were ordinary beggars. The more influential men—these who wanted appointments or help in financial deals—would approach him through Miliukov or through Simanovich—who also dealt with his correspondence.

Rasputin did not object to the constant presence of police spies—they gave him a sense of security. He even made friends with them, and invited them to accompany him to church or to the baths. (Rasputin continued to be a devout churchgoer, and usually went to early mass.) He knew that they paid the concierge a weekly wage to spy on him. Rasputin sometimes slept with a sempstress who lived two floors below, or with a masseuse who lived on the floor above; and he knew that these also kept the police informed of anything they noticed. He felt no resentment; all this spying was merely a part of the bureaucratic system, Russian 'red tape'. (When the Tsarina went out for a drive, police reported her progress for every inch of the way; if she stopped her carriage to talk to an acquaintance, the police would intercept the acquaintance immediately afterwards and say: 'Would you mind telling us exactly what the Tsarina said to you?' It is not surprising that the Imperial Family hated the police.)

He was still received at the palace almost daily. Usually he went of his own accord. Since their family life was so quiet, the Tsar and Tsarina were usually free to entertain him. He entered quietly by the back door, and was received in their private apartments. He would address them both casually and familiarly, clap the Tsar on the shoulder if he wanted to emphasize a joke, and sometimes put his arm round the Tsarina's shoulders and kiss her roughly. If Alexey was present, he often told stories about Siberia. The girls also enjoyed private conversations with him, and he would chaff them about their interest in certain young officers in the Tsar's suite. He still played little part in the appointment of ministers, since most of the men in official positions were his enemies.

The Tsar had many things to worry about in the last months of 1912, and the first part of 1913. The third Duma came to an end in 1912—having lasted out its natural term of office—and a fourth Duma came into existence under the presidency of Rodzianko. Although the Tsar was in theory reconciled to the existence of the Duma, he still dreamed about a strict limitation of its powers. Rasputin was inclined to encourage him in this notion. Public unrest was increasing again. There had been an unpleasant incident at the British-owned Lena Goldfields, when the police had nervously opened fire on peaceable strikers. A brilliant young labour leader called Alexander Kerensky was sent to investigate the incident, and discovered that the man who had ordered the police to fire was drunk and half insane. Once again the government found itself under attack from the Duma. Nicholas probably wished for the good old days, when these little massacres were taken for granted. A wave of strikes and disorders began to spread over Russia again. In 1913 there were nearly three-quarters of a million workers out on strike; a year later the number had doubled. The extreme left naturally took advantage of these disorders. Although assassination never again reached the figure of the earlier years (1905 to 1907, when more than four thousand people died), the revolutionaries were becoming formidably efficient at robbing banks and mail trains to finance the cause. (In 1907, a single coup had netted more than £34,000.) Meanwhile, trouble in the Balkans continued to seethe and bubble, and various Serbian secret societies—the *Narodno Obrana* and the Black Hand—toyed with the idea of assassinating Archduke Ferdinand, heir to the throne of Austria. Without knowing it, Europe was sitting on a volcano.

The Tsar did his feeble best to improve the Russian situation. The centenary of Napoleon's defeat, in September 1912, was celebrated with considerable pomp, and many demonstrations of patriotism. And in 1913 there were even bigger celebrations for the three hundredth anniversary of the Romanov rule. The Tsar and Tsarina travelled to see the first home of the Romanovs on the Volga, taking Rasputin with them. Under the circumstances, this was hardly tactful. Later, there was an open clash between Rasputin and Rodzianko, which reveals some of the feeling of impotent rage and resentment that Rodzianko was beginning to feel towards Rasputin. Rodzianko was a typical Russian official —proud of his position, jealous of his authority. He heard that the Duma had been given seats rather far back in the Kazan Cathedral for the tercentenary celebrations, and demanded better ones. The Duma was allotted new seats at the front, and Rodzianko placed a guard of Duma sergeants round them. As he stood waiting outside the cathedral, a sergeant came out and told him that a peasant had sat down in one of the seats and refused to move. 'Sure enough, it was Rasputin. He was dressed in a magnificent Russian tunic of crimson silk, patent leather top boots, black cloth trousers and a peasant's overcoat. Over his dress he wore a pectoral cross on a finely wrought gold chain.' Rodzianko accosted Rasputin roughly, and roared at him: 'If you address me as "thou" I'll drag you from the cathedral by your beard'. He ordered Rasputin out of the cathedral, although Rasputin showed him an invitation from the Tsar. Rasputin fell on his knees and began to pray, and Rodzianko kicked him in the ribs, shouting: 'Enough of this tomfoolery'. Rasputin groaned and murmured, 'Lord, forgive him his sin', and 'slunk away'.

This episode is hardly creditable to Rodzianko. Rasputin had as much right in the cathedral as he had. It is also plain, from Rodzianko's book, that he boasted of this encounter as a major victory over Rasputin. A member of the Duma mentioned to Rodzianko that Rasputin had told him the story of the clash, and added: 'To tell you the truth, I always thought your story of how you turned him out of the church was a bit of a brag'. From this it emerges that Rodzianko was thought quite capable of bragging and lying.

But from the Tsar's point of view, 1913 was another year of conflict and upheavals. Nicholas seemed incapable of learning. In spite of the universal unrest, he was again day-dreaming of absolute power. The new Minister of the Interior, a diehard conservative called Maklakov, advised Nicholas to go and make a fiery speech at the Duma, then to dissolve it—or at least severely limit its powers. Luckily, Nicholas's cabinet—although they all hated the Duma—were against the idea, so it was dropped. The cabinet spent much time squabbling among themselves, but luckily they had the sense to see that Maklakov's idea would start a revolution.

It is at this point that the sinister name of Stürmer makes its first important appearance. Stürmer had recommended himself to Nicholas many years earlier, when Nicholas was having trouble with the *zemstvos* (land councils); a *zemstvo* at Tver had earned the neurotic Tsar's mistrust by building hospitals and giving the peasants intelligent advice on agriculture. Stürmer —then a petty official—went down and bullied the *zemstvo*, dismissed its members, and replaced them with reactionaries who could be guaranteed to do nothing. Later, Stürmer, whom Pares describes as 'a shallow and dishonest creature, without even the merit of courage', made Rasputin's acquaintance through Maniulov, and lavished flattery on him. Now Nicholas proposed to make Stürmer mayor of Moscow, and the cabinet supported him. But Kokovtsev—who, whatever his defects, knew a syco-phant when he saw one—opposed it, and the Tsar reluctantly gave way. He also made a mental note to get rid of Kokovtsev at the first opportunity. Nicholas's conduct of the government sometimes gives the impression that he had a subconscious longing for suicide.

The trouble was that Rasputin was no judge of character—not because he lacked the insight, but simply because he lacked interest. If a man like Stürmer took the trouble to be nice to him, he took his good faith for granted. Rasputin himself had no ulterior motives; he had no interest in money, and he pos-sessed all the power he needed; consequently he tended to take other people at their face value. There was something horrify-ingly naïve about him. So while the affairs of Russia went steadily downhill, he continued to advise the Tsar to exercise his authority, and used his influence on behalf of creatures like Stürmer. And because an honest—but short-tempered—man like Rodzianko disliked him, Rasputin took sides against the Duma, and made things worse.

1913 was a year in which the clouds gathered, but nothing much happened. In 1914, the storm broke.

In February, Kokovtsev was suddenly dismissed. Typically, Nicholas had an argument with him that ended with the Tsar declaring, 'You are right and I am wrong', and embracing Kokovtsev repeatedly. No one knew where they stood with this irritating man, who agreed with everybody and changed his mind twice a day.

Kokovtsev's successor was the nonentity Goremykin, who had already had a term as Prime Minister after Witte's dismissal. Witte was still alive, and had become a friend of Rasputin: but even Rasputin's friendship was not enough to get him back into office; the Tsar disliked men who knew their own mind. Witte was to die a year later.

The Tsar was still toying with the idea of dismissing the Duma, but his cabinet continued to oppose it. And many people were seriously brooding on the possibility of murdering Ras-putin. Yussupov himself was in Germany, completing his studies. But the monk Illiodor still seethed with resentment, and dreamed of revenge.

One day, Maria Rasputin answered the telephone in the Gorokhovoy, and was addressed by a strange man, who told her that he had seen her in the street, and that he was in love with her. This sixteen-year-old peasant girl was not pretty, but she had a wide mouth, lively eyes and an excellent figure. She had also inherited her father's talent for dancing. She was naïve enough to be thrilled at the idea of love from a stranger, and decided not to tell her father. The unknown rang her up several times, and described walks she had taken with a detail that convinced her that she had been followed closely. But he still declined to give his name, or introduce himself to her.

At the beginning of June 1914, Rasputin decided to go to Pokrovskoe for the summer. The Tsar and his family had gone to Livadia as usual; this time, Rasputin was tactful enough not to follow them. But he was becoming too worried about assassination to stay in St Petersburg. So they began the long journey home—five days on the train, and then two days on the boat from Tobolsk. On the way, Maria Rasputin got into conversation with a young Jew from St Petersburg. He told her that he was a reporter. There was something familiar about his voice, and suddenly he admitted that he was the stranger who had been telephoning her. They continued their acquaintance on the boat, and she found him pleasant enough—voluble and witty—but disappointing in appearance, being short, black-haired and distinctly Jewish in profile. When they arrived at Pokrovskoe, the young reporter puzzled Maria by saying that he would stay for a few days in the village. It was a long way to come simply to be near a sixteen-year-old girl.

They arrived at Pokrovskoe on Saturday, June 27, 1914. At two-fifteen on Sunday afternoon the postman arrived with a telegram for Rasputin. He read it, and hurried out of the house to ask the postman to take a reply. As he did so, a peasant woman approached him. He had already seen her once that day, when she had made a move to accost him as he came from mass. Rasputin stopped to give her a coin; as he did so, she lunged forward and drove a knife into his stomach.[1] Rasputin turned to run, and the woman started to chase him, the knife raised; he

[1] Pares gives the 29th as the date of the stabbing, but Maria Rasputin states that it occurred on the Sunday—the 28th.

decided that attack would be a better policy, seized a piece of wood that was lying in the path, and hit her on the head. Then he dragged himself back to the house, and shouted for the servants. By this time, the half-unconscious woman had been seized by neighbours who had witnessed the attempted assassination, and they dragged her to Rasputin's house. She was screaming: 'I've killed the Anti-Christ'. Maria Rasputin rushed out, and saw the furious peasants dragging along a repulsive lame creature with a huge deformed nose. Her name was Kinia Guseva. (Liepman describes her as 'a beautiful woman'.) She also saw the Jewish reporter, Davidsohn, hesitating on the porch, and shouted furiously at him. Davidsohn rushed off to telegraph his scoop to his newspaper in St Petersburg; this was the last Maria Rasputin saw of him.

Guseva was arrested—Rasputin had some difficulty in saving her from lynching—and Rasputin was taken to the Tioumen hospital. He was badly wounded—the blow had revealed the entrails—but he had no intention of dying. In hospital, he learned that Guseva was an agent of Illiodor—she had just come from seeing the defrocked priest in Norway. Pares describes Guseva as 'a hysterical victim of Rasputin's lust', but this seems to be unfair to Rasputin; he had almost certainly never seen her before. However, he now intervened to prevent her being brought to trial; she was found insane, and interned in an asylum. Davidsohn's exact role in the affair is not known.

On the day Rasputin was stabbed in Pokrovskoe, another assassin was carefully following the movements of his victim. His name was Gavrilo Princip, and he was a young Bosnian who resented Austria's occupation of Bosnia. Archduke Ferdinand, heir to the Austrian throne, had chosen a bad day to visit Sarajevo, for it was Vidovdan, the anniversary of a great Serbian defeat, which was observed as a holiday. Ferdinand knew he was going to die; he had already told his children's tutor: 'The bullet that will kill me is already on its way'. Shortly after ten that morning, a home-made bomb was thrown at the grand-ducal carriage; it wounded several spectators, but left Ferdinand and his wife uninjured. Chabrinovich, the would-be assassin, tried to poison himself with cyanide, but was captured. The Grand Duke and his wife attended a ceremony in the town hall, and left half an hour later. As they were about to get into their car, a photographer snapped them; Ferdinand remarked to his Duchess: 'I've got a feeling there may be more bombs around'. He was right. Gavrilo Princip, the consumptive young student, had a bomb and a Browning revolver with six shots. And yet he almost missed his chance. As the car approached him, he prepared to fire, when the car turned off into Franz Josef Street. Modern history hung in the balance; then some busybody shouted for the cars to stop; the route had been revised. As the Duke's car backed, Princip stepped forward and fired two shots. His aim was excellent; one killed the Duchess, and the other the Duke. Princip was seized and frog-marched off to the police station.

There are fifty degrees of longitude between Sarajevo and Pokrovskoe, which means that eleven o'clock in Sarajevo is about two-fifteen in Pokrovskoe. It is a strange coincidence that two assassins struck at almost exactly the same moment— a coincidence that makes one inclined to doubt the 'blindness of history'. Ferdinand's death made war probable; Rasputin's injury made it certain, for he was the only man in Russia capable of averting it.[1]

While Rasputin lay in hospital, the consequences followed inevitably. Serbia and Austria had been smouldering against one another since 1908; now Austria suspected—rightly—that Serbia was behind the assassination, and sent off an ultimatum demanding huge concessions—including that Serbia should allow Austrian officials to interrogate Serbian officials about the assassination. Serbia refused, and Austria declared war. The Tsar was unsure about what to do in this crisis. Plainly, he ought to go to the aid of Serbia—but then, Germany would probably go to the aid of Austria. He compromised, and ordered a partial mobilization. This was the moment when Rasputin's presence could have saved the situation—he had said often enough that the Balkans were not worth fighting about. Still, it *was* an insult to Russia; after all, the Balkans lay between Russia and Austria, and it was obvious that they should, ideally, remain independent states. Austria had been pushing its luck when their statesman Aehrenthal—a *realpolitik* opportunist of the

[1] As far as I know, this coincidence has never before been pointed out.

Bismarck variety—had duped Russia in 1908. Ever since then, Russia had been nursing the bruise and dreaming of revenge. Now this invasion of Serbia was as insulting as a slap in the face. But worse still, Germany prepared to support Austria in the same insulting, bullying manner, ordering Russia to cease mobilizing immediately. And yet still no one believed it would be war, since no one really wanted war. Serbia had tried to avert it with a soft answer to Austria, proposing compromise, and now Russia tried to avert it by suggesting to the Kaiser that the whole problem could be referred to the Hague Tribunal for arbitration. It was no use. Austria bombarded Belgrade, the capital of Serbia; the Russians heard a false rumour to the effect that Austria had ordered a full mobilization, and the Tsar immediately ordered full mobilization for Russia.

Rasputin was lying in hospital when he heard the news of the mobilization. He immediately sent a telegram to the Tsar, begging him to avert war. The Tsar received it irritably. Everybody in Russia was crying out for blood; there were frenzied waves of patriotism, and the Duma shouted as loudly as the rest. If Rasputin had been able to persuade Nicholas, the two of them would have been the most unpopular men in Russia—but there would have been no revolution in 1917.

As it was, Germany declared war on Russia first, and for the first time in his reign, Nicholas was adored by everyone in Russia. He enjoyed this sudden popularity; the tutor Gilliard says that he was 'like a man transformed'.

Germany delivered an ultimatum also to France and Belgium. The ultimatum to France was as insulting as the one to Russia; Wilhelm was determined to force war. When German troops entered Belgium, Britain entered the war in defence of Belgian neutrality. Japan declared war on Germany, and Italy later entered on the side of the Allies. By early August, while Rasputin was painfully recovering from his wound, half the world was at war.

CHAPTER NINE

THE RAIN OF FIRE

RUSSIA was even less prepared for war in 1914 than England in 1939. The Prime Minister was the vague and incompetent Goremykin, seventy-four years old, who believed that ministers were 'butlers' of the Tsar, and the Minister of the Interior was Maklakov, who actually believed that any national war effort would increase the threat of revolution (for which reason, he discouraged the Zemstvo Red Cross). Russia had vast numbers of men, but no armaments, and—contrary to the general belief— large numbers of men without arms are a positive hindrance to a war effort. The average Russian recruit had to travel enormous distances to reach his unit. The Russians had few aeroplanes, and were short of heavy artillery and ammunition. Communications were bad—through shortage of telephones and wireless— and transport had to be supplemented by the Zemstvo Red Cross. Nearly a million men were without rifles in October 1914.

Yet even so, it was now revealed that some of the troubles of the past ten years had been blessings in disguise. The disasters of the Japanese war had produced reforms in the army and navy—particularly the navy. In the first months of the war, Russia held her own surprisingly well. There were several shattering defeats in August and September—the battles of Zamosc-Komarov, of Tannenberg (after which the Russian General Samsonov committed suicide) and the battle of the Masurian Lakes. Hundreds of thousands of Russians were taken prisoner. On the other hand, the Russians beat the Austrians at the battle of Lemberg, and forced them to abandon eastern Galicia.

Still, it was all a mess. In an excess of patriotism, the Russians changed the name of St Petersburg to Petrograd—its old name had too many associations with the pro-German Peter the Great. But this gesture was somehow typical of the muddled idealism behind the Russian war effort. So was the Tsar's decision to go to the front and take command of the armies himself. However, his ministers persuaded him to give up this idea, and appoint the Grand Duke Nicholas—Rasputin's early patron—instead. (Nicholas had long since regretted his part in bringing Rasputin to court and become an enemy.) The Tsar even decided to ban the sale of vodka because it promoted drunkenness and damaged the war effort, and so great was the nation's patriotic enthusiasm that nobody objected. 'Prohibition' lasted about a year.

And yet the patriotism failed to penetrate to the highest levels. The Minister of War was the old-fashioned General Sukhomlinov, whom Alan Moorehead describes as a 'military fossil'; he boasted that he had not read a military manual for twenty-five years, and said he relied on the bayonet. His pretty Jewish wife—many years his junior—loved spending large sums of money, so the general had to find ways to raise it; it was later suggested that one of these ways was selling his own country to the Germans; another was embezzling money intended to buy arms.

But even the ministers who were not swindlers or traitors were incredibly reactionary. Patriotic enthusiasm did not make them feel warmly towards the Russian peasant; on the contrary, it worried them. The Russian soldier was treated like a convict; he was not allowed to eat in public restaurants or ride in street cars; he was not even allowed to receive newspapers without permission of his officer. He was not allowed to answer 'I don't know' to a question; he had to say 'I cannot know'—because it was assumed that, being a peasant, he *could* not know.

These men were hurled to their deaths in thousands in battles that could not possibly be won. In five months, four million of them died. This was not entirely the fault of the commander, the Grand Duke Nicholas; his hand was forced by the French, who were being quickly overrun by the Germans. But he was not ready to fight, and his ill-judged offensives in East Prussia,

Poland and Galicia were doomed in advance. By early 1915, Russia was in full retreat.

This, then, was the situation that faced Rasputin when he returned to Petrograd[1] in September 1914. The Tsar was angry with him because of his telegram begging him to stop the war. Everybody noticed that Nicholas had become a new man since the war began. But the Tsarina had never felt so much in need of her 'friend and adviser'. She was German by birth, and it was assumed that she was on the German side—although in fact this was totally untrue. A current joke reported the Tsarevitch as saying: 'I don't know which side I'm supposed to be on. When the Russians lose, Daddy looks gloomy, and when the Germans lose, Mama cries.' Her nerves were now so ragged that she found it almost impossible to make a public appearance; the French Ambassador reports that, at a public banquet, her manner was completely wooden, and before the end, was verging on hysteria.

Rasputin was violently against the war—like his friend Witte. Both were widely suspected of being German spies. But Witte died suddenly in March 1915, leaving Rasputin alone to hold the title of the most unpopular man in Russia. It was generally taken for granted that he was a German spy.

The Russian spy mania was not entirely without foundation. A certain Colonel Myasoyedov, a friend of the War Minister Sukhomlinov, was discovered to be a German agent, and executed. Gossip had it that he was no more than Madame Sukhomlinov's lover—but it was inevitable that suspicion should fall on the Minister. A few Jews were also discovered to be pro-German, and this led to a full-scale persecution of the Jews all over Russia and Poland. Thousands of Jews were turned out of Poland to wander in Russia, and many of them died of starvation and exposure.

While all this was happening, the Tsar was once again sole autocrat of Russia. The Duma was not allowed to meet, and its six Bolshevik deputies were arrested. (The sixth, Malinovsky, was a police spy—although he was liked and trusted by Lenin himself.) And, for the first time in ten years, no one objected to this high-handed approach. Everyone was too excited about the

[1] The name was changed on August 31, 1914.

war to bother. It was only when bad news from the front began to leak back all over Russia that this enthusiasm evaporated, and the old dissatisfactions were aroused.

Meanwhile, Rasputin's hold over the Tsarina grew stronger. Feeling herself friendless and misunderstood, she submitted completely to his soothing influence. Rumours began to spread that she was actually hypnotized by Rasputin. (There was a story that Rasputin had started to take lessons from a professional hypnotist in 1913, but that Beletsky had expelled the hypnotist from St Petersburg.) Probably the truth is simply that she now began to feel estranged from her husband—who was basking in his popularity with his subjects, and thought of nothing but the war—so that Rasputin became, for a while, the only receptacle for her strong emotions.

At the beginning of 1915, Rasputin's popularity with the Tsar—which had temporarily revived towards the end of 1914—was again on the wane. The new head of the police department, General Dzhunkovsky, disliked him, and was out to 'get him'. He reported some of Rasputin's activities to the Tsar—particularly late night parties at the Villa Rode, when Rasputin was prone to get drunk, speak disrespectfully about the Tsar (or familiarly, which would be the same thing to a Russian), and sometimes to take off most of his clothes.

So in January 1915, Rasputin was no longer welcome at the palace, and the Tsarina had to meet him secretly in Anna Vyrubov's little house, close to the palace at Tsarskoe Selo.

On January 15, 1915, Anna Vyrubov was on her way into Petrograd to visit her parents when she had a serious accident. The train collided with another one, and Anna Vyrubov's carriage snapped in two. Her legs were trapped in the steam-heating apparatus, while her head was crushed under an iron girder. She was taken out and carried away on a loose door. The Tsarina took her to the hospital of a female doctor, Princess Goidretz, who declared that there was no hope for her life. (Anna Vyrubov believed that the Princess wanted to kill her, and was probably right; she was not popular.) Rasputin heard nothing of this accident, being in disgrace, until twenty-four hours later; he immediately borrowed a car and hurried to the palace. Anna Vyrubov was unconscious, although she occasionally called out for 'Father Grigory' in her delirium. Rasputin went into the room, ignoring the Tsar and Tsarina who stood by the bed, and took the patient's hand, saying: 'Annushka, look at me'. She opened her eyes, and said: 'Grigory. Thank God.' Rasputin continued to hold her hands for a while, staring at her, then said to the Tsar: 'She will live, but she will always be a cripple'. He then walked out of the room. But the effort had exhausted him; he stumbled, and collapsed in a faint outside the door. Anna Vyrubov's slow recovery began from Rasputin's visit.

Perhaps the most interesting part of this story is Rasputin's collapse. This is vouched for both by Anna herself and by Mosolov, the Court Chancellor. 'He tottered from the room and fell outside in a faint, from which he awoke in a strong perspiration, feeling that all his strength had gone from him.' It would seem, then, that what had occurred was another example of Rasputin's healing power—and in this case, it seems clear that he had to lower his own vitality to re-charge hers. It is true that Anna Vyrubov was on the point of death when Rasputin saw her—the doctor had told the Imperial couple to take final leave of her just before Rasputin arrived—so that the effort of re-vitalizing her probably cost Rasputin far more than usual. On the other hand, is it not possible that Rasputin had lowered his own spiritual powers by the debaucheries described by Dzhunkovsky?

Yet even if this is true, the incident again affords us a glimpse of the most important aspect of Rasputin's life. Reading about the inexorable march of events towards catastrophe—particularly the strange coincidence of the attacks on Rasputin and Archduke Ferdinand—it is difficult not to feel that the actors in this story are cardboard puppets, and that the Marxian view of history, as the real force behind human affairs, is the true one. But Rasputin lived—for at least part of his time—in another dimension than history. This was the secret of his power over the Tsar and Tsarina. The façade of 'reality' which imprisons most human beings seemed, at certain points, transparent to Rasputin.

This is a point worth making clear before proceeding further. Human beings all manage to maintain a certain equilibrium between the world—external nature—and the will. A material object is completely subject to the laws of nature; a leaf cannot decide whether it will fall or stay on the tree. Most animals are passive; they merely adjust themselves to nature. Human beings are the only animals who are actively aggressive towards nature; instead of submitting and adjusting themselves, they calculate how they can outwit nature.

Yet although man knows that he can overcome darkness by merely pressing the light switch, the habit of passivity is deeply ingrained. Man never ceases to feel a certain respect and fear for nature, for external reality; a part of his being continues to regard nature as the ruler, the autocrat. Poets and artists go further than most men in this respect; they dream of an ultimate conquest of nature, an ultimate triumph for the spirit of man. Yet most poets—particularly as they approach middle age— cease to feel so aggressive; they adjust.

But the whole spirit of religion—of the inspirational religion of saints and prophets—is a belief in the ultimate power of the spirit. The ordinary man uses his will 'constitutionally', taking into account the laws of nature. This means that when he is confronted by difficulties or misfortunes that seem 'acts of God' —or of chance—he feels peculiarly helpless, passive; he has done his best. Spirit can do no more. The will is immobilized.

A man like Rasputin goes one step further. Only the greatest artists seem capable of defying destiny—like Beethoven shaking his fist at the thunder—as if implying that, although nature may be stronger than spirit, spirit will eventually win from sheer courage and persistence. A Rasputin knows intuitively that there is no such thing as defeat while the will is active—even in the face of a *fait accompli* on the part of nature. For some reason, he is not as passive as most human beings. Instead of collapsing in defeat, the vitality rises to meet an emergency.

Many poets have described this state of the awakening of vitality—the opposite of passivity towards nature. Always, it is described as a kind of awakening from sleep. William Blake symbolized man's passive and animal aspect as 'the spectre', and wrote:

> Each man is in his Spectre's power
> Until the arrival of that hour
> When his Humanity awake
> And cast his own Spectre into the Lake.

Yeats described the same sensation on another level, 'when a man is fighting mad':

> Something drops from eyes long blind,
> He completes his partial mind,
> For an instant stands at ease
> Laughs aloud, his heart at peace.

This is also what Gurdjieff meant by the 'fight against sleep'.

Mrs Eddy—as already described—took the view that man has still not achieved his correct control over nature, because he has an instinctive attitude of mistrust which paralyses his powers. He is like the nervous owner of a dog who can never have full control over the dog because he never ceases to be afraid of it.

Whatever else may be said against Rasputin, he certainly possessed this intuitive optimism and trust, an awareness of the power of the spirit. He could see Russia drifting fatalistically towards catastrophe; he himself could never be a fatalist, for this implies a certain unconsciousness of man's strange autonomy. The Tsarina described his cure of Anna Vyrubov as a miracle. It was not a miracle, if we accept Phineas Quimby's word; it was the utilization of a law of nature. But for the royal family, with their inborn fatalism, their faces pressed suffocatingly into current events, it was undoubtedly a miracle.

The actual event that probably led to the Tsar's temporary coldness to Rasputin in late 1915 has been variously described, and Pares says primly that 'it is perhaps the least offensive illustration we could choose of . . . what harm he did to his sovereign'. In fact, the incident is rather to Rasputin's credit. The police report describes it as follows:[1]

On August 9, 1915, Rasputin, having visited the convent of Tioumen, went on board the steamer *Tovarpar*, which at 11 o'clock started for Pokrovskoe. About 1 o'clock, Rasputin left his cabin drunk, and made friends with some soldiers on board. He gave them twenty-five roubles, and told them to sing. He then returned to his own cabin, and later went back to the soldiers and gave them another 100 roubles. They all sang.

[1] Original Legal Documents Concerning the Murder of Rasputin, offered for sale by Karl W. Hiersemann (Leipzig, 1929).

Rasputin took the soldiers into the second-class dining cabin to give them dinner, but the captain ordered them out. Rasputin molested some passengers, particularly a lady, to whom he barred the way to her cabin. Later, he appeared on deck again and quarrelled with a man from Tioumen, and also with the merchant Michalov from Tioumen. He used certain unfavourable expressions about Barnaby, the Bishop of Tobolsk. He then got into a quarrel with the steward, calling him a thieving rascal, and accusing him of taking 3,000 roubles. After this, Rasputin went into his cabin and leaned out of the window looking over the deck. Hostile passengers shouted: 'Cut off his beard, shave him'. A detective on board requested him to close the window to avert further unpleasantness. At Pokrovskoe, still drunk, he was dragged ashore by four sailors, and his daughters met him in a dogcart and drove him home.

This is the 'shocking incident' at which several writers have expressed disapproval. It is difficult to understand why. Rasputin disliked the way that soldiers were treated as animals, and the whole incident seems to have arisen out of his indignation at the way that the captain and first-class passengers assumed airs of moral superiority over the men who were fighting to defend Russia.

Rasputin's defence was reasonable. He said that he was not drunk, and that the passengers provoked him into being noisy and hostile by their attitude to the soldiers. He argued that the captain knew his identity, and had taken sides against him because of his views on the war—which were generally known in Russia at the time. (It has already been remarked that a large proportion of the Russian people believed that Rasputin and the Tsarina were German spies.)

This absurd incident was brought to the Tsar's attention by Dzhunkovsky, and there was talk of prosecuting Rasputin—on what charge is not clear. There had also been another similar incident on a river-boat when Rasputin had got drunk and noisy, about which details are not known. The police tried to use these two incidents to blackmail Rasputin into making a lengthy tour of monasteries, but the wily *staretz* persuaded them to hand over the evidence against him to Anna Vyrubov, then refused to budge.

His 'resurrection' of Anna Vyrubov had the same effect as his cure of the Tsarevitch in 1912; the Tsar was overawed against his will, and had to agree with his wife that Rasputin possessed extraordinary powers. So for a few months, Rasputin was back in royal favour again, in spite of his outspoken opposition to the war.

Four days after the incident with Anna Vyrubov, Rasputin was walking along the hard snow of the Kamenno-Ostrovsky Prospect when he heard the sound of approaching hoofs; caution made him look round, and he jumped wildly. A sledge that went hurtling by struck him and made him stumble. The sledge skidded, and police agents—who were never far from Rasputin—rushed forward and dragged down several men. (Paléologue, who tells the story, does not specify how many.) Later, these men admitted that they had come from Tsaritsyn, Illiodor's fortress. But it was never discovered whether they had been acting under Illiodor's instructions, or whether it was their own idea to strike down the man who had caused Illiodor's disgrace.

This was the kind of affair that one might expect to be taken seriously—a clear case of attempted murder, with considerable circumstantial evidence. But nothing more was heard of it; presumably the men were released for 'lack of evidence'. Probably Dzhunkovsky muttered under his breath, 'Better luck next time', and turned back to the report on Rasputin's 'disgraceful behaviour' on the river-boat. Being the Tsarina's favourite could be a hazardous business in Petrograd.

The Tsarina herself was enjoying a novel experience—popularity with the Russian army. She had decided to start up hospitals for the wounded, probably on Rasputin's advice, and flung herself into this work with all her nervous energy. She opened up hospitals all over Russia, including one at Tsarskoe Selo, and helped to equip many hospital trains, which bore her name. She then trained as a nurse under the Princess Goidretz, and insisted that Anna Vyrubov and her two eldest daughters should also train. Anna Vyrubov was probably a fractious pupil—this would explain the hostility felt towards her by Dr Goidretz. Her accident cut short her brief career as a nurse, but the Tsarina and her daughters filled Tsarskoe Selo with wounded soldiers, and tended them with a kind of masochistic devotion. For the princesses, probably anything was better than the boredom of sewing tea cosies in the palace. Petrograd society was inclined to sniff irritably about the Tsarina's activities; the anonymous author of *The Fall of the Romanoffs* (who is clearly a woman) wrote: 'Even as a sister of mercy she failed to understand the soldier's sense of what was to be expected from an Empress of Russia. To see her kneeling in front of him, bathing his feet or dressing his wounds, shocked him. . . .' Possibly the Tsarina *was* inclined to go a little far in the part she was playing—but it is clear from other contemporary memoirs that the soldiers were not as upset as the anonymous lady alleges. One dying officer kept himself alive by sheer will-power until the Tsarina could come to his bedside and bless him. This kind of thing gave her a romantic halo in the eyes of the troops—who had only seen photographs of her as a beautiful, mournful girl of twenty, and were unaware that she had turned into a somewhat homely matron suffering from nerves and a persecution mania.

In March, Witte died, and the Tsar went to inspect the front, after being blessed by Rasputin. Rasputin thought of accompanying him, but the Grand Duke Nicholas got wind of the idea, and announced that he would hang Rasputin on sight. Rasputin made a note that there were two more men to be got rid of at the first opportunity—the Grand Duke and the police chief Dzhunkovsky.

The opportunity for this second project came fairly soon. While the Tsar was at the front, there occurred another of these minor incidents that were inflated by Rasputin's enemies into major scandals. On April 8, Rasputin went to Moscow to visit the tombs of the Patriarchs. Pares writes: 'Apparently the praying had been too much for him, or he felt he had some credit in hand. Anyhow, he visited one of the most notorious places of entertainment, Yar . . .' What exactly occurred there is not quite certain. The police report alleges that he sat with his flies undone, exposing his sexual organs to the general public. But Bruce Lockhart, in his *Memoirs of a British Agent*, says that Rasputin was in a private cubicle, from which loud noises ensued, and women's voices. So if Rasputin was in a state of partial undress, the intention was probably not indecent exposure but a rather more normal form of sexual exercise. The manager called the police—he was not willing to eject Rasputin—but the police were equally unwilling to commit themselves, and telephoned the Prefect, who telephoned Dzhunkovsky in Petrograd. Dzhunkovsky told them to arrest Rasputin. This decision probably pleased the manager, whose floor show was being drowned by the noises from Rasputin's cubicle. So Rasputin was arrested and led away, cursing, to cool his temper in the local police station until morning. The police report alleges that Rasputin not only sat with his flies undone, but declared that he could behave in the same way in the presence of the Imperial Family. This is probably no exaggeration, but it was hardly tactful of Rasputin to say so—if, of course, he really said it.

Rasputin was summoned before the Tsar in June, when Nicholas returned from the front. The Tsar was irritable, and Rasputin put on his best Tartuffe manner, and declared that he was a sinful man—which, as Pares remarks, would carry more weight with a Russian than an Englishman. The Tsarina was not informed of the incident. But Dzhunkovsky wondered if it could not be used as the lever to overthrow Rasputin. He was too late. Rasputin had laid his complaints before the Tsarina—and it can be seen that they were real complaints; Dzhunkovsky was inflating minor misdemeanours, and yet omitting to prosecute men who had tried to kill Rasputin. The Tsarina told her husband that Dzhunkovsky would have to go. And in September, Dzhunkovsky went. The dubious Beletzky, whom Dzhunkovsky had dismissed, was now restored to his job as Chief of Police, and played a considerable part in Rasputin's life during the next year. Rasputin did not know it, but he had only another year to live.

CHAPTER TEN

RASPUTIN AS TSAR

HISTORICAL retrospect tempts us to believe that the war made revolution inevitable; and yet a little study of the evidence shows this was not so. In England, Rupert Brooke wrote a sonnet welcoming the war, beginning: 'Now God be thanked, Who has matched us with His hour', and speaking of the conflict as a cleansing bath. And in Russia there was much the same feeling, to begin with. If the Tsar had been able to make peace within the first few months of the war—when the Russian advance was so spectacular that the Austrians were tempted to negotiate—the revolution would have been an impossibility. The Tsar was popular with everyone—even the revolutionaries. The terrorist Vladimir Burtsev, a 'revolutionary detective' who spent most of his time exposing Russian police agents abroad, advised all revolutionaries to support the Tsar in the emergency. He was even rash enough to return to Russia, where he was promptly arrested. (Later he was amnestied.) Only Lenin continued to advise the revolutionaries to use the war as an opportunity for overthrowing the régime; but only extreme left-wing organizations followed his lead, and many of these later supported the war effort with patriotic enthusiasm.

And yet only a year after the outbreak of war, the whole situation had changed. How had this come about?

Much of the responsibility must be laid at the door of the War Minister, Sukhomlinov. He was later accused of being a German agent; but the truth seems to be simply that he believed the war would be over by Christmas 1914, and so did not bother about arms and ammunition. He even refused an offer of arms from the French government, declaring that none were required. The consequence was that the Russians secured many of their victories with the bayonet alone, and at tremendous cost of life. Finally, Rodzianko intervened with the Tsar, and succeeded in getting Sukhomlinov, and also the morose and reactionary Maklakov— Minister of the Interior—dismissed. This was in May–June 1915. The new War Minister was General Polivanov, an honest and efficient soldier.

Rodzianko may have been a self-conceited and fussy man, but he had an ability to get things done. At the head of the liberals, he now proceeded to save Russia from the consequences of bureaucratic vagueness and reactionary stupidity, forming a special defence council and turning all Russia's available industry to the manufacture of arms. When the Duma met on August 1, 1915, there was a remarkably united front, and the War Minister earned applause by declaring that he would co-operate closely with the Duma. It began to look as if Russia would be saved in spite of the Tsar. But six weeks later, Nicholas decided to spoil everything by again closing the Duma until November. All the liberals were furious—naturally—and the workers of Petrograd went on a two-day strike. Pares dates the spirit of defeatism from this moment.

Why did Nicholas take this unfortunate step? He never ceased to be afraid that Russia would be swept into 'constitutionalism'. And yet the Duma were only asking for a 'Ministry of Confidence' —that is to say, for a Prime Minister and Cabinet whom everyone could trust. Goremykin was the worst possible Prime Minister. Not only was he a yes-man; he was a tired old cynic who often talked about his own death, and who had gone past caring what happened to Russia.

And behind all the trouble was the Tsarina, morbidly jealous of her husband's power, endlessly advising him: 'Prove yourself an autocrat'. She was physically worn down by her nursing activities; her heart had been weak ever since the Tsarevitch had been born, and now she often had to move around in a wheelchair. The letters she wrote in 1915 show that her love for her husband and family had never been so intense; her hatred for the Duma was proportionately strong, and she often talked wistfully of hanging 'that horrid Rodzianko' and Guchkov, or arranging a convenient railway accident!

It was the Tsarina who was, through her advice, indirectly responsible for the closing of the Duma in September. She was also largely responsible for another decision that threw both the Duma and the Cabinet into an uproar: the Tsar's decision to become Commander-in-Chief of the army.

There were several reasons behind this drastic step. First, the Tsarina was jealous of the popularity of the Grand Duke Nicholas. Gossips had spread a lying story to the effect that the Grand Duke had referred to himself as 'Nicholas the Third'. At all events, he was more popular than the Tsar in the early months of the war.

Next, Rasputin disliked him. After being Rasputin's earliest patron, the Grand Duke—like so many others—had become one of his bitterest enemies. When Rasputin proposed a visit to the front to dedicate an icon, the Grand Duke telegraphed: 'Come and I'll hang you'.

But third, and perhaps most important, there was Nicholas's tendency to escapism. Petrograd was a city of intrigue where petty problems demanded constant attention. At the front, everything was simpler. The morale of the army was excellent, in spite of heavy defeats. The soldiers were brave, and performed some impressive feats that have been recorded by Pares and others. Nicholas was a military man; he loved the open air. His presence was not necessary at the front; the Grand Duke Nicholas was an excellent commander. On the other hand, the Tsar's presence *was* badly needed in Petrograd, to deal with problems of food distribution and transport. So with his usual genius for doing the wrong thing, Nicholas dismissed the Grand Duke and went to the front, leaving his wife and Rasputin in charge. The Cabinet protested; on the orders of his wife, Nicholas bullied them. The Duma expressed doubts; so the Duma was closed. In effect, Rasputin was now Tsar.

Yet in spite of the criticism he aroused, Rasputin was not entirely a bad influence. Like Rodzianko, he recognized the importance of the railways, and at one point persuaded the Tsar to cancel all passenger trains for three days so that supplies of food and ammunition might reach their destination. In fact, passenger services were suspended for a week; but the chaos and incompetence was so deep-rooted that most of the supplies never reached the places they were intended for anyway.

At this point—the last months of 1915—the sinister Alexis Hvostov again appears on the scene. It will be remembered that Rasputin had been sent to interview Hvostov four years previously, but had found that 'something was lacking'. Since then, Hvostov had become a member of the Duma, and succeeded in being a Rasputin sycophant while pretending to support Rodzianko.

Hvostov was a born intriguer. He now decided that the time had come to seize power. And his plan was bold. It was to get into power by means of Rasputin, then to ruin Rasputin by means of his power.

Hvostov decided that the latter part of his design would require co-operation with the police. He chose for his collaborator the crooked policeman Beletsky, who had once been dismissed by Dzhunkovsky, but was now back in favour since Dzhunkovsky's fall. The two of them worked out their plan. Rasputin would be persuaded to pull the strings to get Hvostov made Minister of the Interior; but publicly, the two conspirators would pretend not to know him. Since they needed an introduction to the palace, they would utilize the services of the homosexual intriguer, Prince Andronikov. If news of their plots should reach the ears of the Duma, Hvostov would explain that he was actually plotting Rasputin's downfall—which was true enough—and was merely trying to get into the enemy camp. Once in power, there was no limit to what they might do. Huge sums of money were lying around, waiting to be picked up. The ex-War Minister Sukhomlinov had managed to divert some of it into his own pocket; but he had been clumsy, and at this very moment the Duma were proposing to put him on trial. (Rasputin's intervention—secured by Sukhomlinov's attractive young wife at a price we can only surmise—finally saved him.) There were rumours that a crank had recently got the equivalent of three million pounds out of the government for experiments on a flame thrower—which had been abandoned only when it had burnt several men to death. Hvostov contemplated the prospects now the government was in the hands of the Tsarina, and could barely restrain his impatience. Like so many others, he underestimated Rasputin.

But to begin with, things went better than he dared to expect. Andronikov got Hvostov into the palace without difficulty, and the Tsarina declared that she was 'yearning to see him'. They were greatly impressed by one another. 'He calls our Friend Grigory,' she told her husband in one of her daily letters. Hvost, in Russian, means 'tail', and the Tsarina now began to refer to the Machiavellian Hvostov as 'my honest Tail'. So in no time at all, Hvostov was Minister of the Interior—which also meant Chief of Police—with Beletsky as his assistant. And for the next five months these two men were virtually Russia's government. Hvostov quickly demonstrated his suitability for his new post by cooking up a plan to rig the elections to the Duma by secretly buying up newspapers and 'directing public opinion'. In some future history of totalitarianism in the twentieth century, Hvostov will deserve a place as an inspired predecessor of Hitler and Mussolini in the propaganda field. (He was a predecessor in the fullest sense, for both he and Beletsky were executed by the Bolsheviks after the Revolution.) Presumably he also directed large sums of government money into his own pocket, for there was later some questioning about the fate of the millions that the government had granted him to rig the elections.

But it must not be supposed that the conspirators were concerned solely with robbing the treasury. Beletsky was penetrating enough to see that the increasing trend towards 'Bolshevism' was due less to socialistic ideas than to the food shortage and consequent rise in prices. He therefore organized food shops subsidized by the government, and probably prevented the Revolution from occurring a year earlier. He also did excellent work in housing the thousands of refugees who were flooding Russia from war-shattered areas. Apart from this, he kept a special branch of the post office busy looking for anti-government remarks in letters, and paid and bullied newspapers into inserting paragraphs about the Tsar's bravery at the front and the Tsarina's saintliness as a nurse.

Rasputin also caused Beletsky some anxiety with his tendency to boast when drinking heavily; he was always supplying his enemies with ammunition, and Beletsky redoubled his police guard, and kept a threatening eye on the liberal newspapers. On one occasion, he had to produce a large sum of money to buy back a somewhat tactless letter that had been stolen from Rasputin's flat and placed in the hands of a left-wing newspaper.

All kinds of unsuitable people were now recommended for official posts, simply because they were friends of Hvostov, or had bought his favour. And at this period, to be a friend of Hvostov usually meant to be a friend of Rasputin. Rasputin made no secret of his aim: to have 'his own man' in every important government post.

It is difficult to understand what happened to Rasputin in late 1915. He was never a man who was interested in money or power for its own sake. And yet now, on the strength of his actions, it is difficult not to believe that his character suffered yet another marked deterioration. Had luxurious living and heavy drinking softened his brain? Or was it perhaps the atmosphere of war-time crisis that produced a lack of restraint in him? Before this, his enemies had been largely mistaken in regarding him as an evil influence; his standards were simply different from theirs. But now it became difficult even for his friends not to feel that he was going too far. Russian politics had turned into something like the Chicago City Hall in the 1920s—a completely corrupt scramble for power—and Rasputin was entirely to blame for having supported Hvostov. According to Simanovich, Rasputin was approached every day by rich women who wanted their sons bought out of military service, or bankers who saw a chance to swindle the government on munitions. Prince Andronikov had constituted himself Rasputin's publicity agent and public relations officer; the only unusual feature of the contract was that, in this case, the agent took a 90 per cent. commission. Beletsky was busy trying to undermine Andronikov by passing information about his sexual perversions to Anna Vyrubov, but this game had to be played carefully, since Andronikov knew too much to be a comfortable enemy. Little by little, Andronikov was edged out, and Rasputin was intro-duced to the care of another 'protector', a corrupt policeman called Colonel Kommisarov, whose job was to accompany

Rasputin everywhere and watch out for assassins. And meanwhile, Beletsky and Hvostov fostered the idea of Rasputin as the ogre behind Russian politics, a new Svengali. A caricature of this period shows a monstrous, menacing Rasputin with the Tsar and Tsarina—two doll-like figures—on his knees. It might have been captioned: 'The puppet master'. Some of the liberals who hated Rasputin would have been surprised to learn that Hvostov and Beletsky regarded him as slightly mentally deficient, and had appointed Kommisarov as a kind of nursemaid to keep him out of trouble.

At one point, Hvostov decided that it was time for Rasputin to go on another 'long journey' to prevent his unpopularity from boiling over. He was supplied with a carriage and several crates of madeira, and given a sum of money for expenses. But Rasputin was comfortable in Petrograd, and gently declined to budge. Threats of legal proceedings about the river-boat incident left him unmoved. Hvostov began to nurse a grudge against the man who had helped him to power.

A curious relation developed between Rasputin and Kommisarov. Like most people brought into constant contact with 'the holy devil', Kommisarov found that there was something endearing about his innocence. Rasputin was basically a child— and frequently a highly embarrassing and difficult child. On one occasion, Kommisarov shook him, and told him he would strangle him if he did not stop disgracing himself. When Rasputin opened his discourses to petitioners with religious sentiments, Kommisarov would interrupt roughly with: 'Now Grigory, skip the theology'.

The most difficult part of Kommisarov's task was to prevent Rasputin from getting too drunk (since he was likely to be summoned to see the Tsarina at any moment) and from raping female petitioners. Most of the petitioners were female, and a large proportion of these came prepared to offer themselves to Rasputin. But others had heard about his reputation as a healer and a holy man, and were unprepared for Rasputin's method of 'testing their souls'. These women could do a great deal of harm by spreading their stories of attempts on their virtue, and Kommisarov did his best to prevent matters from reaching this stage. In one case, Rasputin tried to force his way into a woman's bedroom, and she fled—aided by Kommisarov. Rasputin said resentfully: 'She cheated me'. Another woman was told by Rasputin that he would speak directly to the Tsarina about her petition—provided she gave herself to him. She was too anxious to have her petition granted to refuse directly, and stayed around hoping that he would drive a less hard bargain. Finally Rasputin lost patience and raped her—then decided not to keep his half of the bargain—probably feeling that she had not, after all, 'given' herself.

The strange thing is that in spite of all this, many of Rasputin's admirers continued to believe that the stories told against him were malicious invention. The Golovins—mother and daughter—who had introduced Yussupov to Rasputin, continued to believe in his sanctity. And possibly their faith was not as misplaced as it seems. An incident that took place in mid-December showed that his curious powers were still unaffected. On December 15, the Tsar was starting out for the southern front, accompanied by Alexey, now twelve years old. The boy was standing with his nose close to the window when a jolt threw him forward and caused nose-bleed. As usual, the bleeding could not be stopped. They turned back immediately for Tsarskoe Selo, and a message was sent to Rasputin. But Rasputin was not feeling too amiably disposed towards the Tsar, and decided not to go for twenty-four hours, during which time the boy's condition became serious, and fever began. The moment Rasputin appeared, the bleeding stopped. Rasputin explained to Beletsky that he wanted the Tsar to stew in his own juice for a day before he cut short the anxiety. This makes it clear that he knew he could cure the boy immediately; otherwise the risk of allowing fever to set in would have been too great. The Tsarina reaffirmed her belief that Rasputin was an agent of God, since his healing powers were clearly a gift of the Almighty. It may have been at this time that Rasputin prophesied that the boy's health would improve steadily after his thirteenth birthday—a prediction that proved to be accurate.

On Rasputin's name day, January 23, 1916, his room was filled with expensive presents—furniture, carpets, silver ornaments—all of which were sent to Pokrovskoe immediately afterwards. Anna Vyrubov came to lunch and brought the compliments of the Royal Family; while she was present, Rasputin was well-behaved—perhaps recalling how he had offended her a few weeks previously by getting noisily drunk at her table. As soon as she went home, the gypsy musicians appeared, and the dancing and drinking began. Beletsky states that Rasputin and several women sank unconscious on the floor, but this sounds like an exaggeration inspired by the tales about the Khlysty. At all events, two women certainly spent the night with Rasputin, for this was the occasion when the two enraged husbands were kept at the front door while their wives escaped by the back way.

Meanwhile, the intrigues continued and grew more complicated. The next aim of Hvostov and Beletsky was to get rid of the aged Goremykin; Hvostov had dreams of himself as Prime Minister. Rodzianko unconsciously aided them by losing no opportunity to attack Goremykin's incompetence. But the appointment of Hvostov as Prime Minister would not have suited Rasputin at all. Hvostov was too cunning for his liking. So he gently pointed out to the Tsarina that, even if Hvostov was a clever and trustworthy man, he was still an ex-member of the Duma, and as such, not to be trusted. But who was there who might fill the post of Prime Minister? There was Polivanov, the new War Minister—but he was needed in his present post. If the Tsar had had the courage, he could not have made a better choice than Rodzianko; such a choice would have united the whole country behind the throne, with the exception of the reactionaries. But the Tsarina would never have permitted it; Rodzianko was Rasputin's pet detestation. So the Tsar continued his policy of slow suicide by appointing about the least suitable man in the whole of Russia—Rasputin's stupid, incompetent and cowardly sycophant Stürmer. The only service that Stürmer had ever performed for the Crown was to bully and dismiss a zemstvo at Tver that had wanted to build schools and hospitals; ever since Rasputin's rise to power, Stürmer had hung around him, anticipating—correctly—that a few crumbs of power would fall from the table. On February 2, 1916, Goremykin was dismissed—without warning, as usual—and Stürmer's appointment was announced to a stunned and incredulous Cabinet and a furious Duma. And while Hvostov swore and cursed, Rasputin blandly pretended that this decision had been taken by the Tsar alone. To the people of Russia, it seemed yet another betrayal to the enemy; many believed that Stürmer was—like his name—a German.

And yet Rasputin must have realized that the storm clouds were gathering. The war was going badly. Bulgaria had entered the struggle on the side of Germany, and driven the Russians out of Serbia. Poland had been lost. The general mood was now one of defeatism. In Petrograd, fashionable society was tired of the war, and had decided to pretend that it was not taking place. The champagne parties went on all night as before; cynical epigrams were composed about the government and Rasputin's part in it, but it was taken for granted all the same; no one felt indignant.

Prince Yussupov, who had escaped from Germany at the beginning of the war, was horrified by what he saw in Russia. He assumed—falsely—that Rasputin had been responsible for the Tsar's decision to become Commander-in-Chief of the army, in order that he and the Tsarina could seize power. He also believed that Russia's military defeats were due—to some extent—to Rasputin's spying for the Germans. He began to brood on the idea of murdering Rasputin.

Yussupov was not the only one who was thinking along these lines. Hvostov himself had arrived at the same decision. His reasons, according to Pares, were less creditable than Yussupov's. Rasputin's name was so black that even his closest associates were ashamed to admit his help. So many of them played an elaborate game, pretending not to know Rasputin. Pitirim, for example, the Metropolitan of Petrograd, who had been appointed through Rasputin's influence, always referred to him as 'that awful man'. Hvostov was amused by this pretence, so when his agents informed him that Pitirim was closeted with Rasputin one day, he suddenly made a raid on the place, to the discomfiture of Pitirim and the amusement of Rasputin.

But Rasputin decided to turn the joke on Hvostov, who also made a pretence of being unacquainted with Rasputin. When Hvostov's wife was entertaining her friends, a messenger burst in with a message from Rasputin. Rasputin also took to telephoning Hvostov and Beletsky at their homes, knowing that their wives disapproved of him. Beletsky took the joke good-humouredly. Hvostov, still smarting from Rasputin's refusal to make a tour of the monasteries, and from Stürmer's appointment, decided that it was time that Rasputin disappeared permanently from the political scene. He confided his idea to Beletsky, who secretly thought it a good joke. However, Beletsky pretended to agree, and proposed that Rasputin should be lured into a cab driven by a police agent and quietly strangled in a side street. His body was then to be dropped into the river.

It is not clear what happened to this particular plot. Probably Beletsky simply betrayed it to Rasputin; at all events, Rasputin declined to be lured into a carriage, and the attempt failed.

The attempt now turns into a farce. Hvostov decided to try poison, and asked Kommisarov to buy it. Kommisarov declared he knew just the man in Saratov, and went off. Many weeks later, a telegram summoned the reluctant Kommisarov back to Petrograd, and he went to see Hvostov with a whole chest of white powders, all labelled with skulls and crossbones. Kommisarov spent half an hour explaining their effects to Hvostov, and declared that he had just tried them out on a stray cat, which died instantly. What he did not mention was that the 'poisons' were harmless household remedies, which had been labelled with the help of a cheap book on poisons. Evidently one of the bottles contained real poison, for the next time they called on Rasputin, Kommisarov slipped some of it into the milk for Rasputin's cat, and the cat rolled over and died. For some reason, Rasputin assumed that Andronikov had poisoned the cat, and their somewhat uneasy relationship now came to a definite termination. Andronikov could hardly complain; he had made many thousands of pounds out of the friendship.

Beletsky's peculiar sense of humour found all this funny. Besides, he was getting tired of Hvostov, and saw in this murder plan an excellent opportunity to get rid of him. Now he began to actively counterplot. Hvostov's next idea was to enlist the aid of the monk Illiodor—then living in Norway—in murdering Rasputin. Hvostov's secret funds would supply the money, and Illiodor's followers would carry out the crime. Hvostov exchanged telegrams with Illiodor, and finally dispatched one of his agents, Rzhetsky, to see Illiodor and give him money. But Rzhetsky was a boastful fool, incapable of keeping a secret. He made the false assumption that since Hvostov was sending him, he had 'official' police support. When he was stopped at the Finnish frontier, he dropped mysterious hints about his mission to the authorities there, and ended by ranting bombastically. They telegraphed to Beletsky, informing him of their suspicions, and Beletsky told them to arrest Rzhetsky and send him back. The police, in any case, wanted him for other offences. Beletsky told Hvostov that his agent was a fool, and would ruin everything unless silenced immediately.

Now Hvostov no longer trusted Beletsky. Beletsky advised him to give up the plan for murdering Rasputin, and instead to draw up a report of Rasputin's various misdemeanours, backed by the evidence of Kommisarov. This evidence consisted of detailed accounts of Rasputin's various seductions and rapes, and (according to Yussupov) of photographs of Rasputin actually engaged in sexual orgies. Hvostov and Beletsky drew up the report together, and Hvostov set out to present it to the Tsar. But Rasputin's luck still held. There can be no doubt that this latest report would have finally destroyed his credit with the Tsar. Earlier attempts to undermine him had been based on gossip and hearsay; but in this case the evidence was plentiful and carefully documented. But Hvostov was more concerned with getting rid of Beletsky than with destroying Rasputin; once in the Tsar's presence, he forgot about the report, and asked for Beletsky's dismissal. Later on, he told Beletsky that the Tsar had accepted the report on Rasputin; but Beletsky peeped into his briefcase, and found it still there.

The result of all this double-crossing was that both the conspirators went to Anna Vyrubov and laid their case before her. She was horrified, and rushed to the Tsarina to tell her about the attempt on their beloved 'Friend'. Both Beletsky and Hvostov were questioned, and tried hard to incriminate one another. They only dragged one another down. Beletsky might still have won; the Tsar had appointed him governor of Siberia. But a Petrograd newspaper published an interview with Beletsky in which the murder attempts were made public; the proprietor was naïve enough to assume that an interview with the assistant

Chief of Police could hardly be regarded as 'seditious'. But the Tsar was enraged at this public defiance of his ban on articles about Rasputin. Beletsky's appointment was cancelled. Hvostov was dismissed from his post, which was handed over to the Prime Minister—Rasputin's protégé Stürmer. As the story was whispered around St Petersburg society, people commented that Rasputin had the luck of the devil; he seemed to thrive on plots to overthrow him. Rasputin himself only smiled blandly. He was at least tactful enough not to exult openly.

Reading these accounts of intrigues, it is difficult to understand how Rasputin could have failed to see the writing on the wall. And yet from his own point of view, things were not as bad as they might seem. He still had his followers who believed in him completely. Mounya Golovin, for example—the girl who had introduced Yussupov to Rasputin in 1909—refused to believe a word of the stories about his sexual orgies, and told Yussupov that Rasputin was a saint who humbly endured all slanders and persecutions. (This alone makes it plain that the stories of Rasputin's orgies with his female disciples are largely invention; all the Ohkrana reports indicate that his mistresses were usually prostitutes or actresses.) The Tsarina herself was coming to believe that Rasputin was a reincarnation of Christ, and she wrote to her husband that Rasputin was their only mainstay against disaster.

Rasputin's power was becoming immense. Rightly or wrongly, he attached great significance to his dreams, and sent orders to the Tsar about military operations. At one point, he forbade an attack on the northern front, prophesying disaster. The Tsar was advised to comb his hair with Rasputin's comb before making any major decisions. Rasputin ordered Stürmer about and treated him with open contempt; on one occasion, he threatened to 'put the lid on' Stürmer if Stürmer did not do what 'mama' wished. Rasputin continued to encourage the Tsarina in her ill-judged attempt to keep Russia an absolute monarchy—which meant, in effect, that anyone who showed the least efficiency, honesty or initiative was dismissed at the earliest opportunity. Polivanov, who had filled the post of War Minister with remarkable success, was the next to be dismissed; the Tsarina nagged her husband with constant telegrams until

Nicholas gave way to her. She wrote: 'For Baby's sake we must be firm. . . .' She imagined that all this interference was preserving the Russian throne for her son. (Polivanov's crime was that he had commandeered three official cars that Stürmer had presented to Rasputin.) In retrospect, it seems clear that all the assassination attempts were directed at the wrong person; Yussupov could have saved the dynasty by shooting the Tsarina instead of Rasputin.

To Rasputin's credit, it must be said that he kept exerting himself to improve the situation of the railways and food supplies, recognizing that, if revolution came, it would be due to starvation rather than communism. Prices had continued to rise. The price of butter had doubled, of meat and flour had trebled, while salt cost six times as much as before the war. The fuel crisis was acute, since there was not enough transport to bring coal from the Donets region in the far south. Rasputin tried to get an enormous government grant for the railways, and never ceased to warn the Tsarina that transport was the most crucial of Russia's problems.

In June, Lord Kitchener set out on a secret mission to Russia; his purpose was to see what could be done about Russian arms. The H.M.S. *Hampshire* was mysteriously torpedoed off the Orkney Islands; the full story behind the sinking is still unknown. But another source of potential aid to Russia had been cut off. The Tsarina, as usual, did not recognize disaster when she saw it, and agreed with Rasputin that Kitchener 'might have done Russia harm'. Presumably Rasputin had reached this conclusion in one of his prophetic dreams; it is hard to see how a supply of British guns could have harmed Russia.

The case of the disgraced War Minister Sukhomlinov was preoccupying Rasputin, who found the pleas of Sukhomlinov's pretty wife irresistible. The Minister of Justice, the elder Hvostov (not to be confused with his villainous nephew) was all for prosecuting Sukhomlinov. But Rasputin pulled strings, and Hvostov was removed from his post, and appointed to the Ministry of the Interior. Hvostov was furious, but could do nothing.

The only man who clearly saw where all this muddle and intrigue was leading was Rodzianko. He was invited to a dinner for the Cabinet Ministers, and took the opportunity to hurl denunciations at them, telling them that they were completely out of touch with the needs of the people, and were wasting time on petty squabbles while the country was foundering. Everyone was cowed and impressed—Rodzianko had a loud and deep voice—but no one did anything about it.

Rasputin had made one minor mistake in his latest piece of intrigue. Uncle Hvostov had been appointed to the Ministry of the Interior in order to get him out of the Sukhomlinov affair. But he was an honest man, and immediately proceeded to use his newly acquired powers against Rasputin. Since Kommisarov had been dismissed at the same time as Beletsky and the younger Hvostov, the task of acting as Rasputin's bodyguard and P.R.O. had been taken over by the blackmailer Maniulov, who had been Rasputin's friend for many years. (It had been Maniulov who had thought of the idea of making Stürmer Prime Minister.) Maniulov was using his position to make money in every possible way—most of them illegal. Uncle Hvostov decided to trap him, and concocted a plot involving marked notes, which were offered to Maniulov as a bribe. Maniulov took the bribe, and was promptly arrested. But the super-racketeer was undisturbed; he merely hinted gently that his own trial would involve all kinds of disclosures about Rasputin. The Tsarina was hastily consulted; telegrams flew, and Uncle Hvostov again found himself out of a job. Maniulov went serenely back to Rasputin and continued his swindles and extortions. (Eventually, he was to serve a short term in prison, at the insistence of Uncle Hvostov's successor.)

The post of Minister of the Interior was once again empty. Rasputin took thought, and his decision came to rest upon another nonentity, Protopopov, a strange little man with no particular qualifications, a naïve busybody who could be relied upon to take Rasputin's orders. 'He has liked our Friend for at least four years' the Tsarina told her husband in a letter suggesting Protopopov for minister. Even Nicholas thought that this appointment would be a bad joke, and objected that he could not keep changing his mind once a fortnight. (In fact, this was exactly what he had done throughout his reign.) But she persisted, and the naïve little busybody was appointed on September 10,

1916. He held the post until the Revolution. There is something ironically appropriate about this choice of the last Minister of the Interior of Tsarist Russia. It would be impossible to sink any lower or choose anyone more preposterous. After Protopopov, anything would have been an anticlimax—anything but revolution.

CHAPTER ELEVEN

THE END

ALL over Russia, the discontent was spreading. At the front, the soldiers talked openly about revolution. The munitions situation had improved, through the hard work of a Committee of Defence (for which the Duma was largely responsible), but it was felt that the incompetence of the men in authority was undermining the army. A typical instance, given by Rodzianko, will serve to illustrate the situation:

Our son . . . began to narrate his experiences. Criminal incompetence, lack of co-operation in the higher command . . . had resulted in a senseless slaughter of our crack regiments. Not only officers but the men saw clearly that, in spite of the heroism of the guards, victory . . . was impossible. The Grand Duke Paul . . . disobeyed the order he received to encircle a given point by a flank manoeuvre, and sent the . . . regiments to make a frontal attack on the Rai-Mesto heights. The troops found themselves in a swamp, where many men perished. While they were floundering through the bog, German aeroplanes . . . bombarded them. . . . My son sank up to his armpits, and was with difficulty extricated. . . . The wounded could not be brought out, and perished in the swamp . . . Our artillery fire was weak, and failed to destroy the barbed-wire entanglements; the shells fell short of them and dropped among our own men. General Rauch, instead of obeying orders . . . withdrew his regiments. . . . Nevertheless, the gallant guards fulfilled their task, though bled white, and succeeded in capturing the heights, *which they were then ordered to abandon*' [my italics]. It is not surprising that Rodzianko's son ended by saying: 'The higher command is absolutely rotten. . . . We are willing to die for Russia, but not for the whims of the generals.'

If the Russian government had been half as efficient as the army, Russia would have won the war, and the revolution would never have taken place. General Brusilov made spectacular advances between June and September. For a while, it looked as if the Tsar would be saved in spite of his disastrous home policies.

But in Petrograd, it seemed that nothing could arrest the slide downhill. Depots were full of young troops who could not be sent to the front because there were not enough rifles; and when they finally arrived at the front, they carried with them the mood of defeat, and news of complete chaos at home. There was no meat available in Petrograd or Moscow, and yet sleds loaded with rotting carcases of cattle were openly driven through the streets on their way to the soap factories—meat that arrived rotten at the stations. There were also rumours of whole trains full of meat held up in Siberia—meat that would decay as soon as the thaw set in. But nobody seemed to know what to do about transport.

The new Minister of the Interior was about the strangest candidate yet chosen by Rasputin. Rodzianko declares that his sudden elevation drove Protopopov slightly insane, and he was probably right. Protopopov was a close friend of Rasputin—far closer to him than Stürmer or Hvostov had ever been. He had created something of a scandal in the summer of 1916 by having a meeting in Stockholm with a German financier who was closely connected with the German government. When the press publicized this meeting, Protopopov declared that he had only told the financier that Russia would fight to the death. But it is almost certain that he went as an emissary of Rasputin to talk about the possibility of Russia signing a separate peace treaty with Germany. Rasputin endlessly advised the Tsar to stop the war at any cost—even that of betraying England and France. Now he was appointed Minister of the Interior, Protopopov became a different man. He seemed to walk around in a state of mystical ecstasy, and frequently declared that he felt he had been chosen to save Russia. On the other hand, he was as naïve as a child, and when someone told him he ought to resign, he said: 'How can I resign? All my life I've dreamed of being a vice-governor, and here I am a minister!' But his ideas of how to save Russia were completely vague—in fact, non-existent. He had no idea of how to meet the serious internal crises. His best idea was to try to persuade Rodzianko to become Prime Minister. But Rodzianko—who might have got the post if he had been willing to compromise with Rasputin and the Tsarina—told him that his condition for becoming Prime Minister was that the Tsarina should be confined to the palace at Livadia for the rest of the war. Protopopov could hardly believe his ears, and scurried off back to Rasputin, afraid that a thunderbolt would strike Rodzianko after this terrific blasphemy.

The Tsarina was not getting things entirely her own way. In February 1916, the Tsar had broken all precedents and paid a visit to the Duma, making a speech about co-operation that was wildly cheered. (It is significant that both Rasputin and Rodzianko had advised this visit. The two men had many of the same interests at heart; it was a pity that Rodzianko failed to recognize this.) But the Tsarina felt that her husband's visit to the Duma was a capitulation to the enemy, and exerted all her power over him to make him thwart the Duma and snub Rodzianko as often as possible. Nicholas was weak enough to obey her, and Rodzianko's loyalty to the throne was severely tested.

The new Minister of Justice, Makarov, proved to be as difficult to handle as Uncle Hvostov. He refused to drop the case of Sukhomlinov, so Rasputin plotted to have him dismissed. Eventually, he was replaced by a Rasputin candidate, who lost no time in dropping the cases against Sukhomlinov and Maniulov, Rasputin's confederate. But by that time, Rasputin was dead.

On November 22, to everyone's astonishment—and the delight of most of Russia—Stürmer was dismissed by the Tsar. The reason for this seems to have been a sudden unpremeditated visit paid to the Duma by the Ministers for War and Naval Affairs, who declared their willingness to co-operate with the

Duma. This sign of defection in the Cabinet worried Stürmer, who urged the Tsar—for the tenth time—to dissolve the Duma. He was too late; the Tsarina was enraged at the idea that Stürmer had no control over his ministers, and ordered the Tsar to dismiss him. The French Ambassador, Maurice Paléologue, saw Stürmer shuffling across a snow-covered road after his dismissal, a broken old man. Stürmer was replaced by Trepov, an anti-Rasputin man. At the same time that he decided to get rid of Stürmer, the Tsar had also decided that Protopopov would have to go. But this provoked an outburst of hysteria from the Tsarina, and Protopopov remained—to be executed a year later by the Bolsheviks.

At this time, one of the most brilliant and well-liked members of the Duma was V. M. Purishkevich, an ardent monarchist, who nevertheless hated Rasputin. Purishkevich was known as a wit, and whenever he stood up to speak, members began to smile. He composed a great many satirical verses at the expense of Rasputin, which had a wide circulation in Petrograd. He also coined the phrase 'the ministerial leapfrog' to describe the way in which ministers kept changing.

In early December, Purishkevich delivered a speech in the Duma which was some of the plainest speaking that had ever been heard in that assembly. He poured hatred and scorn on the head of Rasputin, and attacked Protopopov and Andronikov. The speech, and Purishkevich's frantic sincerity, made a tremendous impression. And it made one member of the audience come to a sudden decision. That man was Prince Yussupov, who had for a long time been toying with the idea of Rasputin's murder. He decided that the time had come.

Now comes the strangest part of the story. Rasputin had known for many years that he was likely to be assassinated, and it had apparently never worried him. And yet after Purishkevich's speech, he became moody and silent. He was suddenly aware that the end was near. One day, he went walking by the Neva, and, on his return, said that it was full of the blood of Grand Dukes—which seems to have been a prevision of what would take place a year later. He wrote a letter to his family in which he said that he felt death to be close. And finally, and strangest of all, he wrote an extraordinary, prophetic document, headed:

'The Spirit of Grigory Efimovich Rasputin-Novyhk of the village of Pokrovskoe'. The letter read as follows:

I write and leave behind me this letter at St Petersburg. I feel that I shall leave life before January 1. I wish to make known to the Russian people, to Papa, to the Russian Mother and to the children, to the land of Russia, what they must understand. If I am killed by common assassins, and especially by my brothers the Russian peasants, you, Tsar of Russia, have nothing to fear, remain on your throne and govern, and you, Russian Tsar, will have nothing to fear for your children, they will reign for hundreds of years in Russia. But if I am murdered by Boyars, nobles, and if they shed my blood, their hands will remained soiled with my blood, for twenty-five years they will not wash their hands from my blood. They will leave Russia. Brothers will kill brothers and they will kill each other and hate each other, and for twenty-five years there will be no nobles in the country. Tsar of the land of Russia, if you hear the sound of a bell that will tell you that Grigory has been killed, you must know this: if it was your relations who have wrought my death, then no one in the family, that is to say, none of your children or relations, will remain alive for more than two years. They will be killed by the Russian people. I go, and I feel in me the divine command to tell the Russian Tsar how he must live if I have disappeared. You must reflect and act prudently. Think of your safety, and tell your relations that I have paid for them with my blood. I shall be killed. I am no longer among the living. Pray, pray, be strong, think of your blessed family. Grigory.

This letter, according to Simanovich, was taken by him to the Tsarina, who was asked not to show it to Nicholas. It was later returned to him, he claims, after her death, together with other notes of Rasputin's. Pares, who saw a facsimile of the letter, adds that Simanovich had in his possession the Tsarina's prayer book with her favourite symbol, the swastika (an ironic choice, in view of its later significance as a Nazi symbol) that had been in her possession at the time of her death. The evidence for the authenticity of the letter is therefore strong, and even the sceptical Pares seems inclined to accept it.

Like so many events in the reign of Nicholas, the murder of Rasputin gives a feeling of being somehow predestined. It was in no way carefully planned, and might very easily have been frustrated by an accident. Yussupov approached Purishkevich and laid his plan before him, and Purishkevich immediately agreed. Yussupov decided that they would utilize the help of two of his friends: the Grand Duke Dmitry Pavlovich, who addressed the Tsar as 'uncle', and a young officer called Sukhotin. Purishkevich also recommended a doctor named Lazavert.

But although the conspirators swore to speak to no one, the talkative Purishkevich proceeded to broadcast the plan far and wide. He buttonholed Maklakov in the lobby of the Duma, among a crowd of people, and told him about it. He also told a journalist called Becker and gave her full details of the plot and mentioned the names of all the conspirators. And when Yussupov finally issued an invitation to his house for the night of December 29, Simanovich, Protopopov and Anna Vyrubov all begged him not to go as he would probably be in danger; Protopopov actually extracted from him a promise not to go—which Rasputin later withdrew because he had given Yussupov his word. And two days before the murder, Rasputin's forebodings of death reached a climax in a mood of deep apprehension. Since he had prophesied that he would die before January 1 (a fortnight away —the date would be January 13 in the New Style), it seems incredible that he should have taken such a pointless risk as to visit Yussupov alone at midnight. It can only be explained by Pares' surmise—that he felt a mixture of affection and contempt for the handsome young playboy, to whom he referred as 'the Little One', and could not imagine him as a source of danger. Besides, Yussupov was a close friend of Rasputin's most devoted disciple, Mounya Golovin, whose method of trying to reconcile the two was to assure each of them of the other's admiration.

Besides all this, Rasputin was anxious to meet Yussupov's beautiful wife, the Grand Duchess Irina Alexandrovna. Possibly he saw in her a potential convert. So Yussupov had the ideal bait for luring Rasputin to his palace. He also had an excellent excuse for asking Rasputin to come to the palace secretly and late at night: his father (who was the civil authority in charge of Moscow) hated Rasputin.

The last time Rasputin saw the Tsar, Nicholas asked him for his blessing. Rasputin replied: 'This time it is for you to bless me'. And on the afternoon of November 29, Anna Vyrubov was sent by the Tsarina to take a message to Rasputin at his lodgings. Rasputin mentioned that he had agreed to see Yussupov at midnight, and Anna expressed her doubts about the strange hour. Rasputin assured her that Yussupov's motive was only to keep the visit a secret from his parents. As Anna was leaving him, she must have hesitated, as if expecting something further, for Rasputin said in a strange voice: 'What more do you want? Already you have received all.' It becomes more difficult to believe that Rasputin had no premonition that he was so close to death.

On her return to the palace, Anna mentioned Rasputin's visit to the Tsarina, who said: 'There must be some mistake. Irena (Yussupov's wife) is in the Crimea.' Yet even so, she did not telephone Rasputin to communicate her suspicions, although she was clearly uneasy, and kept repeating: 'There must be some mistake.'

According to Yussupov, the basement room was prepared with bottles of wine and chocolate cake containing potassium cyanide. Powdered cyanide was also dropped into some wine glasses.

At midnight, Yussupov, trembling with nerves, drove to Rasputin's house, and was admitted after being challenged by the concierge. Rasputin was alone, waiting for him. He mentioned that Protopopov had called that evening to beg him not to go out in case he was murdered, hinting broadly that Yussupov was not to be trusted. This in itself seems curious. Perhaps some of the rumours floating about the Duma had come to Protopopov. But Rodzianko mentions several times Protopopov's interest in spiritualism, and says that his closeness to Rasputin was due to a bond of 'mysticism'. Is it possible that Protopopov had the same foreboding as Rasputin?

On arriving at the Yussupov palace, Rasputin heard the sound of a gramophone playing 'Yankee Doodle'. Yussupov told him that his wife had visitors, and would join them as soon as they left. They went downstairs into the basement, and Rasputin was fascinated by a labyrinthine cupboard there. Possibly he was suspicious, for he refused to drink tea or wine at first, although he accepted some biscuits. Yussupov says that he was eventually persuaded to eat some poisoned cake. But at this point, his testimony is dubious. Maria Rasputin says that her father never ate cake under any circumstances; moreover, no poison was afterwards found in the body.[1] Maria Rasputin's surmise may be correct: that Yussupov embellished the sordid and discreditable incident—the murder of an unarmed man by four terrified assassins—with a certain amount of melodrama. For according to Yussupov, Rasputin not only ate cake filled with cyanide, but drank down poisoned wine too. Yussupov waited, and nothing happened. This in itself is enough to arouse the suspicions of anyone acquainted with the action of cyanide; a few milligrams are lethal, and death follows in a matter of seconds, from paralysis of the respiratory centre. Even in the most abnormal circumstances, the fatal dose is a drachm—an eighth of an ounce. From Yussupov's description, it seems clear that Rasputin must have swallowed about an ounce.[2]

Nothing happened. Rasputin asked Yussupov to sing and play his guitar; it must have been difficult for Yussupov to summon the control to handle it properly. Suddenly, Rasputin looked at him with a look of total hatred. Loud noises from above eased the situation, and Yussupov said he would go to see if his wife was ready. He went upstairs to where the conspirators were waiting, and told them that the poison had taken no effect. They talked of going down to strangle Rasputin, but Yussupov was afraid that he might make an uproar when he saw Purishkevich. The Grand Duke gave Yussupov his revolver, and Yussupov descended again. Rasputin was sitting with his head sunk. He said he felt slightly unwell, and that his throat was

[1] According to the Leipzig documents.

[2] Mr Nigel Morland, the well-known writer on crime, has told me that Rasputin was suffering from acute alcoholic gastritis, which thickens the lining of the stomach so that cyanide would take a long time to act. Mr Morland, who was in Russia at the time of the Revolution, received this information from a clerical acquaintance of Rasputin, whom he helped to escape from Odessa. Rasputin had frequently mentioned to his friend that this thickened lining of his stomach allowed him to drink enormous quantities of alcohol without getting drunk. Mr Morland utilized this idea in an interesting novel called *Sparkling Cyanide*.

burning; then, to Yussupov's surprise, suggested that they should go to see the gypsies. 'With God in thought, but with mankind in the flesh,' said Rasputin, winking. Yussupov drew Rasputin's attention to a crystal cross, and said: 'Grigory Efimovich, you had better say a prayer before it'. Rasputin looked at him again with fear and suspicion, but then turned to the crucifix. Yussupov shot him in the back. Rasputin gave a tremendous roar and collapsed on the carpet. The other conspirators rushed into the room, and one of them caught the light switch and plunged them into darkness. When the light went on again, they saw Rasputin lying on his back, his eyes closed. They examined the body, and Dr Lazavert pronounced Rasputin dead. But the doctor's nerves were not in the best condition; he had got into a state of hysteria waiting for Yussupov to come up, and had actually gone outside and fainted in the snow at one point. Two of the conspirators now drove off with Rasputin's coat; Sukhotin was wearing it, apparently to mislead anyone who was watching into believing that Rasputin had left the palace at about 3 a.m. Yussupov and Purishkevich, very elated, went upstairs again. After some time, Yussupov decided to take another look at the body. He had an uneasy feeling that Rasputin had a demonic power of rising from the dead; (he later admitted to Maklakov that he had wanted Rasputin to make the sign of the cross before he died, which would render harmless his demonic powers). He shook the body, but Rasputin lay still. Then the eyelid twitched, and to Yussupov's horror, the 'corpse' stood up and tore an epaulette from his shoulder. Yussupov fled upstairs in terror, and Rasputin followed him, crawling up the stairs on all fours. Rasputin came to a locked door leading to the courtyard, and with tremendous strength, burst it open. Purishkevich rushed after him, firing his revolver. Two shots missed; the next two hit Rasputin, and he collapsed. Then the excitable Purishkevich—a tiny bald man with a snub nose—kicked Rasputin's head—unable to resist the sight of his fallen enemy —and rushed out of the house, to tell two soldiers: 'I have killed Grigory Rasputin, the enemy of Russia and the Tsar'. The two soldiers came and helped drag the body to the house, and Yussupov now fell on it and battered it with a steel press belonging to Maklakov. The whole affair reflects very little credit on either Yussupov or Purishkevich, and this battering of the body suggests a more personal animosity than either of them admitted subsequently, when representing the murder as a patriotic act.

Sukhotin and the Grand Duke now returned with the Grand Duke's car, and Rasputin was bundled into it. A policeman who enquired about the shots was also told that Rasputin had been murdered, although later on the same night, the conspirators changed their story, and declared that they had shot a dog (they did shoot a dog to substantiate this story). Rasputin's body was taken to a spot on the river known as the Little Nevka, and pushed through a hole in the ice. His fur coat was thrown after him, and a snow boot. This boot was actually somehow left on the ice, where it was later found by Simanovich's son, who directed the police to look for the body at this point.

Rasputin was still alive when he was pushed into the river. The conspirators may have suspected this, for they tied his hands before loading him into the car. The cold water roused Rasputin, and he succeeded in freeing one hand. But there was ice above him. He managed to make the sign of the cross before he drowned; when his body was found, his right hand was still against his breast, three fingers raised.

The conspirators believed that, in killing Rasputin, they would turn the tide of Russia's destiny. In retrospect, it is apparent that they only played a small part in that destiny. Rasputin's death made no difference. He had never had the influence that his enemies imagined; the real power had always been in the hands of the Tsarina. After Rasputin's death, the situation remained completely unchanged, except that the Tsar and Tsarina were now more certain than ever that they were about to be engulfed in some inevitable disaster.

On the morning after the murder, the news spread throughout Petrograd. Maria Rasputin rang the Tsarina to ask if they knew the whereabouts of her father. Yussupov denied having had Rasputin to his house, but investigation disclosed bloodstains on the floor of the car and in the cellar and courtyard. The Tsarina ordered Yussupov and the Grand Duke Dmitry to be confined to their houses. Later, Yussupov was sent to his country estate, and the Grand Duke was sent to the Persian front—which saved his life, since he was out of Russia at the time of the Revolution. Purishkevich was allowed to depart for the front. Two days later, Rasputin's body was found, and Maria Rasputin and her sister were called to identify it. 'The thick matted hair was covered with clots of blood. The face was swollen and the eyes already glazed. When the pelisse had been removed, the [frozen] clothes looked like a hard skin which held in places and in others peeled off. But the strangest thing was the right arm [held in] . . . the sign of the cross.' A post mortem was halted by the Tsarina—although it must have been carried out to a certain extent, since the papers concerning Rasputin's death mention that no poison was found in the body. On January 3, a foggy day, Rasputin was buried in the imperial park, with the Royal Family as mourners. The young Tsarevitch—who is often credited with disliking Rasputin—asked furiously whether the murderers were to be allowed to escape.

Nothing changed. The Tsar became curiously apathetic, and no longer bothered about going to the front. The winter weather meant that there was little fighting anyway. The situation could still have been saved—if the Tsar had seized this moment to make a separate peace with Germany. Instead, he stayed at the palace and did nothing. The Tsarina seemed to retreat into herself, and her preoccupation with her family increased.

Rasputin's death caused a widespread sensation, but it only served to deepen the peasants' feeling of dissatisfaction. One of them remarked to Maklakov: 'Yes, only one mouzhik got through to the Tsar, and the Masters killed him'.

The disintegration was now obvious to everyone—so obvious that no one wanted to accept public posts. The Prime Minister, Trepov, was allowed to resign, and a doddering old man called Prince Golitsyn was appointed—much against his will. The Minister of Justice was removed and replaced by Rasputin's candidate, Dobrovolsky, who hastened to obey the Tsarina in everything; the Minister of War was also dismissed, and the Minister of Education allowed to resign. Protopopov spent more time than ever at Tsarskoe Selo. It was said that he was determined to 'step into Rasputin's shoes', and Rodzianko cites a rumour that he was holding seances to get instructions from Rasputin's spirit. Protopopov did his best to raise the Tsarina's spirits by having letters and telegrams sent to her from 'simple people'. This was hardly effective, since she also received many letters threatening her assassination. Pares even cites a report to the effect that an attempt was made on her life while she was working in the hospital. If this actually happened, the news was suppressed. And the petty spites and intrigues went on; the resignations of Ignatyev and Volkonsky—the latter was assistant Minister of the Interior—were refused, but a few days later their dismissal was announced in the press. 'As if to spite the public, all Rasputin's adherents were promoted', says Rodzianko. A man called Kurlov became Protopopov's assistant; he was a police officer suspected of complicity in the murder of Stolypin; this in itself was enough to endear him to the Tsarina.

In the early months of 1917, Rodzianko was twice approached with a plan for a *coup d'état*. A General Krymov summoned an unofficial meeting of the Duma at Rodzianko's house, told them that the army regarded itself as defeated while the Tsarina was in power, and said: 'A *coup d'état* is urgent.' Rodzianko replied that he would never countenance a revolution. Not long afterwards, he was summoned by the Grand Duchess Marie Pavlovna, widow of the Grand Duke Vladimir who had been responsible for the shooting on Bloody Sunday. She said flatly that the Tsarina must be 'annihilated'. Rodzianko expressed horror, and left her.

The revolution now descended like a snowstorm. Already, in the previous October, the police had fired on mobs of strikers, many of whom were killed. But by January, there were strikes and protest marches every day. Protopopov did his best—which amounted to ordering arrests all the time. He had imported a foreign spiritualist now he could no longer rely on the advice of Rasputin. There was no food and no coal, and long queues gave political agitators ready-made audiences. Petrograd was full of discontented troops waiting to be sent to the front, but preparing to support the workers if they were asked to suppress a revolution. There was talk of sending for the Guard Cavalry, but it was discovered that they were also prepared to support an insurrection. Sailors were sent instead. In February, Rodzianko had a last attempt at persuading the Tsar to act. Nicholas seemed tired and apathetic; he was hardly roused to interest even when

Rodzianko told him flatly that the whole conduct of his reign had been one long mistake. In telling of this interview, Rodzianko recalls another occasion when he had presented gloomy reports to the Tsar, and Nicholas had stood at the window, looking out, when he said: 'I was in the woods today. It is so quiet there. One forgets these intrigues and paltry human restlessness. My soul felt so peaceful. One is nearer to nature there, nearer to God.' What is quite clear is that Nicholas was never intended to be a ruler, particularly in such a turbulent age. He would have been happier as a country gentleman, walking over his estate with a gun under his arm. At headquarters, with the country collapsing around his ears, he wrote in his journal: 'I shall take up dominoes in my spare time'.

On Thursday, March 8, the revolution began in Petrograd. Disorders broke out due to lack of bread. It was later said that there was enough bread in Petrograd for several days, but distribution was bad. Two days later, police fired on crowds who were shouting: 'Down with the German woman' (the Tsarina). The next day, more were killed. Then the Volynsky regiment mutinied and killed one of its officers. Other regiments followed, and barricades went up in the streets. On March 14, the Duma decided to step into the breach by sanctioning the formation of a provisional government. The revolution was chaotic, formless. The Bolsheviks had very little to do with it.

The Tsar, hurrying back to Tsarskoe Selo, was advised to abdicate. On joining his wife, Nicholas burst into tears; for the first time, he realized that he was completely alone. Later, when he tried to leave the palace grounds, six soldiers pushed him back with their rifle butts, saying: 'You can't go that way, Mr Colonel'. The Tsarina watched this from a window. This must have been her bitterest moment.

Meanwhile, the Germans were naturally delighted with the news of the revolution; it could only mean that Russia would be forced to make peace on the Kaiser's terms—which, in fact, happened the following year. With the co-operation of the German general staff, Lenin was sent from Switzerland, and crossed Germany by a sealed train. It arrived at the Finland Station in Petrograd on April 16, and Lenin was met by huge crowds and a brass band. He had been in exile for ten years. A member of the 'people's Soviet' made a speech of welcome, and Lenin replied, welcoming 'the victorious revolution'.

In fact, Lenin's victory was still distant. Kerensky was in charge of the provisional government. The 'revolutionary front' was split by squabbles. Lenin wanted to make sure there could be no return to the old system, or anything like it— remembering the lesson of France after 1789; but even the Bolshevists were not sure whether they wanted to see Russia converted to a Marxist state overnight. Finally, Kerensky ordered the arrest of Lenin, who was forced to fly to Finland. But in October he returned in disguise, and in the early hours of November 7, the Bolsheviks struck and seized the principal buildings of Petrograd. The same thing happened in other cities. The civil war was still to come; but for all practical purposes, the revolution was over.

Meanwhile, the Royal Family had been kept prisoners in the palace at Tsarskoe Selo. The British government sent them an offer of asylum, and Kerensky started to arrange for them to leave Russia; then Lloyd George agitated in England, and the offer of asylum was withdrawn. It is doubtful, in any case, whether the Royal Family would have been allowed to escape.

In the first months, the Royal Family had no need to feel much alarm; they were allowed to correspond freely with their friends; there was much talk of sending them to Japan via Siberia; and the officer in charge of them was sympathetic to them.

On August 13, Kerensky had them sent to Tobolsk. They went by train to Tioumen, then by steamer down the river, passing Rasputin's village, Pokrovskoe, on the way. Before setting out, the Tsarina had written in a letter to Anna Vyrubov (who was imprisoned in the Peter and Paul fortress): 'The transfigured spirit of our Friend calls us. . . .' Now they saw Rasputin's house, a story higher than the others, overlooking the river.

Strangely enough, the Bishop of Tobolsk was Hermogen, the man whom the Tsar had exiled. On November 3, he ordered the bells of Tobolsk to peal out in commemoration of Nicholas's coronation.

Maria Rasputin's husband, a strange young theosophist called

Boris Soloviev, decided that they would try to rescue the Tsar, and went to Tobolsk in disguise, followed by his wife. Bishop Hermogen agreed to help them. The idea was simply to get the Tsar and his family to the nearest point where they could join the White Russian army—the loyalists who refused to accept the revolution. The Tsar himself raised objections to this plan; it seemed that, up to the very end, he possessed his faculty for working against himself. He asked for an undertaking that he should not be forced to leave Russian territory; he was still hoping that a revulsion of feeling might place him back on the throne. Evidently he was unaware of the very real danger to his life. On the day when the rescue plot was finally scheduled to take place, Hermogen announced that they had been betrayed, and Maria Rasputin fled to Pokrovskoe. Her husband was arrested, but finally released. Eventually, they reached Berlin, where Simanovich was able to help them—he had also escaped—and Maria Rasputin finally became a dancer in Paris. Her husband died there, leaving her with two children.

In late April, the Tsar was transferred to Ekaterinburg in the Urals, described by Pares as 'perhaps the most vehemently Bolshevik spot in Russia'. On the way there, they changed horses under the windows of Rasputin's house in Pokrovskoe. In May, the rest of his family followed him to Ekaterinburg—the Tsarevitch's illness having delayed them in Tobolsk.

On July 16, the family were told that they were being moved that night. Czechoslovak armies were in the vicinity (they captured Ekaterinburg on the 25th), so this seemed reasonable enough. That evening, they were told to go down to the cellar. Apparently the Tsar suspected nothing, although he had taken an instinctive dislike to their new gaoler, Yurovsky, a Siberian Jew, and wrote in his diary, 'This specimen we like least of all'. The boy was too ill to walk, so the Tsar carried him. The Tsar was given a chair to sit on. Yurovsky stepped forward, and said: 'Nicholas Alexandrovitch, your followers tried to set you free. They failed. Now you are going to be shot.' 'What?' said the Tsar. 'This', said Yurovsky, and shot Nicholas in the chest with a revolver. Nicholas dropped dead. The Tsarina crossed herself. The others opened fire, and the girls dropped on to their knees and were shot in that position. (Bullet marks on the wall were all low down.) The Tsar's doctor, Botkin, was killed by a shot, and also the cook. The maidservant Demidova tried to protect herself with cushions; she tried to fend off the bayonets with these until she was finished off. Anastasia was attacked with the butt end of a rifle and then, according to the usual account, killed with a bayonet. But according to the woman who later called herself Anastasia, she was only knocked unconscious, and assumed to be dead. While all this went on, a lorry revved its engine outside. Finally, the children's spaniel was killed, its head shattered with a rifle blow.

According to an account by Franz Svoboda, a former Austrian prisoner of war, given in 1938, he and a companion then helped to move out the bodies. One of them stirred, and they recognized Anastasia. They wrapped her in a blanket, and managed to load her into a cart outside instead of into the lorry intended for the bodies. Then began her long journey that was to end two years later in Berlin, an attempt at suicide, and the universal sensation that followed the declaration of her identity.

This is no place to tell the story of Anastasia. Pares states flatly that she was an impostor, and it seems possible that history will judge her so. And yet there is a great deal of evidence in favour of her claim, some of which is assembled in the notes (by Roland Krug von Nidda) to *I, Anastasia*, her autobiography. One specimen of this will suffice. Count Carl Bonde, one-time head of the Swedish Red Cross Mission to Siberia, declared in 1952:

> In my capacity as head of the Swedish Red Cross Mission to Siberia, I was travelling in a special train during 1918. At some place, the name of which I have forgotten, the train was stopped and searched for the Grand Duchess Anastasia, the daughter of Tsar Nicholas II. . . . No one knew where she had got to.

It seems certain that the Bolsheviks conducted an extensive search in late July 1918, and the evidence indicates that it may well have been for Anastasia. Gilliard, the Tsarevitch's tutor, at first agreed that 'Anastasia' was the person she claimed to be, but later changed his mind. She never succeeded in establishing her identity, or in gaining access to the millions of roubles that the Tsar had banked in America for such an emergency. If, as seems likely, she was no impostor, then her tragic story is a fitting conclusion to the history of the Tsar's family, of whom more than one historian has said that they seemed to be singled out for misfortune.

The bodies of the rest of the Tsar's family were destroyed with vitriol, and thrown into a mine shaft. Their fate, at least, had been less horrifying than that of other members of the Romanov family. The Grand Duchess Elizabeth, the Tsarina's sister, had been sent to Alapayevsk, not far from Ekaterinburg, together with the Grand Duke Sergius Mikhailovich, three sons of the Grand Duke Constantine and the young son of the Grand Duke Paul. The day after Nicholas and his family had been murdered, this party was taken out to a disused mine shaft and thrown into it while still alive, only the Grand Duke Sergius being shot as he tried to resist. Dynamite was thrown down after them. When the bodies were later recovered, all had severe head injuries, and medical evidence indicated that they had not died immediately.

Many other Grand Dukes were later executed with the excuse of 'reprisals' for the murder of Uritsky, head of the Bolshevik secret police, and for an attempt on the life of Lenin by Dora Kaplan, a Socialist Revolutionary. Several ex-ministers were executed at the same time, including Stürmer, Maklakov, Protopopov, Hvostov (the nephew) and Beletsky. Old Goremykin was already dead, strangled by a mob. Hvostov and Beletsky—who had ended as bitter enemies bringing about one another's downfall—to Rasputin's amusement—ended in the same cell together, in which the revolutionary Burtsev made a third. The blackmailer Maniulov—Rasputin's right-hand man for so many years—helped Burtsev to escape later, and was himself executed, together with Prince Andronikov. The ex-Minister of War, Polivanov, and General Brusilov—who had come near to winning the war in 1916—became Bolsheviks. Many of the leading characters in this story escaped to live abroad, including Rodzianko—who died in poverty in Serbia in 1924 and the Dowager Empress, the Tsar's mother, who lived in England for a period. Purishkevich died of typhus while fighting with the White Army in South Russia. Like Yussupov, he wrote a book describing the murder of Rasputin.

Yussupov himself is perhaps the sole actor in this drama who is still alive at the time of writing (1963). His right to the title of the murderer of Rasputin—which Purishkevich disputed—was established in an American court, when Yussupov sued a film company who had filmed the life of Rasputin. In the film, Rasputin rapes the wife of a prince, who murders him in revenge. This 'prince' was not in any way identified with Yussupov, but Yussupov rightly contended that he was universally known to be the murderer of Rasputin, and that therefore the film was a libel on himself. He won heavy damages.

The Bolsheviks would not allow the body of Rasputin to rest in the royal park. It was dug up, and the coffin burned on a bonfire. It was said that it had suffered all the extremities of water, earth, fire and air.

CHAPTER TWELVE

THE LEGEND AND THE PROBLEM

THE Rasputin legend started with the revolution, when Illiodor hurried back to Russia and published his book *The Holy Devil*. As might have been predicted, Illiodor portrayed Rasputin as a drunken confidence trickster who was able to dominate a hysterical Tsarina and a weak Tsar by force of personality and a certain amount of sleight of hand. Charles Omessa's extraordinary fabrication followed in 1918. Omessa claimed to have talked to 'a certain person' who was able to acquaint him with 'all the secret details of the marvellous adventures of this mystical and rough Don Juan whom a neurasthenic empress aspired to transform into a Mazarin'. Omessa's informant even obtained the Ohkrana reports from 'a former influential Minister'. Omessa does not explain why he has to veil his sources in secrecy; no harm could possibly come to his informant. As to the former Minister, Omessa might well have obtained one of the many reports compiled against Rasputin from any number of ex-Ministers; but again, there could be no possible objection to mentioning his name to provide authenticity. The general trustworthiness of Omessa's book can be judged from its third chapter, in which he tells how the Tsarina's lover, General Prince O——, the Tsar's Equerry, was ordered to leave the country by John of Cronstadt, and was later found dead in a Cairo hotel. Again, Omessa does not explain why he needs to keep the man's name a secret, since both he and the Tsarina were dead by that time.

I dwell on Omessa's book here because such works as this

were the foundation of the Rasputin legend. Many other figures of modern history have been almost blurred out of existence by legends—T. E. Lawrence is an obvious example—but even the most biased books about him—like those by Lowell Thomas and Richard Aldington—are based on fact. Rasputin's 'biographers' were at liberty to invent whatever they pleased, and even the most conscientious of them could seldom resist the temptation.

As far as England and America were concerned, the chief culprit was the 'master of mystery' William LeQueux, the first man to exploit the personality of Rasputin on a large scale. LeQueux published no less than three books on Rasputin in the three years following his murder, only one of which contains anything that could be called 'fact'; not content with this, he introduced Rasputin into a book of memoirs called *Things I Know*, published in 1923, by way of substantiating certain 'revelations' about the identity of Jack the Ripper.

LeQueux's books would deserve no more attention than the one by Omessa, except that his personality and background lent them a certain plausibility. LeQueux had been in Russia during the war—as a secret agent, he claims—and he was a friend of Cabinet Ministers and politicians. *Things I Know* is an orgy of name-dropping.

LeQueux's first book on Rasputin was published in 1917; it was called *Rasputin, the Rascal Monk*. There is little to choose between it and Omessa's book for free invention; but at least it sticks to the basic facts. It must have sold well enough to make LeQueux decide on a sequel, for in 1918, he brought out *The Minister of Evil, The Secret History of Rasputin's Betrayal of Russia*. This book purported to be a translation of a manuscript of Fedor Rayevski, Rasputin's secretary, a young Italian. According to Rayevski, he was working for the government as a kind of secret agent in 1903 when his superior, General Kouropatkin, introduced him to Rasputin. 'All Russia was ringing with Rasputin's renown,' Rayevski declares. (Rasputin, of course, was totally unknown in St Petersburg in 1903.) Kouropatkin told Rayevski that he was to be Rasputin's secretary. The aim was to insinuate Rasputin into the palace. Stürmer and General Kouropatkin finally decided that the affair needed careful pre-

paration; so in the summer of 1903, after the canonization of
St Seraphim of Sarov (whose intervention would, it was hoped,
produce a male heir), Rasputin was told to pray noisily in an
empty church when the Tsarina was about to enter. The Tsarina
was duly impressed by this holy man who prayed so fervently
for a male heir. She did not speak to him, but made enquiries
about him. And later, Rasputin was summoned to an audience
at the palace, where, inevitably, he made an overwhelming
impression. Rayevski was present at nearly all the audiences
with the Tsar and Tsarina, and so is able to give long and precise
reports of intimate conversations. He tells many stories of
Rasputin's misuse of his power; how, for example, a virtuous
lady refused to give herself to Rasputin, and denounced his
Khlysty orgies as impious; so Rasputin had her husband 'framed'
and arrested as a spy. When the wife still refused to surrender
her virtue, the husband was shot.

During the war, Rayevski explains, Rasputin and the Tsarina
worked together for a German victory, and Rasputin and
Rayevski made visits to Berlin, where Rasputin spoke to the
Kaiser (with Rayevski present, of course).

In 1919, LeQueux decided that the world was ripe for more
revelations about Rasputin. This time he decided to be more
cautious and give the book the framework of a novel. *Rasputinism
in London* claims to be an exposé of an erotic religious movement inaugurated by Rasputin. The villain is the Reverend
Stephen Keall, who is introduced to Rasputin in Hampstead,
when Rasputin is on a secret mission to London. Rasputin tells
Keall—through an interpreter—that he possesses the same
power over women as himself, and explains the principle of the
hypnotic stare. Keall applies this, and soon discovers that dark-
haired women find him irresistible. (Fair-haired women are
immune to his charm—LeQueux does not bother to explain
why.) But the head of the Italian secret police is after Keall, and
thwarts every attempt to steal the virtue of the heroine, whom
Keall tries to draw into his orgiastic society. At the end of the
book, Keall is drowned after an exciting chase in a boat. The
book seems to owe more to Matthew Lewis's *The Monk*—both
in style and plot—than to Rasputin. But although the style is
that of a cheap novelette—it is so badly written that it would

not find a publisher today——LeQueux tries to keep up a pretence, for any reader gullible enough to swallow it, that he is writing this as fiction only because the more lurid facts have to be disguised; his real motive, he implies, is moral indignation that these abominations should have been allowed to take place in London.

In 1923, LeQueux published *Things I Know*, and made some more belated revelations about Rasputin. In 1917, he explained, the Kerensky government had given him a large number of papers and manuscripts found in a safe in the cellar of Rasputin's house. (Rasputin, of course, had no cellar—he lived in a flat on the fourth floor.) Among these he found a manuscript entitled *Great Russian Criminals*, written in French at Rasputin's dictation. (Rasputin did not speak a word of French.) This manuscript disclosed that Jack the Ripper was a Russian homicidal maniac called Pedachenko, from Tver, who had been sent to London by the Russian secret police to expose the inefficiency of British police methods. He lived in Westmoreland Road, Walworth, and committed his crimes with the aid of two accomplices, a man named Levitski and a tailoress named Winberg. On his return to Russia, Pedachenko was caught trying to murder a woman called Vogak, and died in a mental home in 1908.[1] LeQueux explains his long delay in making the documents public by saying that he has only recently discovered that there *was* a homicidal maniac called Pedachenko living in Tver in the 1880s. This hardly explains why he made no mention of the Rasputin documents in his earlier books, or why he never attempted to make public such an extraordinary document as *Great Russian Criminals*.

LeQueux is perhaps the most openly malicious and downright dishonest writer on Rasputin—which is saying a great deal, with such competitors as Omessa and Illiodor. He lies and slanders with a cheerful cynicism that is sometimes thought to be an invention of modern scandal sheets. Until Liepman's book, forty years later, no writer on Rasputin treated the facts with quite the same freedom of invention. But most of the books contain

[1] A fuller account of this theory—which occupies only two pages of *Things I Know*—can be found in Donald McCormick's book *The Identity of Jack the Ripper*. Mr McCormick is disposed to accept LeQueux's story; it is evident that he has never read any of LeQueux's other books on Rasputin.

exaggerations and inaccuracies. Vogel-Jørgensen's book, published in 1917, clearly intends to be an honest and accurate account; but in fact, it is almost as misleading as Omessa's. In 1920, Victor Marsden, who was in Russia at the time of the murder, produced a small book called *Rasputin and Russia*. Again, the intentions are obviously excellent; nevertheless, Marsden states with authority that Rasputin's power over the Tsarevitch came from drugs that were administered to the boy by Anna Vyrubov, and that Rasputin was undoubtedly a German spy.

The most widely read book on Rasputin was Fülöp-Miller's *The Holy Devil* (the title borrowed from Illiodor), published in German in 1927. This is an attempt at a full-scale, scholarly work on Rasputin, and has an impressive five-page bibliography of sources at the end, and dozens of excellent photographs. And yet the book contains almost no dates, and ignores most of the historical events that formed the background of Rasputin's career as court favourite. It achieves its considerable bulk by an enormous amount of padding, and by writing up its conversations in the style of a novel. The style itself is hardly reassuring:

> The new saint made a particularly deep impression on the women of the village. When they returned to the light of day, their relations . . . noticed a delicate flush on their faces, such as love alone is wont to paint on the cheeks of young women. A radiant light shone in their eyes and a smile played on their lips. . . .

Where he lacks facts, he is inclined to follow the LeQueux tradition of inventing. But this occasionally obscures more important facts. For example, he explains that Purishkevich, Rasputin's murderer, had been in the habit of coming to Rasputin's flat to beg for a ministerial post, and that Rasputin had obstinately refused to make Purishkevich Minister of the Interior. So Purishkevich took to abusing Rasputin in the Duma, which, however, did not worry Rasputin in the least. The truth is that Purishkevich's final denunciation of Rasputin frightened both Rasputin and the Tsarina, and brought Rasputin his foreboding of death. There is no evidence whatever that Purishkevich ever met Rasputin before the night of the murder, and nothing is less likely than that he would have asked him for a ministerial post.

Many other examples of this kind of distortion could be cited from Fülöp-Miller.

There are also a few interesting minor mysteries connected with his book. Many of the photographs have clearly been touched up. But one of the oddest shows Rasputin having tea with the Tsarina and her son, with a small girl (Anastasia?) standing beside her mother's chair. The woman in the photograph bears no resemblance to the Tsarina, and the man is certainly unlike Rasputin, except for a beard. The tea things on the table have quite obviously been added to the photograph with a pencil, and the perspective of the teapot is so strange that it seems to have been drawn by a child. One is inclined to wonder whether this is one of those faked photographs that Hvostov was accused of manufacturing. If so, its purpose is not apparent.

Aldous Huxley, who read Fülöp-Miller's book the year it appeared, made it the basis of his account of Rasputin in an essay called *Francis and Grigory* (in *Do What You Will*, 1928) which contrasts St Francis of Assisi unfavourably with Rasputin. But Huxley's chief point about Rasputin was that he had none of the pride that made St Francis so intolerable; he was Christian enough not to try to be more than human, and so preached salvation through sin. 'Desiring salvation, Rasputin practised what he preached and sinned—most conspicuously, as was the custom of the Khlysty, in relation to the seventh commandment.' Huxley always showed an unhealthy fascination with adultery, and Fülöp-Miller's Rasputin was ideal material for his illustration in that he could indulge this fascination while appearing to make a point about pride and humility. If Huxley doubted the authenticity of Fülöp-Miller's documentation—as he surely must have, simply on the evidence of his style—he kept his doubts to himself, for the sake of making his point that 'Grigory the moral philosopher is a person who must be taken seriously'.

And yet the aspect of Rasputin that would most have interested the later Huxley—his curious powers—is left unmentioned. Rasputin is simply a man 'with a daemon in his belly'. And the possibility of these powers continues to be ignored in all books about him—ignored, or mentioned as another proof that he was possessed by a 'daemon'.

Anna Vyrubov's memoirs[1] are strangely non-committal on Rasputin—in fact, bafflingly so. She begins her account of him by stating that he was purely a spiritual adviser of the Tsarina, and never at any time discussed politics with her. This is undoubtedly untrue, and Anna Vyrubov must have known it was untrue, since Rasputin used her as a messenger between himself and the Tsarina. The Tsarina's letters to her husband are full of phrases like: 'Our friend thinks that so and so should be dismissed', or 'Our friend thinks that so and so would make a wise Minister of the Interior'. Anna must have known this. She admits only that Rasputin averted the Balkan war in 1912 by advising the Tsar against it.

Anna Vyrubov admits Rasputin's power of second sight, and gives two instances in which he seemed to read the mind of a suppliant. But when she comes to discuss her own serious accident in 1915, she only mentions that Rasputin said: 'She will live', without actually stating that he saved her life. It was Pares who records the story of his effort to recall her from unconsciousness, and his subsequent collapse as he left the room, his source being Mosolov, the chancellor, and the Tsar's diary. It can only be assumed that Anna Vyrubov's aim was to minimize Rasputin's part in the Tsarina's life.

In the 1930s, there were a number of books on Rasputin, several of them in French. The most important of these was a large volume by General A. Spiridovich, who was in Russia at the time of Rasputin. Although full of interesting material, this book in no way replaces Fülöp-Miller's as the standard biography of Rasputin. Simanovich and Rodzianko had also written their accounts of Rasputin by the time this was published.

Perhaps the most misleading volume yet published on Rasputin is Heinz Liepman's *Rasputin, A New Judgement*,[2] since it professes to be a 'new judgement' based upon new materials—in particular, the Ohkrana archives, published in 1956. Liepman invents as freely as LeQueux—I have already cited the matter of Rasputin's first meeting with the Tsarina. There are times when his distortions seem prompted by a curious sense of

[1] *Memories of the Russian Court* (Macmillan, 1923).
[2] Frederick Muller Ltd., 1958.

humour. For example, he solemnly describes how, in 1911, Purishkevich, Hermogen and the other conspirators, ordered Rasputin to go on a trip to the Holy Land. Rasputin says that he will go—if Hermogen is banished too. Rasputin then goes on to say: 'You know that Stolypin has just been assassinated, and you want Kokovtsev made Prime Minister. You know that you will never succeed in getting him appointed without my help. Banish Hermogen, and I will use my influence on his behalf.' Liepman goes on to explain that on March 1, 1911, Hermogen was banished to a distant monastery; two days later, it was announced that Kokovtsev would be the next Prime Minister; ten days later, the newspapers announced that Rasputin would go on a pilgrimage to the Holy Land.

What Liepman does not mention is that in February 1911, Stolypin was still alive—he was not assassinated until September. Hermogen was not banished until almost a year later. (The final clash with Rasputin took place in late December 1911.) Liepman also fails to explain how Purishkevich can bring about Hermogen's banishment. (It was, of course, the Tsar himself who banished Hermogen.)

Liepman's reason for concocting this incredible rigmarole is not apparent—the true version is as dramatic as the one he has invented—and one can only ascribe it to a strange sense of humour.

He also oversimplifies where it suits his purpose. Illiodor is not mentioned once. There is a photograph showing Rasputin, Hermogen and Illiodor, but the caption mentions only Rasputin and Hermogen. Liepman insists that Rasputin was brought to St Petersburg by the Union of True Russians, and was then constantly in touch with a band of conspirators, including Hermogen, Purishkevich and Anna Vyrubov. It is remotely possible—though highly unlikely—that Purishkevich was a conspirator with Hermogen, since he was an extreme reactionary, but quite impossible that Anna Vyrubov should have been involved. And yet Liepman cites whole conversations which were purportedly taken down by the Ohkrana from Purishkevich's dictation. Liepman's aim seems to have been to write a life on Rasputin in clear, sensational scenes, taxing the reader as little as possible. So the historical background is almost completely ignored—even more so than with Fülöp-Miller—and precise dates and times are given for events that never took place at all. For example, Liepman describes an attempt on Rasputin's life on August 27, 1910, when five men waylaid Rasputin. Rasputin picks two of them up and smashes their heads together. 'One man was dead, and the other lay on the ground groaning.' Ohkrana men rush up and seize the four survivors. (Liepman emphasizes Rasputin's enormous physical strength. In fact, he was not unusually strong, as is shown by many instances—as, for example, when two sailors dragged him off the boat at Pokrovskoe, or two officers beat him up at the Villa Rode.) A few pages later, Liepman describes how Rasputin calmed a nervous twitching of the Tsarina's face by stroking her forehead. Anna Vyrubov enters the room and silently withdraws, unnoticed. Liepman implies that the incident is mentioned in Anna Vyrubov's memoirs; in fact, it is not. Perhaps Anna Vyrubov recounted it to Purishkevich, who reported it to the Ochrana.

Surprisingly enough, Rasputin has inspired no notable works of art—unless the books about him are regarded as imaginative fiction. There have been two bad films, and a number of references to him in novels about the Russian revolution—notably Alexey Tolstoy's *Ordeal*, already mentioned, in which Rasputin appears briefly. The only work of any importance treating Rasputin fictionally is Nicholas Nabokov's opera *The Holy Devil* (1958) with libretto by Stephen Spender. Nabokov should be well qualified to write of Rasputin, having studied in St Petersburg at the time of the murder. But in fact, the work is extraordinarily unsatisfactory on every level. Musically, it is curiously nondescript, resembling nothing so much as Menotti's *The Consul* without the flashes of Puccinian melody. The opera takes place in Yussupov's basement and the whole middle section is a flash-back, first to the bedroom of the Tsarevitch, on the evening when Rasputin first saves his life, then to the afternoon before the murder, when Anna Vyrubov warns him not to go to Yussupov's. There is a scene with the gypsies, when Rasputin gets drunk and passes out, then has visions of a chorus of monks calling on him to repent. Then the scene returns to the basement, where the poison is failing to have any effect. Finally, the Prince shoots him—the shooting taking place to absurd marching music. Rasputin collapses, gets up again and knocks out the Prince, then rushes out, to be shot in the courtyard. Inevitably, the end is an anticlimax; operas were intended to end with a bang, not a whimper.

But the faults of the opera throw some light on the whole Rasputin problem. It fails because the librettist, Stephen Spender, has tried hard to keep it authentic, historically accurate. Only Mussorgsky could have treated such a libretto successfully—for he would never have allowed the libretto to dominate the music. The consequence is that nothing of the true Rasputin emerges; he remains as much a caricature as the Rasputin of LeQueux or Fülöp-Miller. Having no opportunity to express himself, he never becomes at ragic figure, like Boris Godunov. But opera is, by its nature, incapable of presenting a man with historical verisimilitude—that is, as a part of the background of his time. Nabokov's opera was bound to be a failure, given Spender's treatment; Rasputin cannot emerge either as a subject or an object.

This also pinpoints the difficulty of writing a book about Rasputin. If he is presented in the Tolstoyan manner—as a mere part of history—the writer finds himself committed to detailing all the complicated and somewhat boring intrigues of the time, and certainly losing the reader's interest. Even Pares' book, as brilliantly written as it is, falls into this trap. The only apparent alternative—and the one chosen by all his biographers—is the subjective treatment; to write 'the Rasputin story' as though it is a novel. But this method produces neither historical accuracy nor psychological truth.

There is a third possibility. It must be clearly recognized that, in studying Rasputin, we are not studying history, but a man whose reality intersects history. The men who belong to history see their destiny from the beginning in terms of history, just as a great financier sees his destiny in terms of money. Even the idealists—the Garibaldis and Lenins—see their destiny in historical terms. At the opposite extreme are the artists who are indifferent to history, totally concerned with the development of an inner world—a Rilke or Van Gogh. Between these extremes stand the men who are, perhaps, the greatest of all: who are concerned with an inner truth, but who see that their truth will come to play its part in the history of their time—or of the next century. In modern times, only the name of Nietzsche comes to mind; but most of the great religious figures of the past enter the category.

By his innermost nature, Rasputin was one of these. Like Nietzsche, he was born free of the diseases of his time. He had the natural crude health and self-belief that characterizes so many men of genius born out of the 'people'. To summarize his early life by saying: 'He was a horse thief and a charlatan' is like saying of Van Gogh: 'He was a neurotic who had the urge to paint without the talent'.

For convenience, we might say that men of talent tend to fall into two groups. The luckiest, in a sense, are those who find no great conflict between their environment and their inner possibilities, whose aspirations are received sympathetically. But it is significant that few of the sons of great artists—or writers or musicians—have also risen to greatness. The sympathetic environment has too little of conflict to harden the greatness.

At the opposite extreme are the men whose environment seems a direct contradiction of their sense of inner possibility. For these men, I suggested the name 'outsider'. Such men, by the nature of their conflict, are made aware of the duality of nature and spirit, environment and will. It is demanded of them that they prefer the invisible to the visible. They are not natural pantheists, seeing nature invested with spirit, regarding the world as the natural background of the spirit, its 'home'. On the contrary, they are inclined to be Manichees, sometimes extreme pessimists. When the inner being stirs and expands, they are aware of 'truth'. The world is usually a lie that denies this inner truth.

This, and this alone, is how Rasputin gained the inner-impetus to become the most powerful man of his time. He may have possessed an element of the charlatan—most of us do. 'Most of us bid for admiration with no intention of earning it' Shaw points out. He was, to some extent, a shrewd peasant with an eye for the main chance. But he was, in the sense defined above, an outsider, one whose environment seems a direct contradiction of his sense of inner possibility. All his significant development took place in the years in Pokrovskoe—the years for which we have no kind of record, least of all the only record that really counts, his own description of what happened. Even if he had been able to verbalize this conflict, there was no one in the Russia of his day who would have understood what he was talking about—with one possible exception, Tolstoy. Illiodor, Maniulov, Simanovich and the rest understood him as little as Zola understood his friend Cezanne (whom he attempted to anatomize in *L'Oeuvre*).

And yet I repeat, these years were the true key to Rasputin's life. These, and not the later years, are Rasputin's true history.

Here it can be seen why all books on Rasputin are necessarily unsatisfactory; relatively sympathetic studies like Fülöp-Miller and Liepman are as far from the truth as Illiodor's libels. To write truly of Rasputin, we would require a personal document relating to his development, the equivalent of the letters of Van Gogh, the diary of Nijinsky or Lawrence's *Seven Pillars of Wisdom*. The problem can be seen clearly in the case of the two last named. There are dozens of books on Lawrence, and nearly as many on Nijinsky. Yet none of the writers seem to grasp the truth that is immediately apparent to any reader of the *Diary* or the *Seven Pillars*. The reality of these men has to be explained in terms of a kind of spiritual geography rather than of the kind of psychology that deals in personal neuroses and conflicts.

Such a document does not exist. And even if it existed, it is doubtful whether most of his biographers would have made use of it; it is difficult not to write Rasputin's life in terms of intrigues and seductions, debauches and rivalries.[1]

But although we possess no confessional documents for a subjective study of Rasputin, the circumstantial evidence is abundant. As Alan Moorehead pointed out, the drooling villain of LeQueux, Yussupov and Rodzianko could never have existed.

---

[1] It is true that Fülöp-Miller has also written interesting books on Van Gogh and Dostoevsky in which he shows himself aware of the 'outsider' factor; and yet his lack of insight can immediately be seen by comparing his book on Van Gogh with Jaspers', or his Dostoevsky study with Berdyaevs'.

Rasputin was no fake or crook. He not only possessed real political shrewdness and insight—as witnessed even by Pares; he also possessed a power to project his inner-reality so that it affected others. It was the indefinable quality of greatness—the same kind that was present in Nijinsky's dancing. Unfortunately, as with Nijinsky's dancing, we have to take the word of those who witnessed it. And Rasputin's greatness was of a kind that aroused far more opposition, was subject to more misinterpretation, than Nijinsky's. Men like Yussupov, Rodzianko, Purishkevich, may have had petty motives for their hatred: jealousy, envy, personal inadequacy; but even without these, it is doubtful whether they could have understood Rasputin. The principle of his motivation, the fuel that drove him, would be incomprehensible to them. (Nor must it be forgotten that, to a large extent, they were right in regarding Rasputin as a bad influence; they had every reason for rationalizing their hatred as idealism.)

On the other hand, it would be interesting to know the reaction of some of his 'disciples' to the posthumous revelations about his character—women like the Golovins, for example. Some may have been inclined to recant, like Anna Vyrubov; but many must have continued to see him as a great man who was never understood, whose essential greatness was unconnected with his weaknesses. Unfortunately, none of these have written books about him—or even left their ultimate judgment on record. The 'monk, satyr and criminal' of LeQueux is virtually unchallenged, except by the inadequate testimony of Maria Rasputin. This would hardly matter—except that the true Rasputin is a great deal more interesting than any of his biographers seem to have realized. His real significance may not be recognized for at least another century—by which time, one hopes, psychical research, telepathy, second-sight and pre-vision will be accepted as simply another branch of psychology. Possibly the word 'abnormal' will have somewhat changed its connotations by then.

The most persistent question about Rasputin is the one that no one is qualified to answer. It is implied in the statement by Charques that I quoted in the introduction: 'Nemesis visibly stalks the . . . reign of the last of the Romanov czars. Neither for this nor for any other period of the past will a determinist reading of history satisfy the imagination.' Since the question admits of no method of meaningful investigation, we can take it that this is one of those casual speculations that even a philosopher is likely to raise at a late hour on a winter evening. And yet the course of Russian history gives it a certain air of validity. Gurdjieff once remarked that most men have no destiny, since they have no inner-reality; they are subject to the laws of chance. A man needs to make a great effort before he crystallizes a certain 'essence' which is also a destiny. Reading a life of Rasputin, one would say that he possessed that essence, while the Tsar's family were victims of the law of chance. And after three centuries of oppression, only a leader with something more than mere personality could have steered Russia away from total revolution. The old order was a rotten tree, asking to be struck by lightning; it is astonishing that it did not collapse under its own weight long before the turn of the century.

As to Rasputin, he undeniably did everything in his power to change the course of history. What is more, he knew that it was simply a matter of time. If the régime could be kept going for another twenty years or so, the time of collapse would be past. Nothing could keep Russia from getting a constitution in any case. In fact, the peasants had already taken the redistribution of land into their own hands before the Bolsheviks made a proclamation to this effect. What we call the 'revolution'—meaning the rise to power of the Bolsheviks and the overthrow of the Romanovs—was only a surface change. The real revolution had been under way since Stolypin's land edict of 1906, and whether Nicholas stayed on the throne or not, it would have been completed by 1920. As Charques pointed out, 'the Bolsheviks had next to nothing to do with the fall of czarism'. 'To change the government is only to change the necktie of the man who picks your pocket', said Malatesta. The Russian people found this out to their cost when they exchanged Nicholas for Stalin. It was no new phase of Russian history; only a continuation of what had been going on for the past three hundred years, complete with terrorism and secret police. And when Stalingrad was renamed Volvograd a few years ago, there seemed a curiously familiar pattern to the event. No one would be surprised if Leningrad one day resumes its original name of St Petersburg, and some Ivan the Terrible of the future pronounces himself Tsar.

In history, no one has the last word. But there is a certain finality to be achieved by standing outside it. Perhaps that is why Rasputin strikes us as a kind of full stop.

BIBLIOGRAPHY

Books about Rasputin:

Fülöp-Miller, René: *Rasputin: the Holy Devil*, Putnam and Co. Ltd, 1928.

Illiodor: *Svyatoy Chort (The Holy Devil)*, Golos Minuvshcago, Petrograd, 1917.

LeQueux, William: *Minister of Evil*, Cassel and Co. Ltd, 1918.
—— *Rasputinism in London*, Methuen and Co. Ltd, 1919.
—— *Rasputin, the Rascal Monk*, Hurst and Blackett Ltd, 1917.

Marsden, Victor E.: *Rasputin and Russia*, 1920.

Liepman, Heinz: *Rasputin, A New Judgement*, Frederick Muller Ltd, 1958.

Omessa, Charles: *Rasputin and the Russian Court*, George Newnes Ltd, 1918.

Purishkevich, V. M.: *Comme J'ai tué Raspoutine*, 1923.
—— *Nous Avons tué Raspoutine*, 1953.

Rasputin, Maria: *My Father*, Cassel and Co. Ltd, 1934.
—— *The Real Rasputin*, John Long Ltd, 1929.

Rodzianko, M. V.: *The Reign of Rasputin*, Philpot, 1927.

Sava, George: *Rasputin Speaks*, Faber and Faber Ltd, 1941.

Simanovich, A.: *Rasputin, Der Allmächtige Bauer*, 1928.

Vogel-Jørgensen, T.: *Rasputin: Prophet, Libertine, Plotter*, Unwin, 1917.

Books in which Rasputin is mentioned or described:

Anastasia: *I, Anastasia*, with notes by Krug van Nidda, Michael Joseph Ltd, 1958.

Anonymous: *The Fall of the Romanoffs*, Herbert Jenkins Ltd, 1918.

Dzhamumova, E. F.: *Mes Rencontres avec Raspoutine*, Petrograd, 1923.

Kerensky, A. F.: *The Catastrophe*, Appleton and Co., 1927.

—— *Letters of the Tzar to the Tzarina*, John Lane Ltd, 1929.

—— *Letters of the Tzarina to the Tzar*, John Lane Ltd, 1923.

Lockhart, Bruce: *Memoirs of a British Agent*, Putnam and Company Ltd, 1932.

Moorehead, Alan: *The Russian Revolution*, William Collins, Sons and Co. Ltd, 1958.

Pares, Sir Bernard: *The Fall of the Russian Monarchy*, Jonathan Cape Ltd, 1939.

—— *Russia*, Penguin Special, 1941.

Rauch, George von: *History of Soviet Russia*, Constable and Co. Ltd, 1957.

Trotsky, Leon: *History of the Russian Revolution* (3 Vols.), Victor Gollancz Ltd, 1932.

Vassili, Count Paul: *Behind the Veil at the Russian Court*, Cassell and Co. Ltd, 1913.

Vyrubov, Anna: *Memories of the Russian Court*, Macmillan and Co. Ltd, 1923.

Books on Russian History:

Charques, R. D.: *A Short History of Russia*, Phoenix House, 1962.

Conybeare, Frederick: *Russian Dissenters*, Harvard University Press, 1912.

Corti, Count Egon: *Downfall of Three Dynasties*, Methuen and Co. Ltd, 1934.

Dillon, E. J.: *Russia Today and Yesterday*, J. M. Dent and Sons, Ltd, 1929.

Geddie, John: *The Russian Empire, Its Rise and Progress*, Thomas Nelson and Sons Ltd, 1885.

Graham, Stephen: *Boris Godunov*, Ernest Benn Ltd, 1930.
—— *Ivan the Terrible*, Benn Brothers Ltd, 1932.

Hodgetts, E. A. Brayley: *Court of Russia in the 19th Century* (2 vols.), Methuen and Co. Ltd, 1908.

Howe, Sonia: *A Thousand Years of Russian History*, Williams and Norgate Ltd, 1915.

Kochan, Lionel: *The Making of Modern Russia*, Jonathan Cape Ltd, 1962.

Koslov, Jules: *Ivan the Terrible*, W. H. Allen and Co., 1961.

Kluchevsky, V. O.: *History of Russia* (5 vols.), J. M. Dent and Sons Ltd, 1911–31.

Molloy, Fitzgerald: *Court of Russia in the 18th Century* (2 vols.), Hutchinson and Co., 1905.

Paleologue, Maurice: *The Enigmatic Tsar* (Alexander I), Hamish Hamilton Ltd, 1938.

Pares, Sir Bernard: *History of Russia*, Jonathan Cape Ltd, 1936.

Platonov, S. F.: *Boris Godounov, Tsar de Russie*, Payot, Paris, 1929.
—— *History of Russia*, Payot, Paris, 1916.

Sumner, B. H.: *A Survey of Russian History*, Gerald Duckworth and Co. Ltd, 1944.

Waliszevski, K.: *Peter the Great*, William Heinemann Ltd, 1898.

APPENDIX

THAUMATURGY AND PRE-VISION

In recent years there has been a great deal of talk about 'spirit healing'—due partly to the serious attention gained by practitioners like Mr Harry Edwards, whose powers seem to be undeniable. The whole subject—including that of psychical research—is no longer looked upon as unmentionable by scientific men. In England, 'logical philosophers' like C. D. Broad and Anthony Flew openly affirm their belief that there is 'something' in psychical research—even if that something is not at all what most Spiritualists believe.

During the writing of this book, I took some trouble to investigate the subject of thaumaturgy, pre-vision, etc. Some of the results were self-contradictory, but they may be worth stating here—on the understanding that I cannot be called in any sense an expert.

I am inclined to accept Phineas Quimby's assertion that most people possess some kind of healing power in a slight degree, and that it cannot be regarded as miraculous, or in any way connected with religion. Mr Noel Macbeth, in an interesting work called *Radiational Physics*[1] suggests that the power possessed by water diviners can be developed by anyone who will take the trouble. The main piece of apparatus required is a pendulum on a piece of cotton.

I conducted a preliminary experiment with the help of two or three friends, including the experimental psychologist John

[1] To which I must thank my friend Martin Delany for drawing my attention.

221

Comley. A subject was told that the pendulum would swing in a circle over a woman's hand and an arc over a man's. This was tried several times, with both men and women, and the pendulum swung in the way described. Then the subject was blindfolded and told that he was holding the pendulum over the hand of a man or woman. The motions of the pendulum became less marked; moreover, it tended to swing in a circle when the subject believed he was holding it over the hand of a woman, even when it was actually being held over a man's hand, or over nothing at all. Finally, the subject was told that we would place our hands under the pendulum without making any noise, so that he could not know whether there was a hand there at all. At this point, the motion of the pendulum ceased altogether.

We concluded that the subject had been deceiving himself, and unconsciously causing the pendulum to swing in the way expected. I myself found that I was able to hold the pendulum completely still over male or female hands; there was no tendency for the pendulum to swing 'of its own accord'.

At this point, however, my wife tried holding the pendulum, and it immediately began to swing far more violently than before, describing enormous circles over female hands and long arcs over male hands. It was obvious that she was doing her best to hold the pendulum still, and was astonished at its motion. When we blindfolded her, these movements again became indecisive, and finally ceased altogether, as with the first subject. We concluded that my wife was unconsciously swinging the pendulum, although she was completely unaware of this, and there was no movement of her fingers to betray that she was swinging it. The experiment at least proved that it is possible for the unconscious mind to cause a pendulum to swing, particularly if the subject is suggestible.

The main question to be decided is whether the 'subconscious mind' only has power to deceive—as in the above case—or whether it may not possess certain powers of which the conscious mind is not aware. The former view is taken by C. J. P. Ionides, the 'snake man', whom I questioned about the activities of witch doctors. He was of the opinion that witch doctors work by suggestion alone, and that their power is solely over the minds of those who believe in them. This view did not correspond to

that of the late Negley Farson, who told me that he had seen a
Liberian witch doctor conjure rain out of a completely clear
sky.

An even more curious story was told to me by Mr Martin
Delany, who was for many years Chairman and Managing
Director of a large company in Nigeria. I have not been able to
obtain corroborative evidence for this story, so as scientific
evidence it is worthless; I repeat it nevertheless. Mr Delany,
having just returned from leave in Europe, was informed by his
European sawmill manager that an extraordinary incident had
taken place in the sawmill a few days prior to Mr Delany's return.
A hen, from a nearby compound, had flown straight into the
large Brenta band-saw and was instantly cut to pieces by the
blade of the saw, which revolves at about 10,000 revolutions per
minute. The Nigerian mill-workers were very perturbed by
this—they knew now that the 'Iron God' was angry and seeking
blood and, unless blood was offered by the witch doctor to
appease the 'God', then he would demand other victims. They
therefore requested that the band-saw should be stopped until
the necessary sacrifice had been made by the witch doctor. Mr
Delany refused their request for two reasons, firstly because an
urgent export order for lumber had to be completed, and secondly
because the sacrifice involved decapitating a puppy dog and
sprinkling the blood over the machine, and this he was most
reluctant to permit. In fact, he hoped that the whole thing was
an isolated incident soon to be forgotten. Two days afterwards
another hen flew into the band-saw. This caused consternation
among the Nigerian workers, who again approached Mr Delany
but were again refused. Four days after this incident the European
manager was asked by the Nigerian foreman in the presence of
Mr Delany if he would come to the band-saw to adjust the saw-
guides as the saw-blade was not cutting evenly; this adjustment
was usually done by the manager. Mr Delany, the manager and
the foreman walked to the sawmill and Mr Delany watched as
the very rigid drill, essential when adjustments or repairs were
made to the band-saw, was carried out. The electricity was cut
off at the mains and the starter switches were put in the 'Off'
position. Then, and only then, was anyone permitted to com-
mence work on the band-saw. Mr Delany watched with interest,

pleased to note that the drill had been faithfully carried out, and turned to leave the mill when suddenly, to his horror, he heard the first sounds which indicated that the saw had commenced to turn. Rushing to the band-saw he discovered that his manager's hand had been badly cut by the saw-blade which had revolved possibly six or seven times. By now, the Nigerian staff were in a state of extreme fear. Mr Delany decided to close the mill for the rest of the day and sent for two European experts, one an electrician, the other a sawmiller. They examined the machine, the starter motors, the mains switches, checking in every possible way, only to state that everything was in perfect order and that it was utterly impossible for the band-saw to start up when the mains and starter motor switches were off. Mr Delany confesses that he was badly shaken by this last incident but still refused to have the witch doctor in because of his natural repugnance to the particular form of sacrifice. He suggested finding blood for the sacrifice from a dead hen or the local meat market, but to this the witch doctor would not agree. The men were persuaded to return to work only by an offer of additional money and the assurance that the machine etcetera were in perfect order, having been checked by the European experts. There was a lull for about two weeks and everyone concerned was beginning to relax when with horrifying and brutal suddenness the 'Iron God' struck. The band-saw had just commenced to saw through a log, the 7-inch wide saw-blade was turning at maximum revolutions when without warning and for no known reason the saw-blade started to peel in a thin strip commencing at the rear. Within a second or so a tangled mass of peeled saw-blade burst out and struck the operator in the chest and face, inflicting serious wounds; in fact, he died before he could be carried out to the waiting estate car. Operators are never protected (i.e. caged in with protective mesh) with this type of saw as normally there is no need, the saws having adequate guards. A Mr Stenner of Stenners Ltd. of Tiverton said some time later that never before in his many years of manufacturing band-saws had he heard of such a thing occurring. Mr Delany then gave way to the demands of his workmen, who would not have worked in the sawmill at any price until the witch doctor had made the sacrifice to the 'Iron God'. The band-saw stopped operating two years ago, but during the eight years from the date of the operator's death it functioned without hitch. The death of the operator was duly recorded in police records. It is interesting to note that when the United Africa Company opened their very large sawmill, costing several million pounds, at Sapele in Eastern Nigeria, the witch doctor was called in to make the appropriate sacrifice to the 'Iron God'.

Mr Delany was not of the opinion that the witch doctor himself had caused these accidents by some form of 'psycho-kinesis'—he described him as an amiable old gentleman. He believed that if the occurrences were not simply accidents, then they were caused by the fear of the natives somehow acting upon the saw—a form of negative psycho-kinesis.

Mr Delany—who himself possesses slight thaumaturgical gifts—told me that he had seen an occurrence similar to the one described by Negley Farson; in this case, the witch doctor predicted that heavy rain would stop for a period of two hours during a party given to the staff of Mr Delany's company when he was about to proceed on leave; the rain stopped a few minutes before the party was due to start, and began a few minutes after it ended. It had been continuous for many weeks. The stoppage was confined to an area of approximately 10,000 sq. yds.

The question of the exact nature of the thaumaturgical gift is a difficult one. Most of us possess suggestive powers over our own bodies; for example, it is possible to stop oneself feeling sick by an act of auto-suggestion (which it is difficult to describe exactly). This act consists in assuming a 'positive' state of mind towards sickness, acting as if one does not feel sick, somehow convincing oneself. It is not an act of *will*, or an act of auto-suggestion in the ordinary sense. There is definitely a psychological 'trick' in it, which could only be put into words by a practised phenomenologist. To some extent, faith healing may be a similar trick of communicating one's own positive outlook to the subject.

Most healers agree that the act of healing seems to involve a certain self-depletion, although the powers can be developed to a point where one can be 'recharged' in a very short period. Mr Harry Edwards describes the feeling of a power—a kind of fluid—flowing down his arm and through his fingertips when he touches an affected part of the patient's body. Mrs Elizabeth Arkle, of Bristol, who also possesses rudimentary healing powers (as well as a certain power of prevision) has described the same sensation to me. She mentioned that she has to be in good health —psychologically as well as physically—to be able to 'summon' her powers; she experiences the thaumaturgic power as a 'kind of fire' in the area of the breast or solar plexus. She mentioned that she had only used it with relatives—where the contact, presumably, is stronger, and that on one occasion, when tempted to use it, she had a strong intuition that it would be wrong, since the person was dying. She could not explain why she felt it to be wrong.

Some degree of prevision seems to accompany thaumaturgic powers, although the reverse is not always true. Mr Hugh Heckstall Smith has told me of two interesting examples of prevision (one of which he has included in his autobiography *Doubtful Schoolmaster*). In one case, his father had brought him a cycling cape to school. As his father started to tell him where he had bought it, Mr Heckstall Smith interrupted: 'No, let me tell you', and described exactly the shop—some fifty miles away— although he knew nothing of the shop. He said that a picture of the shop came clearly into his mind as his father started to talk.

On another occasion, Mr Heckstall Smith was standing beside a piano, listening to an Irish girl playing. He began to look through the music on top of the piano, when the girl said: 'No, it isn't there'. 'What?' 'The Waldstein sonata.' Mr Heckstall Smith had not mentioned the sonata to her, and she had no reason to infer that he was looking for it.

Mr Heckstall Smith, who is a Quaker, says that he would not normally describe himself as a 'psychic', and is not particularly interested in such matters.

My own experiments with mescalin (which I describe at length in an appendix to *Beyond the Outsider*) convinced me that the human mind suppresses a great many of its powers as being unnecessary to survival. Mescalin did not affect me as it affected Aldous Huxley—there were no visual effects—or as it affected Sartre—there were no horrible hallucinations either. I am usually aware of myself as a reasoning mind. My mental world tends to be clear and unconfused, and my chief mental activity is turning intuitions or insights into words. Mescalin destroyed this 'daylight' world and, as it were, took the lid off my unconscious mind. The result was, in some ways, very much like being plunged back into childhood. As a child, my mind was open to all kinds of influences, rather as a sensitive animal can smell all kinds of smells that are undetectable to the human nose. If these influences were good—if, for example, I spent a spring day in the countryside—this sensitivity brought a great deal of pleasure. But since they were more often bad, or indifferent, I found that they occasioned me a great deal of inconvenience. I found that most 'atmospheres' impinged on me far too strongly. I found that the study of chemistry and physics helped to free me from this unnecessarily acute sensitivity, since it was an 'odourless' world. (It is curious that the only sense affected by mescalin was my sense of smell, which became far more acute.) No doubt this was also the reason that I found the work of Bernard Shaw so refreshing at about the same time; his was also a 'daylight world'.

Mescalin made me realize that the daylight world of my own consciousness has been the end product of a long and not entirely conscious discipline. The results were not unpleasant—on the contrary, in a physical sense, they were intensely pleasant and slightly erotic. And yet in the deeper sense, they were intensely unpleasant, since the 'wall' between conscious and unconscious mind had collapsed, and all kinds of feelings and influences were allowed to burst in. It became extremely easy to re-create memories of childhood in detail—in this effect, the effect was like that of Proust's tisane, but more prolonged; even their individual smells and sounds returned.

I shall not dwell on this question of mescalin further, since I have done so at length elsewhere. The main point is that I also had a strong impression that I had become 'psychic'. An analogy will help to make clear what I mean. When a radio has a VHF tuner, it is able to get stations with greater clarity, and to cut out interference; without the VHF tuner, there may be several stations playing at once. My own mind possesses a mental 'cut-out' rather like a VHF tuner, so that when I settle down to write, my whole mind concentrates on the matter in hand; the intuitions that I am trying to turn into words are received quite clearly without interference from other feelings. Mescalin temporarily wrecked this cut-out; it was impossible even to think about writing, because my mind was a jangle of intuitions, all very vivid, but all mixed up. The main intuition was a sense of benevolence—almost of universal love; but although this was reassuring, confirming, as it were, my natural optimism, it was of very little use from the 'survival' point of view, since I normally act upon this assumption anyway. It was merely a distraction.

I have no way of knowing whether I became genuinely psychic, or was only deceiving myself. For example, when my mind turned to the district in which I live (in south Cornwall), I had an overwhelming intuition of witchcraft. Since then, I have made a few enquiries, but I cannot discover that this area was ever connected with witchcraft. The intuition seemed too strong to be imagination; but it may well be that the mescalin somehow 'amplified' my imagination.

The point I wish to make is that I became aware that we discipline our minds to see only certain aspects of the world; life is complicated, and we need all our wits about us to deal with its complexities. There would be no great point in having second sight or thaumaturgic powers for most of us. But it is worth observing that they can generally be developed where needed. Jim Corbett, in his various books on tiger shooting, mentions several times how his intuition warned him of the presence of a tiger. Psychologists used to argue that intuition is merely 'subconscious observation', and this is a matter with which I shall have to deal in a moment, when speaking of my theory of perception; but Corbett records some interesting cases where it is hard to believe that he was merely observing subconsciously.

It seems probable that the ability to see ghosts is of the same kind as the pre-vision I have already mentioned. (I believe there is a gentleman who makes a living by visiting haunted houses, and being able to tell the tenants all about the ghost; some of his customers have tried to test him by showing him the wrong room or corridor, but he unerringly finds the right one.) It is probably true that nervous people tend to believe they see ghosts; but I think there is also a genuine sensitivity to psychic disturbances—which, again, would be quite useless to most of us.

In *Beyond the Outsider*, I have dealt at some length with the

Whitehead-Husserl theory of perception, that seems to me to help to explain pre-vision and thaumaturgy. Whitehead argues that we have two kinds of perception, which he calls 'presentational immediacy' and 'causal efficacy'. According to Hume, the mind works like an adding machine; it is bombarded with sensations, each of which presses a key, and we *infer* 'wholes' from the sum of their parts. This is the only form of perception—immediacy. Now Whitehead states that we have another kind of perception which becomes aware of wholes before it becomes aware of parts. He believes that 'immediacy-perception' is a fairly recent evolutionary development, and that most animals only possess the intuitive 'meaning-perception'. Our ability to focus precisely on some object or idea—which we take for granted—is a sign that we are high on the evolutionary ladder; it is as if human beings possessed in-built microscopes, while animals have to rely on the naked eye. This ability to focus so clearly on the present also means that we are subject to boredom—which has been correctly described as one of the greatest human mysteries. (It will be seen that my own mescalin experiences confirm Whitehead's view; boredom would have been impossible —but so would clear thought; my mind was too aware of *universal meanings* to focus clearly on individual objects or ideas.)

Whitehead's theory of meaning-perception deserves to be studied at first hand in his book *Symbolism, Its Meaning and Effect*. But it will be seen that if Whitehead is right, then human beings possess two kinds of perception that, as it were, work from opposite ends. Immediacy-perception works from particulars, and adds them together inferentially; meaning-perception (which is also the basis of gestalt psychology) grasps things as wholes. And yet some of the consequences would seem to be absurd at first sight. I understand your sentences mainly by immediacy-perception; I add together the meanings of individual words. But this is not all. As you are reading these words, your eye is travelling from word to word, adding together meanings; yet there is a second faculty at work, suspended *above* the page, as it were, not crawling from word to word. Consider the following sentence, taken at random from Whitehead: 'Ingression denotes the particular mode in which the potentiality of an eternal object is realized in a particular actual entity, contributing to the definiteness of the actual entity'. Unless you have studied *Process and Reality* it will be meaningless to you. Your eye follows the individual words, but you will observe now that your meaning-faculty stops working, baffled. The inferential component of your immediacy-perception tries to add meaning to meaning; but the meaning faculty itself is out of order. For a moment, one can clearly recognize that the two faculties are quite different. And yet, as I have said, some of the consequences of this theory seem absurd. It would surely mean, for example, that one would in theory be able to grasp someone's meaning before they had spoken a word, or understand a sentence—or even a page—without reading its individual words. It is difficult to see the way out of this—except to point out that in many cases, we *do* grasp meanings in this way, as Hugh Heckstall Smith grasped his father's meaning before the sentence about the cycling cape was spoken.

All this is open to objections, which cannot be dealt with here. It would also be necessary to describe Husserl's pheno-menology, and his idea of the 'intentional structure of conscious-ness' (which is not as abstract as it sounds—I mentioned above that my own consciousness has developed a kind of VHF system, and therefore has an intentional structure which was not con-sciously developed). But the general idea should be clear: that we possess a second form of perception which does not focus on individual things, but 'spreads out' more like radar, or like a bat's system of 'seeing' in the dark. It is necessary to human evolution—particularly of Aryan man—that he should have a strong sense of individuality, of separation from the rest of the universe, so that his immediacy-perception has been strengthened at the expense of his meaning-perception. And yet man *is*, in a deep sense, a part of the organ of the universe, and is on its general nervous system as well as on his own. Hence Jim Corbett's ability to avoid a man-eating tiger lying in wait for him.

There is one more interesting point that I should make here, since it ties in with what I have written about Mary Baker Eddy, etc. Professor A. H. Maslow, of the psychology department at Brandeis University, U.S.A., has conducted some interesting researches into what he calls 'peak moments'. Professor Maslow says that he grew tired of the Freudian assumption that the study of human beings meant automatically the study of the sick mind, and decided that he would find out the consequences of investigating the healthy mind. He chose the healthiest and happiest specimens he could find—and discovered interesting things about them. Extremely healthy human beings seem to have, as a matter of course, experiences of intense certainty and happiness, a sense of unity with the universe, that were once supposed to be peculiar to mystics. Maslow calls these 'peak moments', and describes many of them in an interesting paper. It also seems possible that these extremely healthy human beings have other faculties developed to an unusual extent—pre-vision, possibly thaumaturgy, although Maslow's researches have not yet confirmed this beyond doubt. What this seems to amount to is that extremely healthy human beings can afford to have a more strongly developed faculty of 'meaning-perception' than the less healthy ones, since they have energy to spare. (Maslow has not yet, as far as I know, gone into the interesting question of the basic mental attitude of healthy people towards life—how far a 'positive' attitude affects them—and possibly the things that happen to them—as the negative attitude of Martin Delany's natives affected the circular saw.)

What is clear is that the whole current of western scientific and philosophical thought tends actively to obscure these questions. If the views of Whitehead and Husserl are ever generally accepted as the basis of our culture—as Descartes views have been for three hundred years—we shall no longer feel that these questions demand an 'extra-scientific' attitude, and Rasputin's healing powers will be as natural a subject for speculation as the influence of cosmic rays on human heredity.

INDEX

Aballakask convent, 31
Akulina, Ivanovna, 40
Alapayevsk, 201
Alexander I, Tsar, 65–7
Alexander II, Tsar, 42, 67–9, 86,
   127
Alexander III, Tsar, 51, 69–70, 81
Alexandra, Tsarina, letters of, to
   Rasputin, 14–15, 133
   Rasputin's power over, 15, 58,
      91–2, 94, 102, 119–20, 124, 126,
      150, 160–2, 164, 176, 181, 194,
      209
   gives Rasputin icon, 34
   influenced by Grand Duchess
      Militsa, 50–1, 87
   spiritualism and, 50–1, 87–8
   character, 76, 113
   religion and, 77
   children of, 78
   first meeting with Rasputin, 89–
      90, 115–16
   and Anna Vyrubov's marriage,
      114–15
   Nicholas's affection for, 141
   hatred of police by, 150
   popularity of, with Army, 166–7
   orders dismissal of Dzhunkovsky,
      168
   hatred of Duma by, 170–1, 187
   ill health of, 170
   meeting with Hvostov, 173

saves Protopopov from dismissal, 188
and Rasputin's assassination, 191,
   195
sees Nicholas humiliated, 197
imprisonment and death, 198–9
Alexis, Tsar, 30, 36, 63–4
Alexis (Alexey), Tsarevitch, and
   Rasputin, 19, 121, 150
birth, 53, 79
accidents and illnesses of, 89–90,
   92, 93–4, 121–2, 142, 176
character and upbringing, 121–3
Rasputin's murder and, 195
imprisonment and death, 188–9
Alice of Hesse, Princess,
   see Alexandra, Tsarina
Anastasia, Grand Duchess, daughter
   of Tsar Nicholas II, 63, 123,
   199–201
Anastasia, Grand Duchess (the
   'Montenegrin'), 50, 78, 87–90
Anastasia, wife of Ivan the Terrible,
   59, 63
Andreyev, Leonid, 47, 73, 111, 126
Andronikov, Prince, 119–20, 172–4,
   179, 188, 201
Angle, Paul, 111 n.
'Anna the Bloody', 64
Anthony, Monsignor, 135, 140
Arkle, Mrs Elizabeth, 226
Artsybashev, 73, 82, 111, 126

Athos, Mount, 33–4
Averzhan, 37
Avvakum, 36

Bashmakova, widow, 50, 147
Badmaev, Peter Alexandrovitch, 93, 116–18
Balik monastery, 32
Barnaby, Bishop of Tobolsk, 32, 138, 149, 165
Belaieff, 74
Beletsky, Chief of Police, 120, 161, 168, 173–81, 201
Belovetchkaya, 93
Berdyaev, Nicholas, 17, 23
Biely, Andre, 73, 111
Birger, Charley, 111
Bismarck, 127
Blake, William, 163
Bogrov, revolutionary, 85
Bolotnikov, Ivan, 63
Bonde, Count Carl, 200
Books, on Rasputin, 11–22, 203–14. See also under specific authors
Borodin, 72
Bosnia, 127–8, 155
Botkin, Doctor, 200
Bourman, Anatole, 74–5
Briussov, 111, 126
Broad, C. D., 221
Brooke, Rupert, 169
Brusilov, General, 186, 201
Bul, Lisaveta Nicholaevna, 48
Burdukov, Master of the Horse, 120
Burtsev, Vladimir, 117, 169, 201

Catherine the Great, 40, 64–5
Chabrinovich, 155
Chaliapin, Fedor, 74
Charques, R. D., 14, 64, 70, 215–16
Chekhov, 29, 42, 72
Comley, John, 221–2
Conybeare, Frederick, 38, 39, 41
Corbett, Jim, 228, 230

Dakin, Edwin F., 97 n.
Damansky, Assistant Procurator, 124, 141

Davidsohn, reporter, 154–5
Decembrist revolt, 67
Delany, Martin, 221 n., 223–5, 231
Demidova, maidservant, 200
Diaghileff, Sergei, 74
Dmitri, Prince, 62
Dmitri Pavlovich, Grand Duke, 190, 192–4
Dobrovolsky, Minister, 195
Donskoi, Dmitri, 37
Dostoevsky, 18, 28, 29, 36, 55, 56, 62, 72, 117, 146
Dowager Empress, the, 139, 201
Dubrovine Praskovie Fedorovna, see Rasputin, Dubrovine Praskovie Fedorovna
Dukhobortsy, the, 146
Duma, the Imperial, formation of, 84, 91
  patriotism of, in Great War, 128, 157
  end of third, 150
  hatred of cabinet for, 152
  Rasputin opposes, 153
  closed by Nicholas in 1915, 170–1
  visited by Nicholas, 187
  meeting at Rodzianko's house, 196
  forms provisional government (1917), 197
Dzhunkovsky, General, 161, 162, 165–8, 172

Eddy, Mary Baker, 94–7, 109, 164, 230
Edwards, Harry, 221, 225
Egorov, sexton, 78–9
Ekaterinburg, 199–200
Elizabeth, Grand Duchess, 77, 83, 201

Fall of the Romanoffs (Anon), 19, 53, 92, 167
Farson, Negley, 223
Fedorov, Doctor, 93–4
Feodor, son of Ivan the Terrible, 62
Ferdinand, Archduke of Austria, 151, 155–6

Flew, Anthony, 221
Florishchevo monastery, 137
Fox, George, 18
Fülöp-Miller, René, 20, 21, 52–6, 90,
    92, 106, 116, 130, 136, 147–8,
    207–9

Gapon, priest, 81, 117
Gilliard, tutor, 121–3, 200
Glinka, 67
Godunov, Boris, 62, 63
Gogol, 67, 111
Goidretz, Princess, 161, 166
Goldberg, B. Z., 42
Golitsyn, Prince, 195
Golovins, the, 176, 181, 190, 215
Goncharov, 111
Goremykin, Prime Minister, 84, 153,
    158, 177, 201
Gorki, Maxim, 29, 42, 72–3, 87
Grass, Karl, 37
Great War, the, 127, 157, 158 ff.,
    169 ff.
Guchkov, President, 138–9
Gunther, John, 17
Gurdjieff, George Ivanovitch, 103–4,
    107–9, 145, 164, 216
Guseva, Kinia, 155

Heckstall Smith, Hugh, 226, 230
Hermogen, Bishop, 54–6, 79, 129–
    31, 135–9, 147, 198–9, 210
Herzogovina, 127–8
Hinduism, 38
Hitler, Adolf, 108–9
Holy Land, Rasputin visits, 34, 133
Husserl, Edmund, 97–8, 229, 231
Huxley, Aldous, 107, 208, 226
Hvostov, Alexis, 139–40, 172–5,
    177–80, 201
Hvostov, 'Uncle', 182–3, 187
Hypnotism, 35, 94 ff., 104–6, 108–9,
    161

Ignatyev, Minister, 196
Illiodor, monk, compared with
    Rasputin, 46, 118
  on Rasputin, 52

character and beliefs, 54–5
first meeting with Rasputin, 55–6
Rasputin's attitude to, 129–30
invites Rasputin to Tsaritsyn,
    130–1
at Pokrovskoe, 131
attitude to Rasputin, 131–2
with Theophan and Hermogen,
    135–6, 139
against Rasputin, 153, 166, 179–80
publishes The Holy Devil, 203
lack of understanding of Rasputin,
    214
Ionides, C. J. P., 222
Irina Alexandrovna, Grand Duchess,
    190
Ito, Japanese statesman, 81
Ivan, son of the Terrible, 61
Ivan the Terrible, Tsar, 17, 37, 59–
    62, 64
Izvolsky, Minister, 122, 127–8

James, William, 129
Jews, position of, in Russia, 113–14
John of Cronstadt, Father, 46, 51–3,
    90, 114, 118, 125, 147, 203
Joseph, Father, of Paris, 107
Journal of a Pilgrimage, 133

Kaliayev, terrorist, 83
Kaplan, Dora, 201
Katkoff family, 50
Kazan, 34, 49, 59, 151
Kennington, Eric, 16
Kerensky, Alexander, 150, 198
Khlysty, the, 28, 32, 35, 37–40, 42,
    43 n., 45, 93, 124 n., 132, 138
Kiev, 134
Kitchener, Lord, 182
Kokovtsev, Prime Minister, 93, 134,
    139, 142, 153
Koliabin, Mitya, 78–9, 136
Kommisarov, Colonel, 174–6, 179,
    183
Kostamarov, 29–30
Kostroma, 38
Krymov, General, 196
Kummer, Rudolph, 21

Kurbsky, 60
Kurlov, 196
Kusmich, Fedor, 66

Landau, Rom, 103–4
Lawrence, T. E., 16–17, 145, 204–7, 214
Lazavert, Doctor, 190, 192–4
Lebedev, Madame, 131
Lee, Doctor, 65
Lena Goldfields, 150
Lenin, 86, 160, 169, 197–8, 201
LeQuex, William, 21, 204, 124–15
Lescalier, Auguste, 21
Liepman, Heinz, 21, 49 n., 51 n., 89–92, 116, 155, 206, 209–11
Livadia, 135, 142, 154
Lloyd George, David, 198
Lockhart, Bruce, 167
Loktin, Olga, 136–7
Lukianov, Procurator, 132, 138, 141

Macbeth, Noel, 221
McCormick, Donald, 206 n.
Makarov, Minister, 187
Makary, hermit, 28–9, 32–3
Maklakov, Minister, 152, 158, 190, 193, 195, 201
Malinovsky, 160
Mamontov, 74
Manicheeism, 37–8, 213
Maniulov, Manasevitch-, 116–18, 126, 152, 183, 187, 201, 214
Marie, Grand Duchess, 123, 199
Marie Pavlovna, Grand Duchess, 196
Marsden, Victor, 207
Maslow, Professor A. H., 230–1
Mescalin, 226–8
Meshchersky, Prince, 117
Mesmerism, see Hypnotism
Micheal, Tsar, 30, 63–4
Militsa, Grand Duchess, 50–1, 77–8, 87, 115, 125
Miliukov, 149
'Miracle workers', 78
Molokanye, the, 146
Moorehead, Alan, 11, 12 n., 90, 159, 214

Morland, Nigel, 192 n.
Moscow, 21, 61, 91, 103, 167, 186
Mosolov, Chancellor, 94, 162, 209
Murat, Princess, 22
Musil, Robert, 30
Mussorgsky, 37, 72
Myasoyedov, Colonel, 160

Nabokov, Nicholas, 211–12
Napoleon I, 108
Netzlin, banker, 75–6
Nicholas I, Tsar, 67
Nicholas II, Tsar, denigration of, in history, 12
    Rasputin's influence on, 14, 102, 116, 119–21, 126, 128, 130, 132, 146, 150, 161, 162, 164, 166
    John of Cronstadt's influence on, 51–2
    canonizes Seraphim, 52, 79
    coronation of, 58
    devotion to Tsarina, 70
    character, 75, 76–8, 197
    first meeting with Rasputin, 78, 86, 89, 115
    approval of force, 82
    in 1905 revolution, 83–5
    dissolves first Duma, 91
    refuses to dismiss Stolypin, 133
    banishes Hermogen, 137–8
    hears Rodzianko's denouncement of Rasputin, 140–2
    and Stürmer, 152–3, 188
    and Serbian crisis, 156–7
    popularity of, in Great War, 157, 160
    at the front, 167–8
    closes Duma (1915), 170
    on appointment of Protopopov, 183
    last meeting with Rasputin, 191
    effect of Rasputin's death on, 194–5
    imprisonment and death, 198–200
Nicholas Nicholaievitch, Grand Duke, 50, 84, 88, 122, 159, 167, 171
Nidda, Roland Krug von, 200

Nietzsche, 14, 19, 47, 126, 213
Nijinsky, Vaslav, 74–5, 82, 214–15
Nikita, King of Montenegro, 50
Nikon, Patriarch, 36
Nilov, Admiral, 119–20
Nizhny-Novgorod, see Novgorod
Nizier-Vachot, Philippe, 51, 78, 88, 117
Novaya Derevnya, 89
Novgorod, 60–1, 63, 139–40
Novoselov, Professor, 138

Olga, Grand Duchess, 123, 166–7, 199
Omessa, Charles, 20–1, 148, 203–4, 206
Optima Pustyn, 78
Orlov, George, 64
Orlov, Madame, 133
Ossipova, Daria, 78
Ostrovsky, 67
Ouspensky, 106

Paléologue, Maurice, 66, 166, 188
Parapsychology, 97 ff.
Pares, Bernard, 19, 26, 51, 54, 75, 77, 85, 89, 113, 117, 125, 133, 136 n., 142, 146, 152, 154 n., 164, 167, 168, 170, 171, 178, 189, 190, 196, 200, 209, 212
Paul, Tsar, 65
Petcherkine, 32, 33
Peter, Father, 32–3, 35, 45, 132
Peter, Grand Duke, 50
Peter the Great, Tsar, 17, 23, 64
Peter the Third, Tsar, 40, 64
Petrograd, see St Petersburg
Philipot, Daniel, 37–40
Pisemsky, 29
Pitirim, Metropolitan, 178
Plehve, V. K. von, 69, 79, 81, 117
Plotitsine, merchant, 41
Pobedonostsev, 69, 79
Pokrovskoe, 13, 23–7, 29, 34, 45, 50, 88, 93, 125, 131–4, 136, 137, 142, 154–6, 164–5, 176, 198–9, 211, 214

Polivanov, General, 170, 177, 181–2, 201
Potemkin, battleship, 82
Powys, Llewelyn, 103
Prokoviev, Sergei, 74
Princip, Gavrilo, 155–6
Protopopov, Minister, 183–4, 186–8, 190–1, 195–6, 201
Pskov, 61, 63
Pugachev, 40
Purishkevitch, V. M., 140, 188, 190, 193–5, 201, 202, 207, 215
Pushkin, 41 n., 67

Quimby, Phineas, 94–7, 109, 164, 221

Rachkovsky, 88, 117
Ramakrishna, 46–7, 107–9
Rasputin, Dmitri (son), 45–50
Rasputin, Grigory, myths and legends concerning, 11–22, 203–17
   history and, 13, 16, 212, 216
   and religion, 14–19, 27–30, 32–3, 43, 44–7, 101–2, 163–4
   birth, 23
   childhood, 24–6
   character and temperament, 30–2, 35, 45–7, 57, 109–10, 213–14
   marriage, 31
   death of first child, 32
   has vision of the Virgin, 33, 34
   visits Holy Land, 34, 133
   hypnotism and, 35, 94, 104–6, 108, 161
   further children of, 45
   and sex, 47, 106, 131–2, 143, 144, 148–9
   period as a wanderer, 49
   physical appearance, 50
   arrives in St Petersburg in 1905, 71, 87 ff.
   first meeting with Tsar and Court, 86, 89–90
   and Tsarevitch's illnesses, 89–90, 93, 116, 121–2, 142, 176
   healing powers of, 93 ff., 109, 130–1, 161–2

gains ascendancy over Tsar and Tsarina, 102
compared to Gurdjieff, 103, 107–8
makes enemies in St Petersburg, 111, 135 ff.
choice of friends, 113, 116
as centre of intrigue, 118 ff., 171 ff.
attitude towards Tsarina, 120
attitude towards Tsar, 120–1
relations with Tsarevitch, 121–2
and with the Grand Duchesses, 123–4
years of triumph, 124 ff.
and Austrian crisis (1908), 127–8
home life of, 134
deterioration of, 144 ff., 174
addresses in St Petersburg, 147–8
continued friendship with Royal Family, 150
clash with Rodzianko, 151–2
attempted assassinations of, 154–5, 166, 181
in hospital, 156–7
attitude to 1914 War, 157, 160, 166, 186
hold over Tsarina increases, 161
temporary unpopularity with Tsar, 161, 164
'cures' Anna Vyrubov, 161–2
restored to favour with Nicholas, 166
as 'Tsar', 171
interest in rail services, 171–2, 182
has premonitions of his end, 188–9
assassination of, 190–5 *and passim*
Rasputin, Maria (daughter), on Rasputin, 12, 20–1, 25, 35, 46, 51, 192, 215
birth, 45
first memory of Rasputin, 50
on Hermogen, 56
on the Tsar's daughters, 123
publishes *Journal of a Pilgrimage*, 133
Davidsohn and, 154–5
and attempted assassination of Rasputin, 155
identifies Rasputin's body, 195
later life, 199
Rasputin, Micheal (brother), 26
Rasputin, Praskovie Fedorovna Dubrovine (wife), 31, 34
Rasputin, Varvara (daughter), 45, 195
Rasputin, Yefimy (father), 24–6, 30, 32
Razin, Stenka, 64, 83
Religion, 14, 18, 27–30, 32–3, 35–43, 44–7, 101–2, 163
Revolution (1905), 81–4
(1917), 197–202
Rhine, J. B., 97
Rimsky-Korsakov, 61 n., 72, 74, 85, 135
Rodionov, 137
Rodzianko, President, 11–12, 91, 118, 124, 135 n., 138–43, 148–53, 170, 182–3, 185–7, 191, 195–7, 201, 209, 214–15
Romanoffs, history of the, 59–70
final fate of, 201
Rosen, Baroness, 120
Rozanov, V. V., 74
Russo-Japanese War (1904), 80–1, 116, 117, 127

Sabler, Procurator, 138
Saborevski, Mileti, 27–9
St Francis, 28, 109, 208
St Louis of Gonzaga, 129
St Petersburg, Rasputin in, 14, 31, 47, 50–7, 87 *and passim*
high society in, 50, 125–6
in 1905, 71 ff.
newspaper attacks on Rasputin in, 131, 133
anti-Rasputin movement in, 135
Rasputin's addresses in, 147–8
name changed to Petrograd, 159
discontent in, 185–6
revolution breaks out in (1917), 197
St Simeon, 28–9
Saltykov, 64
Sarajevo, 155–6

INDEX

Sargant, William, 39
Sarov, 52, 57
Sassonoff, George Petrovitch, 87, 148
Sava, George, 21, 44
Schapov, 30
Schredin, 29, 99
Scriabin, 74
Selivanov, Kondrati, 40
Seraphim, monk, 52, 79
Sergius, Grand Duke, 77, 83, 201
Shodkin, 42
Shuisky, Prince Andrew, 59
Shuisky, Prince (afterwards Tsar), 63
Shukovskaya, Vera, 106
Simanovich, Aaron, on Rasputin, 12, 22, 114, 125, 174, 189, 209
  association with Rasputin, 113, 126, 149, 190
  character and career, 113–14, 118
  aids Maria Rasputin in Berlin, 199
  lack of understanding of Rasputin, 214
Sitwell, Sacheverell, 41
Skoptzy, the, 28, 37, 40–2
Sologub, 29, 42
Soloviev, Boris, 199
Spender, Stephen, 211–12
Speransky, 65
Spiridovich, General A., 209
Spiritualism, 77, 87–8
Stalin, Josef, 17
Staraya, 38
Stenner, Mr, 224
Stolypin, Peter, 84–6, 91, 126, 132–5, 139–42, 210, 216
Stravinsky, Igor, 74
Stürmer, Prime Minister, 118, 149, 152–3, 177–9, 181, 186–8, 201
Sukhomlinov, General, 159–60, 169–70, 172, 182–3, 187
Sukhotin, officer, 190, 192–4
Suslov, Ivan, 40
Suzdal, 41
Svoboda, Franz, 200

Taganrog, 65–6
Tambov, 41

Taneyev, Alexander, 76, 114
Taneyev, Sergei, 114 n.
Tarassov, Doctor, 66
Tatiana, Grand Duchess, 123, 166–7, 199
Tchaikovsky, 72
Thaumaturgic power, 93 ff., 109, 221–31
Theophan, Bishop, 46, 53–6, 79, 129–31, 133–5, 138
Thief, The, 63
Tickers, the, 42
Tioumen, 134, 165, 198
Tobolsk, 31, 48–9, 198–9
Tolstoy, Alexey, 71–2, 211
Tolstoy, Leo, 29, 66, 72, 114 n., 214
Tosno, 142
Trepov, Prime Minister, 188, 195
Trufanov, Sergei, see Illiodor, monk
Tsaritsyn, 130, 166
Tsarskoe Selo, 76, 82, 89, 115, 118, 123, 140, 161, 166, 176, 195, 197–8
Tsuchima, 76
Turgeniev, 72
Tyutchev, Madame, 124

Ulianov, Vladimir, see Lenin

Van Gogh, 100, 213, 214
Vassili, Prince Paul, 80, 111–12, 121–3, 139, 145
Verkhoture, 27–32, 134
Vietroff, Marie, 80
Viscovaty, Prince Ivan, 61
Vladimir, Grand Duke, 196
Vogel-Jørgensen, T., 12, 20, 207
Volkonsky, Minister, 196
Vorontsov, 59
Vyrubov, Anna, 93, 124, 140, 142, 180, 190, 198, 210
  and Rasputin's introduction to Nicholas, 89, 115–16
  character, 114, 118
  Royal Family's attachment to, 114, 116, 119
  marriage, 114–15
  on Rasputin's household, 133–4

239

as intermediary, 149, 161, 191
in railway accident, 161–2
'cured' by Rasputin, 162, 164, 166
memoirs, 209, 211, 215

Wallace, Edgar, 81 n.
Wells, H. G., 100
Whitehead, Alfred North, 229, 231
Whitman, Walt, 46–7
Wilhelm II, Kaiser, 127–8, 157
Witte Sergius, 77, 79–81, 83–4, 117,
 127, 160, 167

Xenia, nun, 136

Yemeljan, 37
Yurovsky, gaoler, 199

Yussupov, Prince Felix, on Pokro-
 skoe, 23–4
on Rasputin, 46, 48, 104–6, 118,
 180
in Germany, 140, 153
introduction to Rasputin, 176, 181
and murder of Rasputin, 178,188,
 190–4
later life, 202
lack of understanding of Rasputin,
 215
Yussupov, Prince (father), 74, 190

Zablin, General, 119–20
Zhelyabov, 68–9
Zhirovetsky monastery, 137